AN EVIDENCE-BASED GUIDE TO COLLEGE AND UNIVERSITY TEACHING

What makes a good college teacher? This book provides an evidence-based answer to that question by presenting a set of "model teaching characteristics" that define what makes a good college teacher. Based on six fundamental areas of teaching competency known as Model Teaching Characteristics outlined by The Society for the Teaching of Psychology (STP), this book describes how college faculty from all disciplines and at all levels of experience can use these characteristics to evaluate, guide, and improve their teaching. Evidence-based research supports the inclusion of each characteristic, each of which is illustrated through example, to help readers master the skills. Readers learn to evaluate their teaching abilities using evidence and how to accumulate, document, and organize that evidence. Two introductory chapters outline the model teaching characteristics followed by six chapters, each devoted to one of the characteristics: training, instructional methods, course content, assessment, syllabus construction, and student evaluations.

The book:

- Features in each chapter include self-evaluation surveys that help readers identify gaps between the model characteristics and their own teaching, case studies that illustrate common teaching problems, discussion questions that encourage critical thinking, and recommended readings for further exploration.
- Discusses the need to master teaching skills such as collaborative learning, listening, and using technology, as well as discipline-specific knowledge.
- Advocates for the use of student-learning outcomes to help teachers better evaluate student performance based on their achievement of specific learning goals.

- Argues for the development of learning objectives that reflect disciplines' core theories and applications, strengthen basic liberal arts skills, and infuse ethical and diversity issues.
- Discusses how to solicit student feedback and utilize these evaluations to improve teaching.

Intended for professional development or teacher training courses offered in masters and doctoral programs in colleges and universities, this book is also an invaluable resource for faculty development centers, college and university administrators, and college teachers of all levels and disciplines, from novice to the most experienced, interested in becoming more effective teachers.

Aaron S. Richmond is a Professor of Educational Psychology and Human Development at Metropolitan State University of Denver.

Guy A. Boysen is an Associate Professor of Psychology at McKendree University.

Regan A. R. Gurung is Ben J. and Joyce Rosenberg Professor of Human Development and Psychology at the University of Wisconsin, Green Bay.

AN EVIDENCE-BASED GUIDE TO COLLEGE AND UNIVERSITY TEACHING

Developing the Model Teacher

Aaron S. Richmond
Guy A. Boysen and
Regan A. R. Gurung

Routledge
Taylor & Francis Group

NEW YORK AND LONDON

First published 2016
by Routledge
711 Third Avenue, New York, NY 10017

and by Routledge
2 Park Square, Milton Park, Abingdon, Oxon, OX14 4RN

Routledge is an imprint of the Taylor & Francis Group, an Informa business

Library of Congress Cataloging in Publication Data
Names: Richmond, Aaron S., author. | Boysen, Guy A., author. | Gurung, Regan A. R., author.
Title: An evidence-based guide to college and university teaching : developing the model teacher / Aaron S. Richmond, Guy A. Boysen, Regan A. R. Gurung.
Description: New York, NY : Routledge, 2016. |
Includes bibliographical references and index.
Identifiers: LCCN 2016001207| ISBN 9781138915244 (hardback : alk. paper) | ISBN 9781138915251 (pbk. : alk. paper) | ISBN 9781315642529 (ebook)
Subjects: LCSH: College teaching. | College teachers–Training of.
Classification: LCC LB2331.R5175 2016 | DDC 378.1/25–dc23
LC record available at http://lccn.loc.gov/2016001207

ISBN: 978-1-138-91524-4 (hbk)
ISBN: 978-1-138-91525-1 (pbk)
ISBN: 978-1-3156-4252-9 (ebk)

Typeset in Bembo
by Out of House Publishing

To Amanda, Stella, Phoebe, and Violet—your unwavering love, kindness, and support allow me to strive to be a model teacher, scholar, father, and husband. I thank you from the bottom of my heart.

Aaron S. Richmond

To my parents for pushing me to be an educated man. To my teachers for making me an educated man. And to Marissa for supporting a man trying to educate himself and others.

Guy A. Boysen

To Liam and Melina—I hope you experience model teachers wherever you go. To my students and teaching friends—you push me to be all we wrote about and more.

Regan A. R. Gurung

TABLE OF CONTENTS

Preface   xiii

    Defining Model Teaching xiii
    Structure of the Book xiv
    Yes, This Book is for You xv
Acknowledgments   xvi
About the Authors   xvii

1   Why Do We Need Model Teachers?   1

    What is Model Teaching? 2
    The Need for Another Definition of Teaching Excellence 3
    Development of the Model Teaching Criteria 4
    An Overview of the Book and the Model Teaching Criteria 5
        Chapter 3: How Do We Train to be Model Teachers? 6
        Chapter 4: What Instructional Methods do Model Teachers Use? 6
        Chapter 5: What Do Students Learn in Model Teachers' Courses? 8
        Chapter 6: How Do Model Teachers Assess Student
           Learning? 8
        Chapter 7: How Do Model Teachers Construct Syllabi? 9
        Chapter 8: How Do Model Teachers Use Student
           Evaluations? 9
    Parting Thoughts 9
    References 10

2   What is Great Teaching?   11

   Case Study: Those Who Can Teach, Teach
      (No Training Required?) 12
   Setting Your Target: Look to Winners 13
      Professors of the Year Are Good Exemplars 13
      Successful College Teachers 14
      Master Teachers 14
      What the Best Teachers Do 15
      What Do Students Think? 19
   Climbing the Teaching Hierarchy 19
      Teaching Fundamentals 101 20
      Sincere Teaching 21
      Scholarly Teaching 23
   Revisiting Your Self-Assessment: Are You Becoming a
      Great Teacher? 24
   Case Study Reexamined: Those Who Can Teach, Teach
      (No Training Required?) 25
   Summary of Best Practices 26
   The Very Busy People Book Club: Your Top Five Must-Reads 26
   References 26

3   How Do We Train to be Model Teachers?   30

   Case Study: A Teaching Artifact 31
   Maintain Expert Knowledge in a Subject Area 32
   Acquire Knowledge About Basic Pedagogical Theory
      and Practice 35
   Maintain Current Knowledge of Pedagogical Theory
      and Practice 37
   Understand How Students Learn 39
      Understand How Students Acquire Knowledge 39
      Understand How Students Solidify Knowledge 41
   Case Study Reexamined: A Teaching Artifact 43
   A Reflection on Your Self-Assessment 44
   Summary of Best Practices 44
   The Very Busy People Book Club: Your Top Five Must-Reads 45
   References 45

4   What Instructional Methods do Model Teachers Use?   49

   Case Study: Professor Padma Amiri's Medical Anthropology
      Course 50

More Than One? Yes, Model Teachers Use Varied Instructional
Methods 51
The Go-to: Active Learning Instruction 52
Problem-based Learning Instruction 53
Interteaching: What a Novel Idea! 55
Model Teachers Use Effective Teaching Skills and Behaviors 56
*On the Importance of Teacher and Student Rapport and
Teacher Immediacy* 60
The Skill of Ethical Teaching 62
Teaching Skills to Engage Students 66
Case Study Reexamined: Professor Padma Amiri's Medical
Anthropology Course 70
A Reflection on Your Self-Assessment 70
Summary of Best Practices 71
The Very Busy People Book Club: Your Top Five Must-Reads 71
References 72

5   What Do Students Learn in Model Teachers' Courses?   78

Self-Assessment Time! 78
Case Study: Assistant Professor of Hubris 79
Key Content Components: Learning Objectives Reflecting
Discipline's Breath of Content 81
Can Content be Standardized? 81
Content Fundamentals 101 83
Key Content Components: Basic Liberal Arts Skills 87
A Focus on Diversity and Ethical Issues 90
Fostering Cultural Literacy 90
Fostering Ethical Literacy 92
Unanswered Questions in the Scholarship of Teaching
and Learning on Content 93
Case Study Reexamined: Assistant Professor of Hubris 94
A Reflection on Your Self-Assessment 95
Summary of Best Practices 96
The Very Busy People Book Club: Your Top
Five Must-Reads 97
References 97

6   How Do Model Teachers Assess Student Learning?   100

Assessment? Who Cares? (Everyone!) 102
Our Work is Never Done: Assessment as a Process 104

Case Study: Someone Call 911! Dr. Mead has an
    Assessment Crisis 104
Students Can't Hit the Mark Without a Target: The
    Importance of Learning Objectives 105
    *Embedded Assessment Plans: All the Fun of Assessment
        With a Fraction of the Work!* 113
Case Study Reexamined: Someone Call 911! Dr. Mead
    has an Assessment Crisis 115
Making the Grade: Evaluation of Student Learning 116
Case Study: The Grade Grubbers 117
    *Evaluation Directness: The Way to Avoid Making Student
        Enemies* 117
    *Evaluation Utility: The Way to Make Lots of
        Student Friends* 119
    Rubrics: Teachers' (and Students') Little Helper 120
    *Feedback Early and Often: Formative Assessment
        Techniques* 125
Case Study Reexamined: The Grade Grubbers 126
Scholarship of Teaching and Learning 127
Case Study: The Tenure Surprise 128
Case Study Reexamined: The Tenure Surprise 132
A Reflection on Your Self-Assessment 133
Summary of Best Practices 133
The Very Busy People Book Club: Your Top Five Must-Reads 134
References 134

7   How Do Model Teachers Construct Syllabi?   138

Case Study: An Offer She Can't Refuse 138
Self-Assessment Time! 139
The Purpose, Elements, Evidence, and Examples of a
    Model Syllabus 140
    The Model Syllabus is a Contract 140
    The Model Syllabus is a Permanent Record 142
    The Model Syllabus is a Communication Device 145
    *The Model Syllabus is a Cognitive Map and
        Learning Tool* 150
The Model Syllabus Requires Planning 153
How Do You Get Your Students to Read and Retain
    the Syllabus? 155
Case Study Reexamined: An Offer She Can't Refuse 157
A Reflection on Your Self-Assessment 158

Summary of Best Practices 158
The Very Busy People Book Club: Your Top Five
    Must–Reads 159
References 159

8   How Do Model Teachers Use Student Evaluations?   162

Case Study: Garbage In, Garbage Out? 164
Zombies and Critiques of Student Evaluation Validity:
    Things that Won't Die 165
Asking for the Truth: Collecting Student Evaluations 167
    This is the End: Summative Student Evaluations 168
    We've Only Just Begun: Formative Student Evaluations 169
    Yes, We are Seriously Going to Talk About RateMyProfessors.com 173
Interpreting Student Evaluation Scores: More than
    Reading Tea Leaves 174
Interpreting Written Comments on Student Evaluation of
    Teaching: Now With 50 Percent Less Crying! 179
Making Improvements Based on Student Feedback 182
    *Steps in an Evidence-Based Model for Using Student
        Evaluations to Improve Teaching* 184
Case Study Reexamined: Garbage In, Garbage Out? 186
A Reflection on Your Self-Assessment 187
Summary of Best Practices 187
The Very Busy People Book Club: Your Top Five Must–Reads 189
References 189

Epilogue   193
Avoid Teacherly Regret: One Last Self-Assessment 193
What is Stopping You? 194
Appendix: The Model Teaching Criteria Scale   196
References 198
Author Index   200
Subject Index   207

PREFACE

What makes a good college teacher? Are you one? Do you know one? These might seem like questions that are impossible to answer objectively, but imagine if there was a clear, researched, and accepted definition of good teaching. That is the purpose of this book. Specifically, we present a set of "model teaching characteristics" that offer evidence-based answers to the question of what makes a good college teacher. The purpose of the model characteristics, and therefore of this book, is to guide, inspire, and reward teachers.

Defining Model Teaching

College faculty at all types of institutions know that good teaching is important, but useful definitions of good teaching are hard to find. Many institutions emphasize student evaluations of teaching as the be-all and end-all measure of teaching quality, and pay scant, if any, attention to the many other indicators of good teaching. Guidelines for tenure and promotion can provide some guidance on what constitutes good teaching, but such documents are often vague; furthermore, they offer no suggestions for how to improve if the standards are not being met. Colleagues, mentors, and supervisors such as department chairs will provide suggestions on how to be a better teacher; their advice is invaluable but incomplete. There are a number of books providing teaching "tips" or arming one with "tools" for teaching, but these tips and tools do not constitute a definition of good teaching. As these examples illustrate, the guidance offered to teachers on pedagogical practices is unfortunately haphazard. However, this book will provide precise, multifaceted, evidence-based guidance on good teaching. In one slim volume, we will provide explicit indicators of model teaching that can guide both novice and experienced teachers in their professional development.

A critical issue for teachers trying to develop their pedagogical skills is the difficulty in evaluating their current skill level. How do you really know if you are a good teacher? Without clear standards, some teachers will be left unskilled and unaware; others will be left skilled but unaware of how they can develop even further. Thus, teachers at all levels of skill and experience can benefit from clear, objective guidelines for defining and measuring quality teaching. To fulfill this need, the Society for the Teaching of Psychology (STP) recently outlined six fundamental areas of teaching competency—model teaching characteristics—and provided detailed definitions of each characteristic. This book describes how college faculty from all disciplines and at all levels of their career can use the model characteristics to evaluate, guide, and improve their teaching.

For each model characteristic we document research supporting the inclusion of the characteristic and suggest evidence that can be used to document the characteristic for tenure, promotion, teaching portfolios, or general professional development. The characteristics and suggestions for evidence offer teachers a method by which they can self-assess their practices against the highest standards of the profession. When teachers find gaps between what they do and the model characteristics, they can engage in professional development by exploring the educational materials found in the supporting references. The criteria for model teaching reflect a multifaceted approach that most clearly differentiates this book from previous efforts to evaluate the quality of teachers. As will be outlined in this book, model teaching is more than just classroom techniques. It is more than the training and preparation. It is more than student evaluations and outcomes. In fact, model teaching is all of these things and more.

Structure of the Book

The book begins with two introductory chapters outlining our argument for the importance of defining model teaching. The next six chapters are each devoted to one of the model teaching characteristics. Specifically, we outline training (Chapter 3), instructional methods (Chapter 4), course content (Chapter 5), the assessment process (Chapter 6), syllabus construction (Chapter 7), and use of student evaluations (Chapter 8). Each chapter has a number of resources to help teachers understand and use the content. One resource is the self-evaluation survey that begins each chapter—teachers can use it to preview the chapter's content and focus on gaps between the model characteristics and their own teaching. Also, case studies throughout the chapters provide examples of teachers facing common problems; we use discussion questions to ask readers about how they would solve the problems and offer our own answers. In addition to the hundreds of references we offer to support our assertions about evidence-based teaching practices, each chapter contains a list of "must-reads," so that busy teachers can focus on the essential sources and continue their understanding of these important model teaching characteristics. Finally, the book is full of examples and illustrations from our own teaching and from disciplines across the academe.

Yes, This Book is for You

Perhaps the most important purpose of the model teaching characteristics is to prompt reflection about teaching strengths and weaknesses, and this applies to teachers at all levels of experience. From a developmental perspective, the characteristics will be a useful educational resource to novice teachers. College teaching courses are available in many doctoral programs and the model characteristics could inform the curriculum of these courses. Although many graduate programs offer teaching courses, access to systematic teacher training in psychology graduate programs is not universal. Furthermore, part-time instructors, graduate students or otherwise, are sometimes thrust into courses with little warning or chance for preparation. For these underprepared novice teachers, the characteristics described in this book can provide not only a basic list of suggestions about quality teaching but also an extensive bibliography of teaching literature on which they can base a self-guided course on college teaching.

More advanced teachers can also benefit from model teaching characteristics. Once individuals have decided to include teaching as part of their regular career responsibilities, they are likely to face expectations to document their teaching abilities. The characteristics offer guidance on the specific characteristics to be documented, the evidence that needs to be accumulated, and a method for organizing evidence. Such explicit guidelines are likely to be especially valuable to pre-tenure faculty. Among well-established teachers who have achieved tenure, the model characteristics can still motivate meaningful reflection. Faculty members have divergent strengths and interests. As such, it will be the rare teacher who meets the highest standards of all of the model characteristics, and the identification of relative weaknesses provides even the most experienced teachers with an opportunity for change and growth. Furthermore, as times change, so do educational practices and knowledge about pedagogy; self-evaluation using the model characteristics is a way to keep fresh and relevant as a teacher.

ACKNOWLEDGMENTS

We are grateful to the many students and colleagues who inspired us to write this book. In particular, we want to acknowledge the members of task forces that helped gather the material for an early version of the characteristics. These include Steve Meyers, Mark Sciutto, Vincent Prohaska, Marie Thomas, Yvette Tazeau, Erin Paavola, and Tara Kuther. We would also like to thank the reviewers who provided valuable input on the initial book plan: Gaynell Green, Texas A&M University—Texarkana, USA; Bibhuti K. Sar, University of Louisville, USA; and two anonymous reviewers. Debra Riegert at Routledge/Taylor & Francis was an enthusiastic supporter of the concept and we are grateful for her support. Writing this book was a blast thanks to co-writers who were passionate, efficient, hardworking, and often humorous—we are glad to have worked on this together.

ABOUT THE AUTHORS

Aaron S. Richmond is a Professor of Human Development and Educational Psychology at Metropolitan State University of Denver. He completed his Master's degree in applied psychology from Montana State University in 2002, and in 2006, received a doctorate in educational psychology with an emphasis on human growth and development from the University of Nevada-Reno.

With more than a decade of professional teaching experience, Dr. Richmond has garnered several awards for excellence in teaching, and his pedagogy focuses on student-centered active learning and engagement with a specific interest in building higher-level thinking skills that students can apply in other classes. He has dedicated his academic career to studying the improvement of classroom practices and learning, and his research explores effective pedagogical approaches to instruction; investigates cognitive and elaborative processes in elementary, secondary, and higher education; and general interest in the scholarship of teaching and learning.

Dr. Richmond is a member of several professional associations and serves as Vice President of Programming for the Society of the Teaching of Psychology and is past-president of the Northern Rocky Mountain Educational Research Association. He currently holds several positions on editorial boards including *Teaching of Psychology*, *The Researcher*, the *Journal of Experimental Education*, and the *International Journal of Technology in Teaching and Learning*. Dr. Richmond has given dozens of invited talks and research presentations throughout the country at annual professional association meetings and conferences.

Guy A. Boysen is an Associate Professor of Psychology at McKendree University. He received his Bachelor's degree from St. John's University in Collegeville, MN, and his PhD from Iowa State University in Ames, IA. Dr. Boysen's pedagogical training has included three courses on college teaching, achievement of Scholar level in Preparing Future Faculty, and numerous training seminars on specific pedagogical approaches.

Dr. Boysen's teaching specialization is clinical and counseling psychology, but he also enjoys courses that cut across the discipline of psychology such as history of psychology and the unconscious. Dr. Boysen's primary areas of research include mental illness stigma, dissociative identity disorder, and the scholarship of teaching and learning. Assessment is another of Dr. Boysen's interests, which is reflected in both his scholarship and in his numerous roles on college assessment committees. Dr. Boysen has been the author of dozens of peer-reviewed research articles and the sponsor of dozens of undergraduate research presentations at professional and undergraduate research conferences, which is a reflection of his dedication to the infusion of teaching and research.

Dr. Boysen has served as a consulting editor and frequent reviewer for the journal *Teaching of Psychology*. He is an active member of the Society for the Teaching of Psychology. His professional service has included membership on several committees and taskforces related to the improvement of teaching in the field of psychology.

Regan A. R. Gurung is Ben J. and Joyce Rosenberg Professor of Human Development and Psychology at the University of Wisconsin, Green Bay. Dr. Gurung received a BA in psychology at Carleton College (MN), and a Masters and PhD in social and personality psychology at the University of Washington (WA). He then spent three years at UCLA as a National Institute of Mental Health (NIMH) Research fellow.

He has received numerous local, state, and national grants and has published more than 100 articles and book chapters. He has a textbook, *Health Psychology: A Cultural Approach*, relating culture, development, and health published with Cengage (now in its third edition) and is also the co-author/co-editor of 12 other books. He has made more than 100 presentations and given workshops nationally and internationally (e.g., Australia, India, Saudi Arabia, New Zealand).

Dr. Gurung is also a dedicated teacher and has strong interests in enhancing faculty development and student understanding. He was co-director of the University of Wisconsin System Teaching Scholars Program, has been a UWGB teaching fellow, a UW System Teaching Scholar, and is winner of the CASE Wisconsin Professor of the Year, the UW System Regents Teaching Award, the UW-Green Bay Founder's Award for Excellence in Teaching as well as the Founder's Award for Scholarship, UW Teaching-at-its-Best, Creative Teaching, and Featured Faculty Awards. He has strong interests in teaching and pedagogy and has organized statewide and national teaching conferences, is a fellow of the American Psychological Association, the Association for Psychological Science, and the Midwestern Psychological Association, and has served as president of the Society for the Teaching of Psychology. He is the newly appointed founding editor of APA's journal *SoTL in Psychology*.

1

WHY DO WE NEED MODEL TEACHERS?

Consider this all-too-familiar story about teaching. Guy was a second-year graduate student in a counseling psychology program with a secret he had been told to keep close to the vest during his doctoral studies: He wanted to be a teacher. Apparently his secret was not that well-kept, because word had gotten out that he was interested in teaching a course. That was all it took. His interest in teaching led to an offer to replace the regular instructor of Learning and Memory. He had not taken graduate work in either of those areas. He had not taken a course on teaching. He had not been trained in pedagogy or assessment or even how to properly construct a syllabus. He had less than 30 days to prep the course.

Why does the story of an underprepared college teacher ring so true? The hard answer is that lack of teacher preparation and development is endemic to colleges and universities. Although pedagogical training is more common than it once was, expertise in a subject area is generally the one prerequisite needed for someone to be given control over a college or university classroom. Frankly, enthusiasm and basic competence may be sufficient in many cases. The great Greek orators of old, the ancient teachers in Indian *Gurukuls* (schools), the Chinese sages bestowing knowledge: all of these teachers focused on their students with passion and dedication but had no formalized training in pedagogy. These teachers did what their own teachers did before them. In the history of modern education, the vast majority of college courses ever offered have been taught by instructors with little formal teacher training (Gurung and Schwartz, 2009). This is not a problem for the history books, however; courses on college teaching are far from universal across the disciplines, and the workaday experience of "covering courses" in many departments illustrates that sometimes the most qualified warm body becomes instructor of record regardless of that person's training as an educator.

All three of us were just such warm bodies early in our careers when different opportunities arose. We leapt at the opportunity. Guy's preparation after learning he would be teaching the Learning and Memory course should also ring true with many readers. He read the textbook and mimicked what he thought were the best techniques of his previous teachers. Learning objectives, pedagogical strategies, outcomes assessment, alignment of evaluation and objectives, syllabus transparency—these are just some of the issues that did not enter his mind when preparing the course. How did it all turn out? As cringeworthy as the course seems in retrospect, his teaching evaluations were fine, and he taught many more classes for the department. Regan and Aaron have similar stories from their early teaching days. Our friends and colleagues in different disciplines suggest that things are similar across the board, and lack of teacher preparation has been a topic of discussion in higher education for decades (Bok, 1991; Boysen, 2011; Weimer, 2010).

The "success" we had in our very first courses illustrates another problem. If higher education lacks basic standards for becoming a teacher, how can we evaluate whether or not a teacher is minimally competent? The status quo for determining competency is subjective analysis of student teaching evaluations, which tend to be as inflated as student grades (Sears, 1983). Our first teaching gigs represented a far-from-sophisticated approach to course design, but it is likely that we would still have teaching jobs today had we chosen to approach every subsequent course in the same way. To summarize, the pedagogical requirements needed to obtain a college or university teaching position are fairly low, and keeping that position is largely determined through unsystematic analysis of student satisfaction surveys—it is amazing we have been able to maintain this as the status quo in a respected and important profession.

What is Model Teaching?

Consider an alternative to underprepared teachers and insubstantial evaluations of performance. What if there was a set of agreed-upon characteristics that defined model teaching? In the case of new teachers, such a definition would provide guidance on their minimum qualifications. For established teachers, such a definition would provide a rich means of evaluation. Perhaps most important, for both new and established teachers it could provide much-needed direction in what should be a continual process of professional development. Higher education needs clear guidelines on what it means to be a competent teacher—we need a definition of model teaching.

Our goal in this book is to provide a detailed outline of the criteria that define model teaching and a guide to the development of those criteria. What do we mean by "model teaching"? Models serve as idealized examples to be emulated. In the current context, we use the term "model" in reference to teaching practices generally accepted as ideal in higher education. We believe that teaching practices are ideal if they can be scientifically shown to increase desirable student outcomes such as learning or if they are otherwise considered foundational best practices in higher education. In terms of what counts as teaching, we conceptualize it broadly. Teaching includes activities that occur inside and outside of the classroom; specifically, it includes preparation to teach, instruction in the classroom, and evaluation of learning and teaching effectiveness. As with any definition, there may be disagreement about the particulars of what is and is not included, and we are certain that our definition will evolve with the accumulation of pedagogical knowledge. Nonetheless, we are also certain that individuals who meet all of the criteria outlined in our definition would be difficult to describe as anything other than model teachers.

The Need for Another Definition of Teaching Excellence

This book is far from the first effort to outline effective teaching practices or define what it means to be a good teacher. There are many high-quality sources of information about best teaching practices, but they are too piecemeal to be useful as standards for model teaching. Take the example of the Teacher Behavior Checklist (Keeley et al., 2006). The TBC lists 28 ideal teacher behaviors and requires students to rate how frequently their instructor exhibits each behavior. Some items ask students to rate how frequently their teacher "speaks clearly," "dresses nicely," and "makes the class laugh through jokes and funny stories." Great teaching is copiously represented on the TBC, but it is ultimately hampered by its reliance on the limited perspective of students (more on the TBC in Chapters 2, 4, and 8). Model teaching includes behaviors not visible from a classroom desk.

There have been efforts to expand upon the limited perspective offered by student evaluations. For example, Bernstein and colleagues (2010) described the ideal teacher as conforming to a scientist-educator model. Scientist-educators do not simply disseminate information. They intentionally design courses based on known principles of learning and examine student performance systematically to assess and improve learning. In a more far-reaching effort to define the quality as a whole, Chickering and Gamson (1987) famously set forth "seven principles for good practice in undergraduate education." According to their principles, good teachers do things such as set high expectations, frequently interact with students, and respect diversity. From a completely different angle, Bain (2004) interviewed students and award-winning teachers in order to synthesize the elements of excellent teaching. He outlined many attributes shared by the best teachers, such as organization and caring for students.

Each of these definitions of teaching excellence is purposefully narrow; their creators have intentionally left out fundamental aspects of teaching. Thus, model teaching reflects not just one of these definitions, but all of them. Is a model teacher someone with a high score on the TBC who engages in teaching as a scientist-educator and complies with the principles of quality? We are not going to argue that there is a simple mathematical formula such as A + B + C = model teaching, but the idea of integrating various components of quality in one model is precisely the direction we are heading in.

Teachers cannot be expected to piece together the entire pedagogical literature on their own. The novice teacher has to focus on course preparation. Experienced teachers may have knowledge of the pedagogical literature, but relatively few of them will have the comprehensive knowledge possessed by faculty who specialize in the scholarship of teaching and learning. Other teachers, having received no pedagogical training, may be completely unaware of the extensive literature that could be informing their teaching. Lack of time, expertise, and awareness are just some of the reasons why teachers are unlikely to construct complete knowledge of model teaching on their own. What is needed is one comprehensive guide to basic teaching competencies that spans from initial training, to course planning, to teaching techniques, and finally to evaluation of outcomes. Such a resource now exists.

Development of the Model Teaching Criteria

Our story starts in the discipline of psychology. For the first time, psychologists have a comprehensive definition of model teaching. A Society for the Teaching of Psychology Presidential Taskforce was charged to develop a list of basic characteristics possessed by model teachers (Richmond et al., 2014). The Taskforce worked for two years to reach consensus and integrated the literature on basic pedagogy, higher education, curricular design, and scholarship of teaching. What emerged was a list of six general criteria that break down into 19 more specific sub-criteria (see Table 1.1) and a self-assessment tool to measure these characteristics (Richmond et al., 2014). The model was reviewed by the American Psychological Association's Board of Educational Affairs and the Society for Teaching of Psychology, and endorsed in 2014.

Following early formulation of the model criteria, we (Aaron, Guy, and Regan), modified and expanded the self-assessment tool and conducted research to explore its validity (Boysen et al., 2015). We asked a nonrandom sample of 208 psychology teachers from colleges across the United States to report their ability to document the practices represented in the characteristics. Teachers, on average, reported meeting the model's six general criteria 77 percent of the time. Teachers reported meeting characteristics related to syllabus construction most frequently (91 percent) and the instructional methods characteristics least frequently (69 percent). The characteristics shared positive correlations among themselves even when controlling for separate measures of teaching quality and personality. We talk more of these findings in later chapters, but the point for the time being is that the high percentage of teachers engaged in these practices strongly suggests that they are truly fundamental to college teaching (Boysen et al., 2015).

Although our story begins in psychology, there is reason to believe that what we learned generalizes across disciplines. To begin, the three of us have rolled out this framework for model teaching to numerous faculty workshops across the disciplines—Aaron playfully refers to it as *America's Next Top Model* (perhaps revealing too much about his TV-watching habits). We used the feedback from teachers from different disciplines to fine tune and refine the characteristics. It is important to note that this is not a how-to book that outlines specific teaching techniques that might apply to one discipline and not another. Rather, we describe the general characteristics shared by model teachers and leave it up to the readers to determine how those practices best fit into their classrooms. For example, we will advocate for the use of active learning as a model practice, but we do not dictate how active learning should occur in an English seminar versus a chemistry lab. How did we even reach a conclusion that active learning should be advocated for all teachers? The basic principles of human learning are universal, and the model criteria are largely based on practices known to increase learning for people in general, not just for people studying one subject. Better learning outcomes is a goal all teachers should be able to support. Another source of model criteria were well-established best practices in higher education. Some practices—engagement in the assessment process, for example—are so fundamental in higher education as to be inescapable; they are, therefore, applicable to all teachers. Finally, it is important to acknowledge that teachers from different disciplines have more that unites them than is commonly acknowledged—we share students, we share a commitment to fundamental educational goals such as increasing knowledge and analytical skills, and we share common means of evaluating our performance such as student satisfaction and learning. Given all of this, we believe that the Model Teaching Criteria will be useful to teachers across the academy.

In addition to being useful across disciplines, we believe that the model characteristics can offer guidance to everyone from novice teaching assistants to experienced professors who are seeking to become better teachers. Is simple exposure to a list of teaching characteristics enough to improve teaching? We think it is a good start, but additional guidance is needed. Teachers need an in-depth explanation of the Model Teaching Criteria, and they need suggestions for how to pursue their professional development related to each criterion—this is exactly the type of guidance we offer in this book.

An Overview of the Book and the Model Teaching Criteria

This book is organized around six model teaching criteria (see Table 1.1). After a brief discussion in Chapter 2 of the many approaches to defining teaching greatness, we devote each subsequent chapter to detailed discussions of one model criterion and the specific teaching practices that make up its sub-criteria.

Each chapter will provide similar tools to help readers learn and develop model practices. Readers begin by using a survey to self-assess their current consistency with model teaching practices. Then the bulk of each chapter is devoted to defining the model practices, summarizing research on the model practices, and presenting practical examples of the model practices in action. To illustrate the major points of each chapter, we include case studies and examples, as well as discussion of how they relate to the model criteria. Finally, each chapter ends with summary points and our top-five list of must-reads related to the chapter's topics.

There are six areas of teaching represented in the model criteria: training, instructional methods, course content, assessment process, syllabus construction, and student evaluations. What follows are brief introductions to each criterion and its corresponding chapter. If these descriptions spark your interest, feel free to jump to the relevant chapter for the full description of criterion and the research that supports its inclusion as a model practice.

Chapter 3: How Do We Train to be Model Teachers?

Model teachers are well-trained and up-to-date in their knowledge and methods. Both discipline-specific and general training are essential because teaching excellence is built on a foundation of content knowledge and general expertise in pedagogy. In addition, the ever-changing nature of higher education and technology requires an ongoing commitment to learning about the craft of teaching. In this chapter, we discuss how model teachers maintain expert knowledge in a subject area, acquire knowledge about basic pedagogical theory and practice, and maintain current knowledge of pedagogical theory and practice.

Chapter 4: What Instructional Methods do Model Teachers Use?

Masterful classroom teaching is elusive. Two individuals may teach the same material using the same method but have widely varying success. Alternatively, two teachers might be equally successful covering the same material using different methods. As such, model teaching does not require the use of one specific teaching method. However, excellent classroom teaching shares some common features no matter what method is being used. The features can be divided into broad pedagogical approaches and specific teaching skills. This chapter explains how model teachers demonstrate effective use of various teaching methods (e.g., collaborative learning, interteaching) and demonstrate excellence in specific teaching skills (e.g., listening, use of technology, rapport, preparedness, etc.).

TABLE 1.1 Model Teaching Criteria Definitions

Criterion	Definition
Training	**Model teachers:**
Subject knowledge	• Develop and maintain expertise in their chosen content area.
Pedagogical knowledge	• Possess knowledge of basic pedagogical and learning theory.
Continuing education in pedagogical knowledge	• Continually develop their teaching practices by maintaining current knowledge about effective pedagogical practices.
Instructional methods	**Model teachers:**
Pedagogy	• Use varied instructional strategies (e.g., active learning, interteaching, collaborative learning).
Teaching skills	• Use effective teaching skills (e.g., student rapport, effective communication, technology, preparation).
Content	**Model teachers:**
Disciplinary literacy	• Cover the main habits of mind of the discipline, and share how the discipline creates knowledge.
Knowledge base and application	• Share core and foundational content, and develop students' skills that relate to the discipline.
Liberal arts skills	• Foster the development of general skills such as information literacy, communication skills, and critical thinking.
Values	• Build students' appreciation for values characteristic of strong citizenship such as respect for ethics and diversity.
Assessment processes	**Model teachers:**
Student learning goals and objectives	• Set learning objectives that are clear and measurable before facilitating learning.
Assessment of student learning outcomes	• Collect evidence of student achievement of learning objectives.
Reflection on assessment	• Use the results of assessment to make changes that improve teaching and learning.
Evaluation directness, evaluation utility	• Align their evaluations of student learning (e.g., tests, assignments) with learning objectives and give students prompt and useful feedback on their success at meeting learning objectives.
Scholarship of teaching and learning	• Share the results of what they have learned from the assessment process with peers in order to advance pedagogical knowledge.
Constructing syllabi	**Model teachers:**
Syllabus is a contract	• Incorporate contract elements (e.g., detailed calendar, explicit grading, attendance, revision or redoing policies, etc.) in their syllabi.
Permanent record elements	• Include learning objectives, evaluation procedures, and course content in their syllabi.

(continued)

TABLE 1.1 (*cont.*)

Criterion	Definition
Effective communication device	• Treat the syllabus as a way to communicate with their students by including contact information, behavioral expectations for the student and teacher, and a teaching philosophy.
Syllabus is a cognitive map and learning tool	• Treat the syllabus as a tool to help students learn by including elements such as tips for success, common mistakes, and information about student support services.
Course planning	• Carefully plan the content, layout, and organization of syllabi.
Student evaluations of teaching	***Model teachers:***
Student feedback	• Solicit feedback from students formatively during the semester and summative at the conclusion of the semester.
Reflection on student feedback	• Interpret feedback from students systematically in order to make changes to course design and teaching style.

Note: Information in this table is modified from Richmond et al. (2014) and Boysen et al. (2015).

Chapter 5: What Do Students Learn in Model Teachers' Courses?

Disciplines vary substantially in content and instructors bring a wide variety of backgrounds, perspectives, and prior knowledge to the classroom. As such, the specific content of individual courses varies widely. Nonetheless, there is some consistency in the learning goals set by model teachers of all backgrounds and teaching specialties. In this chapter, we discuss how model teachers establish learning objectives reflecting the agreed-upon core of their discipline. Furthermore, model teachers recognize that some learning goals are so fundamental as to cut across all courses; thus, they foster student development of basic liberal arts skills and infuse ethical and diversity issues throughout their teaching.

Chapter 6: How Do Model Teachers Assess Student Learning?

A sign of quality in higher education is systematic and intentional assessment of student learning at the college and program level. Engagement in the assessment process at the classroom level is also considered an essential part of good teaching. Throughout this chapter, we discuss model teachers' engagement in assessment, including creation of learning objectives, assessment of learning outcomes, and use of assessment outcomes to improve teaching and learning. Teachers who organize their courses according to this basic assessment process are also able to evaluate student performance based on their achievement of specific learning goals and give them prompt, meaningful feedback; we also discuss these model practices in the evaluation of students. An evidence-based approach to teaching lends itself to public dissemination of lessons learned from assessment outcomes and other teaching-related research; thus, we also outline model teaching practices related to the scholarship of teaching and learning.

Chapter 7: How Do Model Teachers Construct Syllabi?

A syllabus represents the teacher who created it. Students understand this relation between syllabus and teacher, and they make judgments about teachers based on syllabi characteristics. Model syllabi establish a set of abilities that students will have the opportunity to develop, they explain to students the process by which they can develop the abilities, and they establish the benchmarks by which the teacher and student will evaluate progress as it relates to the abilities. We will discuss how model teachers create complete, clear, and well-thought-out syllabi; the chapter also outlines ways to increase the number of students who actually read and use syllabi.

Chapter 8: How Do Model Teachers Use Student Evaluations?

Student evaluations of teaching are a contentious subject in higher education. Although there is some disagreement about their appropriate interpretation and use, student evaluations are the most common and well-validated measures of teaching effectiveness. Recognizing this, model teachers solicit and utilize feedback from their students. We will explain how model teachers collect formative and summative student feedback on teaching and how they utilize this information to improve teaching and learning.

Parting Thoughts

Are great teachers born, or are they made? As is so often the case for thought-provoking questions such as this—and much to the frustration of students everywhere—the answer is likely "both!" Certainly there are teachers who know nothing of pedagogy but are nonetheless masterful in their ability to motivate students and facilitate learning. Natural geniuses exist. Few will ever write like Fitzgerald, blow like Coltrane, or theorize like Darwin; but that does not mean the rest of us should not strive to be better writers, musicians, or scientists. Likewise, all of us mere mortals can study the craft of teaching in order to hone the best methods at our disposal and build on less-than-perfect talents.

We will end this chapter with some good news and some bad news. The bad news is that teaching is an incredibly complicated profession that requires a number of wide-varying competencies, and there is no one thing that you can do to instantly transform your teaching. The good news is that a great deal of knowledge has accumulated about those wide-varying competencies, and this book summarizes that knowledge in a way that will help you along the path to being a model teacher. In the pages ahead we take responsibility for introducing you to the concept of model teaching. The rest is up to you!

References

Bain, K. (2004). *What the best college teachers do*. Cambridge, MA: Harvard University Press.

Bernstein, D., Addison, W. E., Altman, C., Hollister, D., Komarraju, M., Prieto, L., and Shore, C. (2010). Toward a scientist-educator model of teaching psychology. In D. F. Halpern (ed.), *Undergraduate education in psychology: A blueprint for the future of the discipline* (pp. 29–45). Washington, DC: American Psychological Association.

Bok, D. (1991). The improvement of teaching. *Teachers College Record*, 93, 236–251.

Boysen, G. A. (2011). The prevalence and predictors of teaching courses in doctoral psychology programs. *Teaching of Psychology*, 38, 49–52.

Boysen, G. A., Richmond, A. S., and Gurung, R. A. R. (2015). Model Teaching Criteria for psychology: Initial documentation of teachers' self-reported competency. *Scholarship of Teaching and Learning in Psychology*, 1, 48–59.

Chickering, A. W. and Gamson, Z. F. (1987). Seven principles for good practice in undergraduate education. *AAHE Bulletin*, 39, 3–7.

Gurung, R. A. R. and Schwartz, B. M. (2009). *Optimizing teaching and learning: Practicing pedagogical research*. Oxford: John Wiley & Sons.

Keeley, J., Smith, D., and Buskist, W. (2006). The Teacher Behavior Checklist: Factor analysis of its utility for evaluating teaching. *Teaching of Psychology*, 33, 84–91.

Richmond, A. S., Boysen, G. A., Gurung, R. A. R., Tazeau, Y. N., Meyers, S. A., and Sciutto, M. J. (2014). Aspirational Model Teaching Criteria for psychology. *Teaching of Psychology*, 41, 281–295.

Sears, D. O. (1983). The person-positivity bias. *Journal of Personality and Social Psychology*, 44, 233–250.

Weimer, M. (2010). *Inspired college teaching: A career-long resource for professional growth*. San Francisco, CA: Jossey-Bass.

2

WHAT IS GREAT TEACHING?

Is great teaching identified by outstanding student course evaluations? Will a high rating on RateMyProfessor.com (and a chili pepper for good measure) signify good teaching? Or is it that your students are challenged and learn? Is being a great teacher innate or a set of behaviors and characteristics that can be learned? There are many ways to define great teaching and this chapter provides a broad overview of them to set the stage for our discussion of Model Teaching Criteria. Whereas both course evaluations and online teacher rating sites are correlated with other measures of good teaching (Martin et al., 2008) what really makes a great teacher?

Novice and expert teachers alike have many resources to turn to when they want to improve their teaching. One can be inspired by sage advice and inspirational stories from passionate educators such as Parker Palmer, pick up tips and tools from well-known books (Brookfield, 2006; Davis, 2009; Roth, 1997; Svinicki and McKeachie, 2013; Weimer, 2010), or peruse disciplinary teaching journals (e.g., *Teaching of Psychology, Teaching Artist Journal, The Writing Instructor, American Biology Teacher*, etc.). A large research literature exists surrounding the effectiveness of specific teaching techniques, and it can inform decisions such as whether to use cumulative exams and whether classroom response systems help learning. There are also a number of books describing what the best or master teachers do. Our Model Teaching Criteria (MTC) provide an evidence-based, multidimensional answer to this question. While incorporating many of the answers to this question, it stands on the shoulders of years of research aiming to unpack good teaching. In this chapter we review the many different extant answers to this basic question of what makes great teaching and the related though distinct question of what makes a great teacher. We first discuss common approaches to examining these questions

TABLE 2.1 Self-Assessment of What Constitutes Good Teaching

Take a moment and jot down your answer to the following questions:

1. What makes a good teacher?
2. What are characteristics of the best teachers you have had?
3. What are characteristics of the worst teachers you have had?

and review some characteristics attained to date. We then describe a teaching hierarchy, focusing on the pinnacle in our view, the scholarship of teaching and learning (SoTL).

Before we fully unpack the different forms of training, as practitioners of science, we need to establish a baseline measurement of your training activities to date, so please take a moment and complete the self-assessment in Table 2.1.

CASE STUDY: THOSE WHO CAN TEACH, TEACH (NO TRAINING REQUIRED?)

Now that you have assessed your training activities to date, let's take a look at an example of a prototypical junior faculty member. Consider this case study:

Sarah and Samantha were great friends. Both women wanted to be teachers. Sarah always knew she wanted to teach kids. From her first day of college she set her sights on the education program and worked towards her teaching certification. She even knew where she wanted to do her student teaching. Samantha also wanted to teach, but she wanted to be a college professor. She sat in her psychology classes and knew that she wanted to be just like her teachers who she found so inspiring and motivating. But how exactly would she do that? When Sarah and Samantha talked about their career challenges, they noticed that only one of them had a clear path to teaching excellence. Whereas Sarah's accredited education program made it really clear what she had to do to be a good teacher, all Samantha knew about college teachers was that they had to have advanced degrees. The professors she talked to did not have much more insight than Samantha. The only step ever mentioned on the road to being a good college teacher was "getting your doctorate." Her academic advisor quickly let her know that good teaching in college was hard to define. He even went so far to say that good teaching did not really matter that much because being a professor was mostly about doing research. Samantha concluded that as long as she knew her material well and was enthusiastic and caring, she would eventually become just as good as the professors who inspired her.

Take a moment to answer these questions. We will revisit your answer at the end of the chapter. And yes, you may change your answers after reading the chapter.

1. How clearly does Samantha understand the training needed to be a good college teacher?
2. What would you tell Samantha to do?
3. How do you compare K-12 teaching to college teaching?

Setting Your Target: Look to Winners

You may look at the title of this chapter and exclaim, "Great? Who wants to be *just* great? I want to be the very best!" We understand. Not surprisingly, the majority of published books on the topic of college teaching head straight for the top. Why not aim to be the very best? Perhaps you would rather the moniker "Master Teacher" to our more modest "Model Teacher"? Or perhaps you would settle for just being considered "inspiring." These are all labels you will find in the literature on quality teaching. A short trip through some of the findings from the diverse literature on teaching is well worth the time.

Professors of the Year Are Good Exemplars

If you want to know what good teaching is, where's an easy place to look? At recipients of major teaching awards of course. After all, award committees field a large number of nominees, go through some sort of rigorous sifting and winnowing of the candidates, and then proclaim a winner. Many scholars have focused on award-winning teachers to investigate what makes great teaching. One of the most prestigious teaching awards in the United States is the Council for Advancement and Support of Education (CASE)'s Professor of the Year program. Supported by the Carnegie Foundation for the Advancement of Teaching, college and university faculty have a shot at winning one of four Professor of the Year awards at the national level, or a state-level award (one of us was State Professor of the Year a few years ago). The process is involving. Each college can nominate one faculty member. Candidates then complete a lengthy application (teaching statement, testimonies from past students, and more), and a Carnegie-selected grand jury selects winners after a multiple-stage judging process. This complex procedure yields a pool of candidates who provide us with a good place to start identifying characteristics that good teachers share.

In order to tap into the insights of winners, first Beidler (1986) and then Roth (1997) edited a volume of essays written by past winners sharing their insights. The title of the latter, *Inspiring teaching*, clearly adds another goal to the list of what we as teachers can aim for, to inspire. The essays in both collections span a wide range of topics, and while they are exclusively anecdotal, they still provide food for thought. For example, one essay listed ten things good teachers do: They want to be good teachers, take risks, have a positive attitude, never have enough time, think of teaching as a form of parenting, try to give students confidence, try to keep students (and themselves) off-balance, try to motivate students by working within their incentive system, listen to their students, and treat student evaluations with suspicion (Beidler, 1997). Of course we can debate each one of these anecdotal suggestions, but most of them make good intuitive sense. In fact, subsequent chapters will show that many of them are borne out by empirical evidence.

Successful College Teachers

Sharon Baiocco and Jamie DeWaters (1998) conducted a series of studies described in their book, *Successful college teaching*. In one study, they surveyed 50 members of the American Association of University Professors and asked them what they thought characterized distinguished teaching. They also surveyed 30 local, state, and national award-winning faculty. Based on the surveys and a review of the literature, they identified many major traits consistently cited in classical philosophy, education, and psychology. Successful teachers were enthusiastic, sociable/friendly, organized, conscientious, and optimistic. Other factors on this list included: loving the subject, rigorous, having the ability to inspire, available and generous with their time, skilled in active-learning techniques, knowledgeable, and valuing student ideas (Baiocco and DeWaters, 1998). These characteristics pop up frequently in research on excellent teaching (Centra, 1979; Cronin, 1992; Jarvis, 1991; Keeley et al., 2006; Lowman, 1995; Weimer, 1993), including our own model laid forth in this book.

Master Teachers

Bill Buskist carried out one of the most rigorous recent studies of teaching excellence (Buskist and Keeley, 2015). He also adds another term to our goal setting lexicon: *master teacher*. Buskist wanted to discover the key elements that underlie master teaching. So he embarked on a long journey. He searched the literature. He scoured the countryside talking to master teachers. His search revealed many lists of qualities of excellent teachers but did not reveal any specific or learnable behaviors. Look at the list in Table 2.2. Can you teach someone to be enthusiastic? He decided to flex his psychological research skills and create a new way to measure mastery. Buskist first asked 114 students at Auburn University to describe their best teachers. He defined best as the "most effective," teachers from whom the students learned much and enjoyed the process of learning. This resulted in 47 categories. He then asked 184 more students to take each term and add a descriptor consisting of an observable behavior. For example, the general quality of "manages class time" yielded the specific behavioral descriptor of "arrives to class on time/early."

Now we are getting somewhere. The results of the two rounds of student surveys yielded 28 behavioral categories. Buskist and his collaborators subjected the resulting scale, which they called the *Teacher Behavior Checklist* or TBC for short, to substantial validity and reliability checks, and the result was a handy tool for teachers who want to document the behaviors associated with good teaching (Keeley et al., 2006; 2012). Table 2.2 shows all items of the TBC and their corresponding behaviors.

Overall, the TBC provides some valuable information but we need more. Note that similar to other student-based evaluations, the TBC leaves out some essential aspects of teaching that happen outside of the classroom. Teachers also have to plan the course, design assessment, and participate in continued professional development. You will not be surprised to learn that students and teachers can have dramatically different perspectives on what constitutes good teaching. For example, research using the TBC illustrates that critical thinking is highly valued among teachers but generally seen as unimportant among students (Buskist et al., 2002). The *Model Teaching Criteria* on which we base this book was indeed inspired by the TBC, but the criteria provide a broader perspective on teaching by including practices that occur before, during, and after classroom instruction. Not surprisingly, a teacher's rating on TBC is associated with our Model Teaching Criteria (Boysen et al., 2015). Specifically, self-reports on both measures share statistically meaningful correlations. Such trends illustrate that definitions of good teaching, including our own, tend to converge.

What the Best Teachers Do

Around the same time Buskist was devising the TBC, another researcher was hard at work culling together various clues as to what highly effective teachers do. Using a more qualitative approach, interviews, videotapes of teachers teaching, examples of their assignments, and even a careful consideration of learning objectives, Bain's (2004) *What the best college teachers do* provides a treasure trove of information and shapes many components of our MTC. Although not a conventional empirical study on what makes exceptional teachers, Bain studied a total of 63 teachers combining the tactics of an investigative journalist with those of a narrative historian. He describes that the best teachers are guided by seven common principles of teaching. Specifically, Bain suggests that teachers "create a natural critical learning environment" (p. 99). Table 2.3 summarizes Bain's observations. For strategies to help you accomplish these principles jump to our chapter on instructional methods and check out Table 4.2.

In Bain's research, he found that model teachers create a learning environment that is natural by making it authentic; that is, connecting content to

TABLE 2.2 Teacher Qualities and Corresponding Behaviors

1. **Accessible**—posts office hours, gives out phone number and email information.
2. **Approachable/personable**—smiles, greets students, initiates conversations, invites questions, responds respectfully to student comments.
3. **Authoritative**—establishes clear course rules; maintains classroom order; speaks in a loud, strong voice.
4. **Confident**—speaks clearly, makes eye-contact, and answers questions correctly.
5. **Creative and interesting**—experiments with teaching methods; uses technological devices to support and enhance lectures; uses interesting, relevant, and personal examples; not monotone.
6. **Effective communicator**—speaks clearly/loudly; uses precise English; gives clear, compelling examples.
7. **Encourages and cares for students**—provides praise for good student work, helps students who need it, offers bonus points and extra credit, and knows student names.
8. **Enthusiastic about teaching and about topic**—smiles during class, prepares interesting class activities, uses gestures and expressions of emotion to emphasize important points, and arrives on time for class.
9. **Establishes daily and academic term goals**—prepares/follows the syllabus and has goals for each class.
10. **Flexible/open-minded**—changes calendar of course events when necessary, will meet at hours outside of office hours, pays attention to students when they state their opinions, accepts criticism from others, and allows students to do make-up work when appropriate.
11. **Good listener**—doesn't interrupt students while they are talking, maintains eye-contact, and asks questions about points that students are making.
12. **Happy/positive attitude/humorous**—tells jokes and funny stories, laughs with students.
13. **Humble**—admits mistakes, never brags, and doesn't take credit for others' successes.
14. **Knowledgeable about subject matter**—easily answers students' questions, does not read straight from the book or notes, and uses clear and understandable examples.
15. **Prepared**—brings necessary materials to class, is never late for class, and provides outlines of class discussion.
16. **Presents current information**—relates topic to current, real-life situations; uses recent videos, magazines, and newspapers to demonstrate points; talks about current topics; and uses new or recent texts.
17. **Professional**—dresses nicely (neat and clean shoes, slacks, blouses, dresses, shirts, ties) and no profanity.
18. **Promotes class discussion**—asks controversial or challenging questions during class, gives points for class participation, and involves students in group activities during class.
19. **Promotes critical thinking/intellectually stimulating**—asks thoughtful questions during class, uses essay questions on tests and quizzes, assigns homework, and holds group discussions/activities.
20. **Provides constructive feedback**—writes comments on returned work, answers students' questions, and gives advice on test-taking.
21. **Punctuality/manages class time**—arrives to class on time/early, dismisses class on time, presents relevant materials in class, leaves time for questions, keeps appointments, and returns work in a timely way.

22. **Rapport**—makes class laugh through jokes and funny stories, initiates and maintains class discussions, knows student names, and interacts with students before and after class.

23. **Realistic expectations of students/fair testing and grading**—covers material to be tested during class, writes relevant test questions, does not overload students with reading, teaches at an appropriate level for the majority of students in the course, and curves grades when appropriate.

24. **Respectful**—does not humiliate or embarrass students in class, is polite to students (says thank you and please, etc.), does not interrupt students while they are talking, and does not talk down to students.

25. **Sensitive and persistent**—makes sure students understand material before moving to new material, holds extra study sessions, repeats information when necessary, and asks questions to check student understanding.

26. **Strives to be a better teacher**—requests feedback on his/her teaching ability from students, continues learning (attends workshops, etc. on teaching), and uses new teaching methods.

27. **Technologically competent**—knows how to use a computer, knows how to use email with students, knows how to use overheads during class, and has a web page for classes.

28. **Understanding**—accepts legitimate excuses for missing class or coursework, is available before/after class to answer questions, doesn't lose temper at students, and takes extra time to discuss difficult concepts.

Source: Keeley et al. (2006).

students' individual history and experiences. Teachers can accomplish this task by asking students what is intrinsically motivating to them, and then connecting course material to those motives. He also suggests that the learning environment should encourage critical thinking because it is important to get students to move beyond rote memorization of course content. So you may ask, "How do you get your students to think critically?" One way is to ask elaborative questions (i.e., elaborative interrogation; Martin and Pressley, 1991). That is, ask "why?" questions. For instance, a teacher of literature might ask students, "Why does Fitzgerald return to the green light on the dock repeatedly in *The Great Gatsby*? How does the light relate to the characters and their motivations? What is your 'green light' in life?" In this process, the best teachers get their students to connect what they are learning to what they already know. Often, this process leaves students with the compulsion to seek and understand more information.

Bain (2004) also suggests that the best teachers get students' attention and then keep them focused. As many a cognitive psychologist would attest, getting students' attention is central to getting them to learn. Bain found that many teachers grabbed the attention of their students, but few could sustain it over a class period—only the best ones could. In order to get students' attention, you need to know them. Thus, Bain also concluded that great teachers "start with the students

TABLE 2.3 A Summary of Ken Bain's (2004) Answer to "What do the Best College Teachers do?"

- Know their subject matter extremely well
- Prepare for their teaching sessions as serious intellectual endeavors, as important as research and scholarship
- Expect more from students
- Understand and study how humans learn
- Put a lot of preparation into their teaching
- Create a natural critical learning environment
- Treat students fairly
- Check progress and evaluate efforts
- Seek comments
- Help students to learn outside of class
- Engage students in disciplinary thinking
- Create a natural critical learning environment
- Create diverse learning experiences

Source: Adapted from Bain (2004).

rather than the discipline" (p. 110). The best teachers understand that students bring a wealth of knowledge to the classroom and that their experiences are integral to the learning process. Recognizing this fact, the best teachers, using the Socratic method, asked students what they know about the course content before they discuss it.

What do the best teachers do with that attention once it is captured? Bain (2004, p. 114) found that they "engage students in disciplinary thinking." It is important to teach students to think within the bounds of your discipline—that is, teach them to think like a scholar! Whether their specialty is physics, art, or sociology, the best teachers will discuss what it means to be a scholar within that discipline and model how to analyze, apply, evaluate, and synthesize information. They tend to self-reflect and explicitly share this process with students. How they share that process with students is varied, however. Bain suggests that model teachers "create diverse learning experiences" (p. 116). Splendidly, Bain observed the best teachers use varied instructional strategies. By varying their instruction, model teachers demonstrate respect, acceptance, and ways to modify instruction to account for individual differences and celebrate diversity. See Chapter 4 for detailed discussion.

This is a lot to ask of students; thus, Bain (2004) suggests that the best teachers "seek commitments" from their students (p. 112). That is, teachers communicate that they themselves are deeply committed to the class and that their students should also be committed to the course as well. The best teachers ask their students to be committed to learning and the class from the very first class meeting. Bain asserted that the best teachers model commitment not only by being dedicated classroom teachers but by "help[ing] students learn outside of class" (p. 114). Some teachers lecture for a 75-minute period and forget about their students until the next class, but Bain suggests that the best teachers approach teaching fundamentally differently; that is, they try to find ways to help their students learn beyond that 75-minute class period. Examples might include assigning homework based on principles known to increase learning, explicitly teaching learning strategies to students, and simply being available outside of class to help students.

Our model and Bain's findings have a lot in common. Most importantly, both approaches emphasize that good teaching involves a great number of characteristics that must be woven together and simultaneously maintained. The main difference, however, is that our goal is not just to describe those characteristics but to help you develop them.

What Do Students Think?

Beyond the accumulated wisdom of experience from award-winners and pedagogical research, it also is useful to look to students directly. We conducted a simple, non-scientific, survey of students using Facebook. You may be surprised by what students think of when they consider the issue of good teaching. Table 2.4 shows some unedited responses.

Anything jump out at you from these responses? Students had no preparation for this little exercise whatsoever. Regan just had the impulse to put out the question while he was working on this chapter. He was surprised to get these responses, and more, within an hour of the posting. Students wanted to respond. We all noticed how much the students wrote about passion and wanting connection. Students wanted to be inspired. Students wrote about relationships. We were surprised that expertise, knowledge, and content did not come up in detail, if at all. Try this with your students the first day or week of class. Perhaps hand out notecards and have them answer the same question anonymously and see what you get.

Climbing the Teaching Hierarchy

"Master," "inspirational," "effective," "successful," "the best"—all of these are labels to strive for, but the reality is that few teachers will ever be all of these things. We are not ashamed to admit that we are still working toward them. Before reaching for these pinnacles, however, we firmly believe that it is important to look at the fundamentals of being a model teacher. Not everyone is going to be a "master," but you can work on the fundamentals. Let's use golf as an analogy. Very few of us will ever drive the ball as far or straight as Tiger Woods or Jack Nicklaus (in their primes, that is), but that does not mean you should not develop the basic

TABLE 2.4 Student Responses to the Question: "What Makes a Good Teacher?"

- Engaging learners, reinforcing their response and acceptance of feedback, modeling what you are teaching.
- Hands-on. Critique. Letting us take tests over and over so we get a deeper understanding of the material.
- Acknowledging that we exist and that we try despite full-time jobs, students, and multiple other factors.
- When the teacher is passionate about the information they're delivering and when they're really caring and understanding about their students!
- Patience with a willingness to explain/demonstrate the same concept in multiple ways in order to achieve understanding
- Igniting the life-long learner in all of us—if I leave a formal or informal "classroom," thinking about phrases that were said verbatim, and find myself going down a rabbit-hole of my own thoughts.
- Pushing/encouraging/mentoring students to places they never knew existed.
- A professor who cares so much about students (not only grade-wise but personally as well) that it shows in everything they do, teach, and encourage. Taking the time to explain things and really being invested in their success.
- A good teacher leaves questions unanswered. They leave their students with a sense of longing for that answer and the drive to find it for themselves. A good teacher does not simply lecture; they teach their students how to help themselves and be self-sufficient problem-solvers and world citizens.
- Connecting with the students.
- Incorporates recent events into the material. Uses current technology, like Prezi instead of traditional PowerPoint!
- Good teaching is essentially mentoring. My best learning experiences in the educational and professional world so far have been when people are doing so much more than simply teaching a lecture or giving a tutorial.

skills: keep your eye on the ball, arm straight, build strength. Tiger may have some tangible and intangible characteristics that you do not, but you can still strive to nail the foundational skills of the game. There is a clear developmental aspect to teaching and developing teaching competence that is not something that happens automatically. We believe that there is a clear pathway to model teaching and a relatively clear-cut series of steps to get you there. Whereas being a "master" is one end of the spectrum, there are some fundamentals to talk about first.

Teaching Fundamentals 101

We take a big-picture view to teaching and conceptualize teaching as a journey with three main stages. At the onset, there are the fundamentals of teaching. Returning to sports, even the most skilled athletes cannot skip on knowing the fundamentals. Aaron Rodgers of the Green Bay Packers is one of the best quarterbacks in the National Football League. Hardly a game goes by without announcers commenting on how—in addition to arm strength and accuracy—he has the basic fundamentals down pat. Model teachers likewise need to get the fundamentals down. There is a wealth of resources to help with the fundamentals.

Two of the most used resources on the fundamentals are Barbara Gross Davis's (2009) *Tools for teaching,* and Marilla Svinicki and Bill McKeachie's (2013) *McKeachie's teaching tips.* Both of these books take readers through each step of the teaching process from the first day of class to the last. All of the nuts and bolts are introduced. Every beginning teacher should have these books on their shelves with a plethora of sticky notes jutting out of the pages. The good news for you is that we have taken many of the important bits from these resources and woven them together for you in one place—this book.

For teachers who want to go beyond the basics but still want to learn about different practices in higher education, Groccia et al.'s (2012) *Handbook of college and university teaching* and Buskist and Benassi's (2012) *Effective college and university teaching* also provide good ways to strengthen fundamentals. Both these books are edited volumes with a number of different chapters on different aspects of teaching. Teachers who have some experience in the classroom will better absorb the material here, but there is some helpful advice for the novice. In the chapters ahead, we will refer to these books as sources for additional information if there are elements of teaching that you want to delve into deeper.

Far too often starting teachers make rookie mistakes. When we taught our first courses, we all had a tendency to first pick a textbook and then plan out the classes and assignments. In actuality, designing a course should begin with developing course learning objectives based on departmental and disciplinary goals and then picking ways to assess whether or not students have achieved those outcomes. Only after these initial steps is it time to select content (textbooks, readings), methods of delivery (lecture, discussion), and assignments (papers, presentations). These are the basic stages of "backward design" (Fink, 2003; Wiggins and McTighe, 2005). Although proper use of backward design may be a fundamental skill, many instructors, novice or not, have never used the approach. Two handy guides for elements of backward design include Linda Suskie's (2009) *Assessing student learning* (a great aid for writing student learning outcomes), and Stevens and Levi's (2011) *Introduction to rubrics*; we also expand on this critical topic in Chapter 6.

Sincere Teaching

Once you are comfortable with the fundamentals, it is time to take it up a notch. Sometimes called sincere teaching (Gurung and Schwartz, 2009) this step involves reflection and reading the pedagogical literature. Too many teachers do not take the time to self-reflect, to ask, "what do I do when I teach?" Answering this question sets the stage for the even more important question of "why?" Self-reflection

TABLE 2.5 Question the Whats, Hows, and Whys of Pedagogy

• How do you use space?
• How do you handle discussion?
• How well do you listen to student answers?
• How does participation work?
  • How long do you wait before calling on someone?
  • What strategy do you use when an answer is wrong?
• How do you deal with incivility?
• How do you start/end class?
• What do you do with your hands?
• What would you best like your students to get from your class?

Source: Adapted from Weimer (2010).

and a direct look at what justifies teaching policies, practices, and behaviors are a key part to developing as a teacher (Brookfield, 1995; Weimer, 2010). Table 2.5 lists some sample questions to drive your own self-reflection.

It is important to be clear about what you do in the classroom and examine various parts of your teaching. Do you have a detailed description of *how* you teach? How easily can you answer the questions in Table 2.5? Read through them and jot down your answers.

You may be surprised by how difficult it is to answer some of these questions. Some of the answers you discover may also make you ponder your practices. It gets better. Once you have a strong sense of what you do, it is time to unpack *why* you do it. Most of the time we do things automatically. We prepare our material to cover for the day, create a slideshow to illustrate the key points, and then we stride in and deliver the material. Sure, we pay attention to whether students are getting it, how they respond to our questions (when we remember to ask them or if the Socratic method is part of our pedagogical repertoire), and how we end classes, but being a sincere teacher involves explicitly examining the assumptions that underlie what we do. "Becoming critically aware of our own presuppositions involves challenging our established and habitual patterns of expectation" (Mezirow, 1990, p. 12).

Look at your course policies. What do you say about attendance, classroom civility, and participation (to name but a few policies)? Do you set strong deadlines? Deadline policies assume that learning can be made to conform to a timeline, that students cannot/will not manage their own time well, and that students will learn time management by you managing it. How about attendance? If you require attendance you may be assuming that what happens in the classroom is essential to learning, that a teacher and other learners contribute to efforts to learn, that all students find a formal, structured learning environment beneficial, or that students won't come to class unless they are required to (Weimer, 2010). Now, some of these may be accurate (e.g., attendance policies increase attendance; Snyder et al., 2014), but not all automatic assumptions that we make are supported. To use a clichéd example, the assumption that students have attention spans lasting only ten minutes could influence how you design your class presentations, but it does not have much support in the literature (Wilson and Korn, 2007). The bottom line is that assumptions underlying teaching choices, what is often called a "teaching philosophy," bear examination and reexamination. A written philosophy statement both guides what we do as teachers and shapes our identity (Korn, 2003; Palmer et al., 2010). If you have not written one yet, Korn (2012) provides a great starting point, as does the exercise in the next paragraph.

There are other ways to examine underlying teaching assumptions (Beatty et al., 2009). One exercise begins with 84 cards that contain keywords and concepts from traditional education philosophies on one side (available at www.obts. org/JME_supplemental_materials/JME_TP_cards_907.doc). The other side contains the names of educational philosophies and philosophers associated with the words and concepts on the first side. For example, for the concept "learning by doing," the flip side has "Locke (empirical method); Pestalozzi (observing environment); Spencer; Dewey (problematic encounters)" (Beatty et al., 2009, p. 117). To conduct this exercise, you first review the cards and select those that most represent your own ideas about teaching, discarding the cards that do not relate. Next you sort the cards again, grouping the cards into clusters that represent common themes such as "problem-solving," "team learning," or "democratic classrooms." Each resulting stack signifies the key components of your own teaching philosophy and can help you better craft a full philosophy document. Try it. You may find you will modify your syllabi or even some of your assignments once you modify and reflect on your teaching philosophy.

Scholarly Teaching

Once we are comfortable with our fundamentals and have taken the time to reflect on our teaching, it is time to go further. The intuitive next step is to dive into the rich body of pedagogical research on teaching and learning that fosters evidence-based teaching (e.g., Davis, 2009; Schwartz and Gurung, 2012). Looking into the published literature on teaching in order to reflect on and improve one's own teaching is referred to as *scholarly teaching* (Richlin, 2006; Smith, 2012). A scholarly teacher is "constantly researching how her students are experiencing learning and then making pedagogical decisions informed by the insights she gains from the students' responses" (Brookfield, 2006, p. xi).

Reflection on student learning may lead to productive changes in teaching, but the process does not need to end there. There may also be a formal or informal assessment of the effectiveness of changes; this can be a form of scholarship in and of itself. Good teaching becomes *scholarship of teaching and learning* (SoTL) when teachers critically assesses their own teaching and share their findings with peers. SoTL entails methodologically rigorous scholarly work conducted to enhance teaching and advance learning (Gurung and Landrum, 2014). It is commonly described as intentional, systematic reflections on teaching and learning resulting in peer-reviewed products made public (Gurung and Schwartz, 2010; Smith, 2012). Boyer (1990) popularized the term "scholarship of teaching," although caring and master teachers have practiced the kind of work it refers to for many years. Huber and Hutchings (2005) further developed SoTL and describe it as "viewing the work of the classroom as a site for inquiry, asking and answering questions about student learning in ways that can improve one's own classroom and also advance the larger profession of teaching" (p. 1).

SoTL improves student learning by stimulating faculty to think deeply about teaching and learning and stimulating the exploration of pedagogical questions by enhancing the knowledge base on teaching and learning, and enriching one's own teaching experiences (Bishop-Clark and Dietz-Uhler, 2012; Nelson, 2003). Conducting SoTL is a critical part of faculty development as the rigor and intentionality of SoTL cannot but make one a better teacher, a finding not without empirical support (Hutchings et al., 2011). Moreover, SoTL is actually the practice of teaching the broader community of teachers to be more effective at what they do.

Although SoTL can be seen as the pinnacle of excellent teaching, it is conceptually orthogonal to what constitutes excellent teaching. A teacher who gets poor student evaluations may still be a successful SoTL researcher. Likewise, an excellent teacher may be a scholarly one, practicing evidence-based teaching (Dunn et al., 2013) but may not take the time to present or publish the work (i.e., SoTL). SoTL plays a large role in being a model teacher, as we discuss more in Chapter 6.

Revisiting Your Self-Assessment: Are You Becoming a Great Teacher?

We have covered a wide swatch of the education landscape on the topic of good teaching. How do you know if you are one? Of course we trust many of you read the preceding pages and nodded to yourself ("Yes, I do that, Yes, I do that" or "Hmm, I should try that"). Some of you may say, "Most of my students get As so they must be learning and I must be good." The proof of the teaching should be in the learning, but teaching is only one of the factors influencing learning (accounting for approximately 25 percent of the variance; Hattie, 2015). We trust that by this point in the chapter you have a good answer to the first question in Table 2.1 (What makes a good teacher?). Perhaps your recollection of your best teachers resonates with many of the findings we reviewed in the preceding pages.

In higher education, explicit answers to the question that heads this chapter are few and far between. You may keep a finger on the pulse of your own teaching and have a sense of whether you are good (subjective and not always reliable). You may hear the buzz on you or lurk on RateMyProfessor.com (eye-opening). You may, like many schools, let it all ride on student evaluations (pros and cons here as you see later in Chapter 8). Our goal is to provide you with an organized way to assess yourself. In addition to measuring single components of your teaching such as teaching behaviors (Keeley et al., 2006), student engagement (Handelsman et al., 2010), or student–professor rapport (Wilson and Ryan, 2013), the model teacher criteria (Boysen et al., 2015; Richmond et al., 2014) provides you with a comprehensive measure. Whereas there is much to learn from the research on master, skillful, successful, and inspiring teachers, few of those sources provide an objective and detailed method to assess your own teaching. The six components underlying the Model Teaching Criteria highlight the many critical elements of what it takes to be a good teacher and provide a helpful roadmap for your professional development.

CASE STUDY REEXAMINED: THOSE WHO CAN TEACH, TEACH (NO TRAINING REQUIRED?)

1. *How clearly does Samantha understand the training needed to be a good college teacher?* She does not understand the training at all, and it appears that her advisor similarly buys into some basic myths about college teaching (e.g., all you need is content knowledge). If Samantha follows the advice she is getting from faculty, she clearly will have no training to teach once she obtains her doctorate.

2. *What would you tell Samantha to do?* Whereas many faculty may be gifted orators and have natural abilities to convey information and help others to learn, training is essential to be a model teacher. Reading the some basic pedagogical literature is a good start, so of course we hope that you would urge Samantha to run out and get a copy of this book. There are a number of suggestions in Chapter 3 on training that will put her on the right path.

3. *How do you compare K-12 teaching to college teaching?* It is important to note that K-12 teaching and college teaching require significantly different levels of training. For the former, individuals often major in education, go through the hoops for certification, and often spend one college semester teaching students. There are few mandated teacher-training programs for college teachers. Think about this for a second. Why should there be such a gulf between the training requirements for two different types of teachers? Aren't the goals of both to foster student learning? We hope that college teaching will someday require a portion of the rigor devoted to preparing K-12 teachers.

Summary of Best Practices

Oh, if Samantha could only read this chapter and this book, she would have a whole different understanding of what it takes to be a teacher. In fact, we hope this book *does* make it into the hands of many undergraduates considering teaching and just not graduate students and teachers. The fact is that teaching involves many different skills. Teaching is also very different based on where you do it. Sarah and Samantha, in our opening case study, are heading to two different environments. K-12 teaching preparation is far more involved than college training. In contrast, for the most part there is no training to teach in college. If Samantha just got her PhD and expected to be well-prepared to be a teacher, she would be the same as many college teachers, but she would not be well-positioned to be a model teacher.

As you see in this chapter, there are many different indicators of good teaching. Many studies and interviews of award-winning teachers highlight some of the major characteristics and behaviors needed to be master teachers. Some of what makes a master teacher is behavioral in nature; some is attitudinal in nature. All of it takes work. The Model Teaching Criteria that we unpack in each of the next six chapters provide you with an in-depth look at all the components of good teaching. This one conceptualization presents an advance over other attempts to define good teaching in that it incorporates many different components, behaviors and attitudes. Our definition of good teaching does not endorse one scale over another, behaviors over attitudes, interviews over awards. We believe the only way to be a model teacher is to go beyond the fundamentals and develop all elements of the craft.

The Very Busy People Book Club: Your Top Five Must-Reads

Bain, K. (2004). *What the best college teachers do.* Cambridge, MA: Harvard University Press.

Buskist, W. and Benassi, V. A. (2012). *Effective college and university teaching: Strategies and tactics for the new professoriate.* Thousand Oaks, CA: Sage.

Royse, D. (2001). *Teaching tips for college and university instructors: A practical guide.* Needham Heights, MA: Allyn & Bacon.

Svinicki, M. and McKeachie, W. J. (2013). *McKeachie's teaching tips* (14th edn). Belmont, CA: Wadsworth.

Weimer, M. (2010). *Inspired college teaching: A career-long resource for professional growth.* San Francisco, CA: Jossey-Bass.

References

Bain, K. (2004). *What the best college teachers do.* Cambridge, MA: Harvard University Press.

Baiocco, S. A. and DeWaters, J. N. (1998). *Successful college teaching: Problem-solving strategies of distinguished professors.* Boston, MA: Allyn and Bacon.

Beatty, J. E., Leigh, J. A., and Dean, K. L. (2009). Finding our roots: An exercise for creating a personal teaching philosophy statement. *Journal of Management Education,* 33(1), 115–130.

Beidler, P. G. (1986). *Distinguished teachers on effective teaching: Observations on effective teaching by college professors recognized by the Council for Advancement and Support of Education*. San Francisco, CA: Jossey-Bass.

Beidler, P. G. (1997). What makes a good teacher? In J. K. Roth (ed.), *Inspiring teaching: Carnegie professors of the year speak* (pp. 2–12). Boston, MA: Anker.

Bishop-Clark, C. and Dietz-Uhler, B. (2012). *Engaging in the scholarship of teaching and learning: A guide to the process and how to develop a project from start to finish*. Sterling, VA: Stylus.

Boyer, E. L. (1990). *Scholarship reconsidered: Priorities of the professoriate*. San Francisco, CA: Jossey-Bass.

Boysen, G. A., Richmond, A. S., and Gurung, R. A. R. (2015). Model Teaching Criteria for psychology: Initial documentation of teachers' self-reported competency. *Scholarship of Teaching and Learning in Psychology*, 1, 48–59.

Brookfield, S. D. (1995). *Becoming a critically reflective teacher*. San Francisco, CA: Jossey-Bass.

Brookfield, S. D. (2006). *The skillful teacher: On technique, trust, and responsiveness in the classroom*. San Francisco, CA: Jossey-Bass.

Buskist, W. and Benassi, V. A. (2012). *Effective college and university teaching: Strategies and tactics for the new professoriate*. Thousand Oaks, CA: Sage.

Buskist, W. and Keeley, J. (2015). Becoming an excellent teacher. In D. Dunn (ed.), *The Oxford handbook of undergraduate psychology education* (pp. 99–112). New York: Oxford University Press.

Buskist, W., Sikorski, J., Buckley, T., and Saville, B. K. (2002). Elements of master teaching. In S. F. Davis and W. Buskist (eds.), *The teaching of psychology: Essays in honor of Wilbert J. McKeachie and Charles L. Brewer* (pp. 27–39). Mahwah, NJ: Lawrence Erlbaum.

Centra, J. A. (1979). *Determining faculty effectiveness*. San Francisco, CA: Jossey-Bass.

Cronin, T. E. (1992). On celebrating college teaching. *Journal of Excellence in College Teaching*, 3, 149–168.

Davis, B. G. (2009). *Tools for teaching* (2nd edn). San Francisco, CA: Jossey-Bass.

Dunn, D. S., Saville, B. K., Baker, S. C., and Marek, P. (2013). Evidence-based teaching: Tools and techniques that promote learning in the psychology classroom. *Australian Journal of Psychology*, 65, 5–13.

Fink, L. D. (2003). *Creating significant learning experiences: An integrated approach to designing college courses*. San Francisco, CA: Jossey-Bass.

Groccia, J. E., Alsudairi, M. A. T., and Buskist, W. (eds.) (2012). *Handbook of college and university teaching: A global perspective*. Thousand Oaks, CA: Sage.

Gurung, R. A. R. and Landrum, R. E. (2014). Editorial. *Scholarship of Teaching and Learning*, 1(sup), 1–2.

Gurung, R. A. R. and Schwartz, E. (2009). *Optimizing teaching and learning: Pedagogical research in practice*. Malden, MA: Blackwell.

Gurung, R. A. R. and Schwartz, B. M. (2010). Riding the third wave of SoTL. *International Journal for the Scholarship of Teaching and Learning*, 4(2). Retrieved from http://digitalcommons.georgiasouthern.edu/ij-sotl.

Handelsman, M. M., Briggs, W. L., Sullivan, N., and Towler, A. (2010). A measure of college student course engagement. *Journal of Educational Research*, 98, 184–192.

Hattie, J. (2015). The applicability of Visible Learning to higher education. *Scholarship of Teaching and Learning in Psychology*, 1, 79–91.

Huber, M. T. and Hutchings, P. (2005). *The advancement of learning: Building the teaching commons*. San Francisco, CA: Jossey-Bass.

Hutchings, P., Huber, M. T., and Ciccone, A. (2011). *The scholarship of teaching and learning reconsidered: Institutional impact*. San Francisco, CA: Jossey-Bass.

Jarvis, D. K. (1991). *Junior faculty development: A handbook.* New York: MLA.

Keeley, J., Smith, D., and Buskist, W. (2006). The Teacher Behaviors Checklist: Factor analysis of its utility for evaluating teaching. *Teaching of Psychology*, 33, 84–91.

Keeley, J., Christopher, A. N., and Buskist, W. (2012). Emerging evidence for excellent teaching across borders. In J. E. Groccia, M. Al-Sudairy, and W. Buskist (eds.), *Handbook of college and university teaching: Global perspectives* (pp. 374–390). Thousand Oaks, CA: Sage.

Korn, J. H. (2003). Writing a philosophy of teaching. In W. Buskist, V. W. Hevern, B. K. Saville, and T. Zinn (eds.), *Essays from excellence in teaching*, Vol. 3. Society for the Teaching of Psychology, http://teachpsych.lemoyne.edu/teachpsych/eit/eit2003/index.html.

Korn, J. H. (2012). Writing and developing your philosophy of teaching. In W. Buskist and V. A. Benassi (eds.), *Effective college and university teaching* (pp. 71–80). Thousand Oaks, CA: Sage.

Lowman, J. (1995). *Mastering the techniques of teaching.* San Francisco, CA: Jossey-Bass.

Martin, J. H., Hands, K. B., Lancaster, S. M., Trytten, D. A., and Murphy, T. J. (2008). Hard but not too hard: Challenging courses and engineering students. *College Teaching*, 56, 107–113.

Martin, V. L. and Pressley, N. (1991). Elaborate-interrogation effects depend on the nature of the question. *Journal of Educational Psychology*, 83, 113–119.

Mezirow, J. (1990). How critical reflection triggers transformative learning. In J. Mezirow and Associates (eds.), *Fostering critical reflection in adulthood: A guide to transformative and emancipatory learning* (pp. 1–20). San Francisco, CA: Jossey-Bass.

Nelson, C. E. (2003). Doing it: Selected examples of several of the different genres of the scholarship of teaching and learning. *The Journal on Excellence in College Teaching*, 14, 85–94.

Palmer, P. J., Zajonc, A., and Scribner, M. (2010). *The heart of higher education: A call to renewal.* New York: John Wiley & Sons.

Richlin, L. (2006). *Blueprint for learning: Constructing college courses to facilitate, assess, and document learning.* Sterling, VA: Stylus.

Richmond, A. S., Boysen, G. A., Gurung, R. A. R., Tazeau, Y. N., Meyers, S. A., and Sciutto, M. J. (2014). Aspirational Model Teaching Criteria for psychology. *Teaching of Psychology*, 41, 281–295.

Roth, J. K. (ed.) (1997). *Inspiring teaching: Carnegie professors of the year speak.* Bolton, MA: Anker.

Schwartz, E. and Gurung, R. A. R. (2012). *Evidence-based teaching in higher education.* Washington, DC: American Psychological Association.

Smith, R. A. (2012). Benefits of using SoTL in picking and choosing pedagogy. In B. M. Schwartz and R. A. R. Gurung (eds.), *Evidence based-teaching for higher education* (pp. 7–22). Washington, DC: American Psychological Association.

Snyder, J. L., Lee-Partridge, J. E., Jarmoszko, A. T., Petkova, O., and D'Onofrio, M. J. (2014). What is the influence of a compulsory attendance policy on absenteeism and performance? *Journal of Education for Business*, 89(8), 433–440.

Stevens, D. D. and Levi, A. (2011). *Introduction to rubrics: An assessment tool to save grading time, convey effective feedback, and promote student learning.* Sterling, VA: Stylus.

Suskie, L. (2009). *Assessing student learning: A common sense guide* (2nd edn). San Francisco, CA: Jossey-Bass/Wiley.

Svinicki, M. and McKeachie, W. J. (2013). *McKeachie's teaching tips* (14th edn). Belmont, CA: Wadsworth.

Weimer, M. (1993). *Improving your classroom teaching.* Newbury Park, CA: Sage.

Weimer, M. (2010). *Inspired college teaching: A career long resource for professional growth*. San Francisco, CA: Jossey-Bass.

Wiggins, G. and McTighe, J. (2005). *Understanding by design* (2nd edn). Alexandria, VA: Association for Supervision and Curriculum Development.

Wilson, J. H. and Ryan, R. G. (2013). Professor-student rapport scale: Six items predict student outcomes. *Teaching of Psychology*, 40, 130–133.

Wilson, K. and Korn, J. H. (2007). Attention during lectures: Beyond ten minutes. *Teaching of Psychology*, 34, 85–89.

3
HOW DO WE TRAIN TO BE MODEL TEACHERS?

We can all remember our first forays into the classroom. We were nervous. We were excited. We felt (mostly) underprepared. Regan in particular, had never taken a 'how to teach' class and had no specific training to teach. He was not required to teach as an undergraduate, graduate, or postdoctoral student. In graduate school he gave one guest lecture and was a teaching assistant. As a postdoc, Regan taught his first two courses, building them from the ground up mostly using class notes from when he took the same class years before! Consequently, his move to a school with a seven-course load was quite the transition. Thanks to great colleagues and friends in the Society for the Teaching of Psychology, he had attended great talks by master teachers. He had even thumbed through a copy of *McKeachie's teaching tips*. But is that enough training to teach?

Teaching is both an art and a craft. Parini (2005) explores the "art" aspect of this duality and Brookfield (2015), Palmer (1998), and Weimer (2010) provide thoughtful explorations of some of the more abstract elements of teaching that do not lend themselves to being trained. Thankfully, there are also many concrete elements of teaching that can be learned. Some could argue that teachers are born and not made and if you have it, you have it; if not, bad luck. Although we agree that some folks may have a greater predisposition—or even a calling—to teach, there are many skills that can be developed (see all subsequent chapters, especially Chapter 4). Our research shows that training is one part of the Model Teaching Criteria that could be improved. Instructors in our study met the model's training criteria 71 percent of the time (Boysen et al., 2015). Not bad you may say, but this is actually quite disappointing given that everyone in our sample was an active teacher. Shouldn't everyone who teaches be trained? We believe so; thus, this entire chapter will focus on the training experiences of model teachers.

CASE STUDY: A TEACHING ARTIFACT

Professor Joanne Owens did her doctoral work at a large Midwestern university that prided itself on scholarship and innovation. Joanne's dissertation in art history focused on a famous Italian patron of the arts and her area of interest is the Italian Renaissance. She was a teaching assistant once in graduate school but was never an instructor of record. She now teaches at regional public university in the East. She typically teaches both introduction to art history and some upper-level courses in her specialty area. With four years of teaching under her belt, she is approaching tenure and is working hard to get out as many publications as she can. She regularly attends art history conferences in the US and abroad and presents a paper every time she attends.

Joanne's teaching style is somewhat of a historical artifact itself—dated and static. Two classes a week she reads a prepared lecture to students (mostly based on her conference papers), and on the third day she writes four or five discussion questions on the board and leads a discussion—rather, she attempts to lead a discussion but fails to realize that she is still talking 75 percent of the time. Assignments in her classes consist of a midterm and a final. In advanced classes she also requires a term paper about a course topic of the student's choosing that is due on the last day of class.

Students find Joanne extremely interesting, warm, and enthusiastic about her subject. Her student evaluations are dominated by comments such as "nice," "knowledgeable," and "easy-going." Most of the means on her teaching evaluations are at or above those in her department, but the items related to "learning" and "intellectual challenge" are significantly lower than those of her peers. Wanting to make sure she had a slam-dunk case for tenure, Joanne went to the campus Center for Teaching and Learning to discuss ways to improve her student evaluations. The teaching specialist began by asking "What is your pedagogical approach?" Joanne said she mostly lectured and required essays but wasn't sure if that was the right answer. The specialist followed up by asking "Does a lecture and essay format best match how students learn art history?" She had never considered it. Joanne began to wonder if there was still a lot for her to learn about being a professor.

1. How would you characterize Dr. Owens's training to be a professor of art history?
2. How would you characterize Dr. Owens's training to be a teacher?
3. What recommendations would you make to Dr. Owens if you were the teaching specialist at the Center for Teaching and Learning?

We will cover a wide variety of 'training'. There are two main domains, content and skills, and model teachers should be trained in regard to both. There are also discipline-specific skills and knowledge and general knowledge and pedagogical expertise (Dinham, 1996; Shulman, 1987). Of course, you can never be done. Changes in higher education, varying cohorts of students, and technological innovation necessitate a consistent commitment to stay abreast of developments in pedagogy. This chapter explores different forms of training starting with a discussion of how teachers need to maintain expert knowledge in a subject area, acquire knowledge about basic pedagogical theory and practice, and maintain current knowledge of pedagogical theory and practice. We also provide a basic overview of how students learn.

Before we fully unpack the different forms of training, as practitioners of science, we need to establish a baseline measurement of your training activities to date. Please take a few minutes and reflect back on your past teaching experiences, and then complete the self-assessment in Table 3.1. After completing this self-assessment, keep your results in mind while you read the chapter. Revisit your self-assessment at the end of the chapter and see what you feel like you are doing well and what you can improve upon.

Maintain Expert Knowledge in a Subject Area

It almost goes without saying that excellent teachers know their disciplines well. But it should be said, has been said, and the data bears this out (Buskist et al., 2002). When we serve on a search committee, we want good teachers, but we also want teachers who have shown distinction in specialized disciplinary knowledge and who are well-versed with their own discipline's habits of mind—the basic skills, values, and methods of their disciplines (Haynie et al., 2012). There is no substitute for knowing your area of study well. It may be a small part of your discipline, the area encompassed by the many pages of your dissertation, but that will do for starters. Graduate programs in most disciplines also tend to require students to acquire a breadth of knowledge in the field that serves the students well when it is time to teach. We all had distribution requirements in graduate school and the extent of the depth and breadth of your graduate education is clearly illustrated by your graduate transcript, a key piece of evidence in establishing your knowledge in the subject area. When talking about training, the first area teachers needs to be well-versed in is their subject area. An ongoing program of research, reading current issues of journals, and attending conferences can maintain this knowledge.

The need for subject-specific expertise is officially recognized in several ways. At the most basic level, teaching positions have minimum requirements for degrees and degree specializations. In addition, some disciplines have explicit recommendations regarding teaching from national bodies. In our home discipline of

TABLE 3.1 Self-Assessment of Your Training Model Teaching Criteria

*Directions: Please indicate on the scale below how often you take part in these efforts/
activities to improve your training.*

Scale: 5 = Always, 4 = Often, 3 = Sometimes, 2 = Rarely, 1 = Never   *Your score*

1. You teach only courses that are related to your professional degree.	
2. You teach only courses for which you have documented graduate coursework.	
3. You give presentations at regional or national conferences related to content areas taught.	
4. You publish peer-reviewed research related to content areas taught.	
5. You utilize pedagogical training that stems from credit-bearing courses you have completed on teaching.	
6. You present at regional or national conferences on topics related to teaching.	
7. You publish peer-reviewed research related to pedagogical strategies (e.g., SoTL articles).	
8. You participate in continuing education related to content areas taught.	
9. You participate in continuing education related to pedagogical strategies.	

Note: This self-assessment is adapted and modified from Richmond et al. (2014) and Boysen et al. (2015).

psychology, the American Psychological Association's (2011) *Principles for quality undergraduate education* state that instructors should not be given responsibility for courses outside of their training or knowledge, and it is considered unethical to teach outside of one's area of competency. In contrast to disciplinary guidelines, different universities institute their own guidelines for teaching. For example, the University of Michigan's Center for Research on Teaching and Learning has principles of teaching evaluation that suggest what comprises quality teaching. Thus, model teachers instruct courses for which they have adequate knowledge and training. Basic knowledge of a subject is just a starting point for the best teachers, however (Buskist et al., 2002). Teachers should stay up-to-date in their field. They should also have salient examples and real-life illustrations of their subject matter. Model teachers remain intellectually engaged in their subject going beyond what they are doing research on. It does take some discipline but it is important. Because this is the type of knowledge that is traditionally gained in graduate school and naturally maintained by faculty to ensure promotion, tenure, and for merit raises, we do not dwell on it as much. We focus more on training related to pedagogy.

Going beyond basic subject knowledge, it is important for instructors to be aware of ways to teach the content of the discipline. The understanding and skill to teach the discipline, what Shulman (1987, p. 8) calls "pedagogical content knowledge" varies widely. In what can be seen as the "second wave of SoTL"

(Gurung et al., 2009; p. xvii; Gurung and Schwartz, 2010), many scholars have taken an almost metacognitive look at the scholarship on how their disciplines create knowledge.

In the early 2000s, Donald (2002) examined how different faculty in various disciplines conduct research and scholarship in their disciplines. She compared various disciplines and showed that how one teaches a science is very different from how one teaches English or history. One needs to modify one's pedagogy based on the uniqueness of each discipline. Shulman (2005) catalyzed this form of scholarship with his introduction of the notion of signature pedagogies, the way each discipline teaches students to think like the professionals in that discipline. Around the same time, Pace and Middendorf (2004) took a more thorough look at student learning within a discipline. In addition to the differential creation of knowledge by experts in each field, both Pace and Middendorf, and Donald clearly note that how students learn differs significantly across disciplines and that this notion is rarely presented to students explicitly. Students often encounter conceptual or procedural obstacles to learning, "bottlenecks" (Meyer and Land, 2005), which the model teacher needs to work to free up. Bottlenecks prevent students from moving on and continuing with additional learning.

Knowing one's discipline well thereby helps a teacher better identify what a student may find difficult in the discipline. Dewey (1983, pp. 285–286) noted that "every study or subject thus has two aspects: one for the scientist as scientist; the other for the teacher as teacher. These two aspects are in no sense opposed or conflicting. But neither are they immediately identical." Grossman, Wilson, and Shulman (1989) outline three aspects of knowledge in the discipline. In addition to being knowledgeable about content that enables them to look credible and making teaching personable, encouraging discussion, and fostering student confidence (Dinham, 1996), teachers also need to understand a discipline's substantive structures, "the explanatory frameworks or paradigms that are used both to guide inquiry in the field and to make sense of data" (Grossman et al., 1989, p. 29). The fact is our fields are often filled with jargon and cumbersome topics. We need to be watchful for topics that our students have trouble with. Whereas paying close attention to exam responses to see what topics students get wrong often is good, we should aim to be mindful in the classroom. For a long time, Regan made the assumption that "correlation" was a concept that could be easily and quickly explained. It is just an association between two or more different things after all. Easy for him to say! Not so easy for a first-year student to grasp but a basic research element for most of the sciences. In time, Regan added more and more examples to explaining this potential bottleneck concept. Much higher-level understanding builds on the basic understanding of a correlation. To get to this level of understanding, a teacher must understand the ways knowledge in the field is created as well.

There are a number of concrete ways to stay up-to-date with both subject knowledge and pedagogical content knowledge. Each of us does it a little differently but the bottom line is we ensure that we are reminded to do this. You can set monthly or bi-weekly recurring reminders in your calendar so you are prompted to read up on happenings in the field. You may want to go so far as to block out an hour or so where you will peruse the latest issue of journals in your field. Most journals allow you to set up electronic reminders and even send you the table of contents of each new issue. Having this electronic list and even abstracts sent to your email provides easy access. Every once in a while we even take a look at the latest editions of introductory textbooks, so we get a quick overview of any new developments. The best place for new developments is the conference program of your disciplinary conferences. Look over the program for a sense of what scholars in the field are working on.

Acquire Knowledge About Basic Pedagogical Theory and Practice

The process of becoming a model teacher is doubly challenging because it requires development of expertise in a specific content area and in the general area of pedagogy, the method and practice of teaching. An important aside: Whereas the term "pedagogy" is often commonly used to describe the method and practice of teaching, some educators make the distinction between "pedagogy" and "andragogy," where the latter is used to specifically refer to adult learning (Knowles, 1973, 1980). Given that adults and children have different motivations, and may vary in readiness to learn, this distinction is important but given our discussion covers learning for both children and adults, we will use the more general term "pedagogy."

What should college teachers know about teaching? Whereas faculty from schools and colleges of education, educational psychologists, and thoughtful, well-read practitioners of SoTL may be able to provide some quick answers, this is not an easy question for people without such specialized expertise. However, a number of different sources point to some concise answers.

In one of the first grand syntheses designed to collect key principles on undergraduate education, Chickering and Gamson (1987) enumerated seven good practices. In their view, quality pedagogy encourages contact between students and faculty, develops reciprocity and cooperation among students, encourages active learning, gives prompt feedback, emphasizes time on task, communicates high expectations, and respects diverse talents and ways of learning. Seven is a popular number. In a recent review of the scientific literature on learning, Ambrose, Bridges, DiPietro, Lovett, and Norman (2010) list seven principles that help facilitate learning. The principles, which apply to all learning situations, are prior knowledge, motivation, social interactions, context, experiences, organization, and practice (Ambrose et al., 2010). Each principle has implications for teaching and, correspondingly, has pragmatic implications. For example, the principle that prior knowledge affects learning suggests that teachers need to think about how to activate prior knowledge, identify for students when that prior knowledge may be accurate but insufficient, or determine when the prior knowledge is inappropriate or inaccurate. Pragmatic techniques related to this principle include talking to colleagues teaching prerequisite courses to learn about what students should know, administering diagnostic tests of knowledge, having students assess their own prior knowledge, or using techniques such as concept mapping (Ambrose et al., 2010).

Whereas these principles are helpful and there are extensive suggestions on how to implement them in easily available books (e.g., Ambrose et al., 2010), there are a variety of additional ways to acquire the knowledge needed to teach. Completing a graduate course on teaching is a standard method for improving pedagogical knowledge and skills (McElroy and Prentice-Dunn, 2005; Prieto and Meyers, 1999; Prieto and Scheel, 2008). Courses on teaching allow individuals to develop basic skills, such as deciding on learning outcomes, lecturing and leading discussion, writing a syllabus, selecting a textbook, using different forms of evaluation, grading, providing feedback, and motivating students. As described in Chapter 6 on assessment, it takes training to differentiate between evaluation (a judgment of performance) and assessment (a process of documenting and improving learning).

In the event that one has not taken a course on teaching in graduate school, campus faculty development center workshops and teaching conferences provide additional ways to increase teaching skills. Most campuses have mentor programs where new faculty are paired up with seasoned teachers who can conduct peer observations and provide valuable tips on teaching. Some professional societies also have mentoring programs where faculty can pair up with a teaching mentor from a different campus or early career faculty activities to shore up pedagogical knowledge.

The good news for anyone interested in becoming a model teacher is that there are a number of different resources to peruse to pick up pedagogical tips (see Chapters 2 and 4 for more information on this topic). From a pragmatic standpoint, you can either take a class on teaching, examine your discipline's options for continuing education in teaching, or self-train. Reading this book is great self-training and we hope you also follow up on the many references we provide at the end of each chapter.

The key is to have a guideline to select among the many different selections that exist. One criterion is to search for evidence-based pedagogical tips (Schwartz and Gurung, 2012). Teachers should utilize scientifically justified methods of instruction; they should specifically design lessons to take advantage of the methods known to promote learning (American Psychological Association, 2011; Bernstein et al., 2010). Teachers who approach pedagogy from a scientific perspective are referred to as scientist-educators (Bernstein et al., 2010). The most advanced type of scientist-educator integrates both knowledge of their field's content and knowledge of effective pedagogy into the design of learning experiences. Thus, model teachers are trained as scientist-educators who put pedagogical knowledge into practice.

Maintain Current Knowledge of Pedagogical Theory and Practice

Model teachers also possess pedagogical knowledge that goes beyond specific teaching techniques. Because the student population and disciplines themselves are increasingly diverse, model teachers seek to increase their multicultural competency in terms of knowledge and ability to engage in effective cross-cultural interactions (Littleford et al., 2010). In addition, rapidly changing technology means that teachers need to stay abreast of possible new ways to improve learning or accessibility through the use of technology (Millis et al., 2010). For example, incorporating the "flipped classroom" using online e-learning websites (e.g., Blackboard, Moodle, etc.) to teach can increase student learning (Wilson, 2013).

Once armed with a basic knowledge of theory and practice, the model teacher needs to ensure they establish mechanisms (or habits) to stay current on this topic. Bernstein and colleagues (2010) argued that development of teaching competency is an ongoing process for scientist-educators. Just as our fields of expertise are constantly developing as new scholarship emerges, pedagogy changes with the production of new knowledge. To illustrate, recent research placed doubt on the ability of learning styles to influence actual learning outcomes (Pashler et al., 2008) and on the ability of technology (e.g., course response systems) to improve learning in teaching methods that are already pedagogically sound (Anthis, 2011). Knowledge of these results could lead to dramatic shifts in teaching. Up-to-date pedagogical knowledge can even be considered an ethical responsibility. The American Association of University Professors (2015) states that ethical "professors devote their energies to developing and improving their scholarly competence" (see Chapter 4 for more on ethical teaching). Considering the evolving nature of pedagogy, model teachers engage in continuous efforts to learn about teaching.

Continuing education in pedagogy takes many forms. Model teachers read books and journals on education, attend teaching conferences, and participate in professional development opportunities on their own campuses. Most disciplines now have pedagogically oriented journals and a number of cross-disciplinary journals exist as well. For a great list of these, check out the list maintained by Kennesaw State University's Center for Excellence in Teaching and Learning at http://cetl.kennesaw.edu/teaching-journals-directory. College teachers can be informed of pedagogy in their disciplines by making it a point to read these journals (yes, it means setting aside time on a regular basis). Some examples from the different disciplines include:

- *College English* publishes articles about literature, rhetoric-composition, critical theory and others relating to the teaching of English.
- *CBE Life Sciences Education* publishes peer-reviewed articles on life science education at all levels and is aimed to serve biology teachers in all environments.

- *Operations Management Education Review* publishes refereed teaching materials and articles on key developments in teaching methods and technologies.
- *Philosophy of Music Education Review* publishes articles addressing philosophical or theoretical issues relevant to music education.
- *Physics Education* is an international journal reflecting the needs and interests of teachers in secondary school and at the introductory undergraduate level.
- *Scholarship of Teaching and Learning in Psychology* publishes empirical articles on teaching, research reviews specifically tailored for teachers, and updates on educational topics that cut across disciplines.

There are also national resources and organizations to help teachers. One example is the Reinvention Center, established in April 2000 as the only national organization to focus on undergraduate education exclusively at research universities. The Reinvention Center represents and advocates the distinctive kind of undergraduate education only research universities can provide. A unique consortium of 65 institutions, both public and private, the Center integrates and disseminates the educational insights and successes research faculties have developed and are devising (http://reinventioncenter.colostate.edu). Another great example is Writing Across the Curriculum and in the Disciplines at Sand Francisco State University (http://wac.sfsu.edu). "Writing across the curriculum" and "writing in the disciplines" refer to a national movement in higher education, now 40 years old, where writing receives curricular or pedagogical attention from faculty outside an English composition program.

Resources clearly exist, but the challenge is to make the time to keep abreast of the new developments. Model teachers schedule times to read journals on teaching, peruse books on pedagogy, and participate in teaching-related conferences. Sometimes these workshops may be online in the form of webinars. Sometimes teachers may be able to take advantage of teaching-related programming that is part of larger disciplinary conferences. One large national conference is the annual meeting of the Modern Language Association. A giant hub for English and language faculty from around the nation teaching different areas of literature and language, the conference has a special track for the teacher of language and literature. Similarly, whereas there are two national conferences on teaching in psychology—the National Institute of Teaching of Psychology and the Society for the Teaching of Psychology's Annual Conference on Teaching—the two largest disciplinary conferences (Association for Psychological Sciences and the American Psychological Association's Annual Meetings) also have teaching programming as part of the main conference. The bottom line is that model teachers have many opportunities for professional development, and they must find the time needed to keep abreast of pedagogical advancements and reflect on their teaching.

Understand How Students Learn

Whereas teachers learn about their disciplines en route to earning their degrees, and can add pedagogical content knowledge and pedagogical skills, the model teacher can benefit from a detailed understanding of how their students learn.

Understand How Students Acquire Knowledge

"Learner-centered teaching" is a phrase that has been bandied about widely. This phrase nicely focuses attention on a worthy (if not the sole) target of an instructor's energy—the student. Learner-centered teaching focuses attention on what the student is learning, how the student is learning, the conditions under which the student is learning, whether the student is retaining and applying the learning, and how current learning positions the student for future learning (Weimer, 2013). Looking at students as learners and being concerned about their learning directly influences teaching success (Boice, 1992). Beyond working itself into the gestalt of contemporary pedagogical philosophy and writing, learner-centered teaching also begs a focus on the process of learning, both in terms of how students approach learning and what predicts learning. Basic and applied research indicates that there are fundamental ways that people learn, and teachers should be aware of these basic learning principles (American Psychological Association, 2011; Worrell et al., 2010).

A substantial body of pedagogical writing bears on the ways that people acquire knowledge (National Research Council, 2000; Shell et al., 2010). For example, Bloom, Englehard, Furst, Hill, and Krathwohl (1956) initiated the modern examination of learning by proposing that optimal learning is achieved by having students analyze, evaluate, synthesize, and apply knowledge and otherwise go beyond just remembering and comprehending it. Anderson and Krathwohl (2001) and Krathwohl (2002) adapted this list, usually referred to as Bloom's Taxonomy, so that the skills included having students remember, understand, apply, analyze, evaluate, and create. Words to live by, and to design learning outcomes by. Model teachers consider this taxonomy when planning all of their educational activities. Before determining how content will be covered, you must ask yourself how high you want to take students up this hierarchy. The answer to that question has specific implications for how you choose to facilitate and evaluate students' learning (see Chapter 6).

In a somewhat different approach, a number of scholars have pointed out that all students are not the same. One of us (Guy) frequently teaches about the various approaches to psychotherapy. He has noticed that students universally enjoy the topic, but introductory students want to know what the "right" approach is, whereas advanced students revel in the fact that they can argue for their pet theory being "best." What's going on here? Although there are many similarities between students, they often think in different ways and have different understandings of how knowledge is created. Perry (1970), and those who updated his theory (Belenky et al., 1986), discussed different types of students, distinguishing dualistic students (for whom knowledge is certain and for whom right or wrong is acquired from authority) from students who are uncertain (who replace the right-or-wrong dichotomy by separating knowledge into what is known versus unknown) and students who use relativistic thinking (for whom some knowledge claims are better than others and for whom knowledge is validated by evidence relevant to context).

Perry's model, although valuable, may not reflect the development of all students in our classrooms (Belenky et al., 1986). For example, culture can impact teaching and learning preferences. Tweed and Lehman (2002) focused on cultural diversity and organized a wide body of findings about culturally Chinese and culturally Western learners. They compared the Socratic method of learning (exemplified by questioning one's own and others' beliefs, evaluating others' knowledge, having high esteem for self-generated knowledge, and focusing on error to evoke doubt) with the Confucian method of learning (exemplified by effortful, pragmatic, and respectful learning; behavioral reform; and the acquisition of essential knowledge). Tweed and Lehman (2002) suggest that teachers need to keep in mind what method of learning students may be using. If students are expecting dialogue but you just unload information, then the student is going to be less motivated to learn. Likewise, if a student is not used to discussion and the Socratic method, then they will require preparation for that different style of teaching.

There are other in-depth discussions of cognitive development as it relates to higher education (see Gurung and Schwartz, 2009 for a review). For example, Magolda (1992) distinguishes between *absolute knowers* (who acquire information from authorities), *transitional knowers* (who focus on understanding knowledge via others' views regarding uncertainty or via being forced to think), *independent knowers* (who decide their own opinions, focusing on either peer views or their own views), and *contextual knowers* (who construct knowledge by judging the evidence and others' views). King and Kitchener (1994) posited seven stages of knowing ranging from Stage 1, where knowledge is certain, and authorities' beliefs are accepted, to Stage 7, where some knowledge claims are valued over others on the basis of critical evaluation of the evidence.

Such extensive frameworks of knowing and knowledge acquisition provide educators with pragmatic innovations to enhance education. If we approach our classes with a one-size-fits-all model, we will leave some students behind. This brief review of the scholarship on ways of learning and knowledge formation provides topics for continuing education. Most instructors (perhaps outside of education) have not been instructed in these differences. What can we do? We believe that being cognizant of these differences can help us better design our classes and our assignments. Are your assignments aimed more towards one type of learning than another? Does your teaching style allow for a wide range of students? Perhaps you want to have special assignments prepared for students at either end of the developmental spectrum.

Understand How Students Solidify Knowledge

Moving beyond such general models of knowledge acquisition, a model teacher should also have a strong understanding of how learning works. Learning is best defined as "permanent changes in comprehension, understanding, and skills of the type that support long-term retention and transfer" (Soderstrom and Bjork, 2015, p. 176). The previous section focuses more on developmental differences in cognition and naturally occurring variance in students' mental capacities and understanding. Layered on top of these cognitive differences are the ways in which students solidify new material in memory. Luckily, model teaching practices can be guided by the huge research literature on how people learn.

Many different factors have been linked to learning and general academic performance in college (National Research Council, 2000; Robbins et al., 2004; Shell et al., 2010). Numerous factors such as achievement motivation, goals, social involvement, and perceived social support are associated with students' academic performance (Hattie, 2015; Robbins et al., 2004). In particular, factors such as effort, ability, and self-efficacy are strongly related to academic performance (Credé and Kuncel, 2008; Komarraju and Nadler, 2013). Not surprisingly, a student's cumulative college GPA, ACT score, and high school GPA also predict learning in a university setting (Komarraju et al., 2013). But wait, does this mean that learning is totally dependent on student characteristics—good students learn, bad ones don't? No, in fact there is much room for teachers to affect learning.

A large body of academic literature identifies key factors influencing learning (Credé and Kuncel, 2008) and what learning techniques work well (e.g., Dunlosky et al., 2013). If teachers know the behaviors that lead to learning, they can utilize methods that lead students to study using those practices. Study techniques are important because they predict academic performance over and above standardized tests and previous grades (Gurung, 2015) and allow faculty a direct route to help students learn material better.

In one of the most comprehensive reviews of study techniques, Dunlosky and colleagues (2013) closely examined ten learning techniques most commonly used by students. The authors described each technique, specified why it should theoretically improve learning, considered if use of the technique would generalize across contexts, highlighted real-world research with the technique, and also pointed out how the technique could be misused. The authors then rated the techniques. They created a "utility" or effectiveness level (high, medium, low) based on a number of key factors, specifically how well the technique generalized to different learners, forms of testing, and educational contexts. For example, high utility techniques are "robust and generalize widely" (Dunlosky et al., 2013, p.7). Low or moderate utility techniques only work when learning certain kinds of material, or lack empirical evidence. All ten techniques improve learning, although they vary in utility with some being low (e.g., highlighting) and others being high utility (e.g., spaced practice).

Five techniques did not fare well in the rating. Summarization, highlighting, keyword mnemonics, rereading, and using imagery for text learning got a 'low' rating (Dunlosky et al., 2013). One particular surprise was highlighting. Whereas students use this a lot and those who can highlight the most relevant material do better on exams (Bell and Limber, 2010), this technique overall is not recommended. Elaborative interrogation (generating an explanation for why a concept is true), self-explanation (relating new information to old information), and interleaved practice (studying by mixing different kinds of material within a single study session) got a moderate utility rating.

Only two techniques got top billing because of their high utility. Practice testing (or practice retrieval) and distributed practicing (or spaced practice) earned top marks from Dunlosky and colleagues (2013). Furthermore, students should be able to recall correctly more than once, at least twice (Karpicke, 2009) or better still, three times (Rawson et al., 2011). Spreading out studying, a technique referred to as "distributed practice" is particularly useful (Dunlosky et al., 2013). Get your students to use flashcards as it gets them to both practice test and space out practice over time (Wissman, 2012). You can also let your students know they will perform better on tests if they space out their studying over time rather than cramming it just before the test (Bain, 2012).

Few studies compare the techniques head-to-head simultaneously in a single study. One recent exception measured students' use of all ten techniques tested that best predicted exam scores (Bartozewski and Gurung, 2015). More than 300 students took part and their instructors provided exam scores to assess learning. The use of many techniques was correlated but only elaborative interrogation predicted exam scores. It is possible the use of certain techniques may be tied to how the techniques are recommended and required by instructors. In Bartozewski and Gurung's (2015) study, the role of the teacher was clear. Practice testing was used the most in one of the two classes in the sample. A close look showed that the instructor of that class rewarded practice testing and assigned 10 percent of the course grade for it. Savvy teachers can get their students to practice more. Students who use online assignments connected to the textbook more, perform better on exams (Gurung, 2015). In short, teachers should educate themselves on these different techniques and explore different ways to get students to use them.

Clearly, learning is a complex endeavor. The three of us have been reading the literature on learning for some time and it is still hard for us to keep everything straight. The bottom line seems to be that people best learn by practice (doing something repeatedly, spacing repetitions over time), testing (practice tests, retrieval without cues), observing a model (copying behavior, following demonstrated behaviors), deep processing (thinking of meaning, making connections, relating information to the self), and collaboration (sharing individual knowledge to increase group knowledge). One of these, deep processing, a particularly important and well-validated approach to learning, is one that does not really get enough attention in teaching circles. It is especially important as it probably underlies why active learning works. Having students think deeply about course material is a great teaching approach because it ties directly into how people learn. The more ways you can get your students to think deeply about what you are teaching the better.

The findings and variables reviewed previously provide a vivid picture of just how many different factors play a role in learning. An integral part of training to be a teacher is to develop an understanding, or at minimum a recognition, of these factors. A wonderful overview of the main factors is available in recent trade publications discussing how learning takes place (Brown et al., 2014; Carey, 2014). The model teacher can then build on this overview with knowledge of the pedagogical theories and practices that facilitate learning.

CASE STUDY REEXAMINED: A TEACHING ARTIFACT

Did Dr. Joanne Owens sound familiar? We all know many faculty members who fit the profile we amalgamated into the case study. Let's take a look at how key components of this chapter align with the questions we asked about the case study.

1. *How would you characterize Dr. Owens's training to be a professor of art history?* There is no doubt that Dr. Owens has the training to be an art history teacher. Her degree specialization is perfectly matched to the courses that she teaches. In addition, she keeps up-to-date in her area through both her research and her attendance at conferences, both of which are reflected in her lectures. Even students perceive her expertise as indicated by their comments on her course evaluations.

2. *How would you characterize Dr. Owens's training to be a teacher?* Well, her training to be a teacher seems to be at the opposite end of the spectrum from her art history qualifications. Dr. Owens has received no official training to be a teacher. Furthermore, there is no evidence that she has engaged in professional development on her own to develop her knowledge of pedagogy. Dr. Owens's teaching style is decidedly old school. No advancements in knowledge about pedagogy or how people learn seem to have made their way into her classroom.

3. *What recommendations would you make to Dr. Owens if you were the teaching specialist at the Center for Teaching and Learning?* We would begin by suggesting that Dr. Owens put herself through an unofficial course on college teaching. She should study some or all of the recommended

readings at the end of this chapter. Another important recommendation is for Dr. Owens to attend some conferences with programming related to teaching; it could be conferences devoted entirely to college teaching or a history conference with special programming on teaching. Of course, she should take advantage of professional development opportunities on her own campus as well. Once Dr. Owens feels that she has a strong grasp on pedagogy and the science of human learning, we would recommend that she redesign her courses so that they take advantage of her newfound expertise.

A Reflection on Your Self-Assessment

Going beyond Dr. Owens, how did you do on your self-assessment? This is a good time to go back to scores from the early pages of the chapter to see what more you can do. Make a concrete plan to do it. Perhaps schedule some time every few weeks to read up on journals in your field. Look for a good teaching conference you can attend. Sign up for electronic notifications for journals so you can be fresh with new developments. None of the Model Teaching Criteria in this section are necessarily difficult. The challenge is to fit them into your already busy life. The good news is creating time for all of this will pay off many times over.

Summary of Best Practices

Unlike the field of education—where future teachers take courses in teaching, do a student internship in a school, and then get a teaching certificate—college faculty do not have to take any specific courses on teaching before they step into the classroom. Whereas some uninformed members of the lay populace may mistakenly believe that all it takes is people skills, patience, and some level of content knowledge, teaching requires a lot more. In this chapter we reviewed some of the key components of teacher training. Although many elements discussed fall into the category of teaching fundamentals (see Chapter 2), there are many different elements of training model teachers should pay attention to. Model teachers should:

- understand how students learn;
- acquire knowledge about basic pedagogical theory and practice;
- maintain current knowledge of pedagogical theory and practice; and
- maintain expert knowledge in a subject area.

Whereas all four components can benefit teachers at any stage of their careers, the sooner instructors gain basic knowledge, the better. Furthermore, even seasoned instructors can benefit by keeping abreast of the changes in higher education in general but, more specifically, the growing body of research on teaching and learning.

The Very Busy People Book Club: Your Top Four Must-Reads

Ambrose, S. A., Bridges, M. W., DiPietro, M., Lovett, M. C., and Norman, M. K. (2010). *How learning works: 7 research-based principles for smart teaching.* San Francisco, CA: Jossey-Bass.

Brown, P. C., Roediger, H. L., and McDaniel, M. A. (2014). *Make it stick: The science of successful learning.* Cambridge, MA: Harvard University Press.

Dunlosky, J., Rawson, K. A., Marsh, E. J., Nathan, M. J., and Willingham, D. T. (2013). Improving students' learning with effective learning techniques: Promising directions from cognitive and educational psychology. *Psychological Science in the Public Interest,* 14, 4–58.

Shell, D. F., Brooks, D. W., Trainin, G., Wilson, K. M., Kauffman, D. F., and Herr, L. M. (2010). *The unified learning model: How motivational, cognitive, and neurobiological sciences inform best teaching practices.* New York: Springer.

References

Ambrose, S. A., Bridges, M. W., DiPietro, M., Lovett, M. C., and Norman, M. K. (2010). *How learning works: Seven research-based principles for smart teaching.* San Francisco, CA: Jossey-Bass.

American Association of University Professors (2015). *Statement on professional ethics.* Retrieved from www.aaup.org/report/statement-professional-ethics.

American Psychological Association (2011). *Principles for quality undergraduate education in psychology.* Washington, DC: American Psychological Association. Retrieved from www.apa.org/education/undergrad/principles.

Anderson, L. W. and Krathwohl, D. R. (eds.) (2001). *A taxonomy for learning, teaching, and assessing: A revision of Bloom's Taxonomy of educational objectives.* New York: Longman.

Anthis, K. (2011). Is it the clicker, or is it the question? Untangling the effects of student response system use. *Teaching of Psychology,* 38, 189–193.

Bain, K. (2012). *What the best college students do.* Cambridge, MA: Harvard University Press.

Bartoszewski, B. and Gurung, R. A. R. (2015). Comparing the relationship of learning techniques and exam score. *Scholarship of Teaching and Learning in Psychology,* 1, 219–228.

Belenky, M. F., Clinchy, B. M., Goldberger, N. R., and Tarule, J. M. (1986). *Women's ways of knowing: The development of self, voice, and mind.* New York: Basic Books.

Bell, K. E. and Limber, J. E. (2010). Reading skill, textbook marking, and course performance. *Literacy Research and Instruction,* 49, 56–67.

Bernstein, D., Addison, W., Altman, C., Hollister, D., Meera, K., Prieto, L. R., Rocheleau, C. A., and Shore, C. (2010). Toward a scientist-educator model of teaching psychology. In D. Halpern (ed.), *The NCUEP: A Blueprint for the Future* (pp. 29–46). Washington, DC: American Psychological Association.

Bloom, B. S., Englehard, M., Furst, E., Hill, W., and Krathwohl, D. (1956). *Taxonomy of educational objectives: Handbook I. Cognitive domain.* New York: McKay.

Boice, R. (1992). *The new faculty member.* San Francisco, CA: Jossey-Bass.

Boysen, G. A., Richmond, A. S., and Gurung, R. A. R. (2015). Model Teaching Criteria for psychology: Initial documentation of teachers' self-reported competency. *Scholarship of Teaching and Learning in Psychology*, 1, 48–59.

Brookfield, S. (2015). *The skillful teacher: On trust, technique, and responsiveness in the classroom.* San Francisco, CA: Jossey-Bass.

Brown, P. C., Roediger, H. L., and McDaniel, M. A. (2014). *Make it stick: The science of successful learning.* Cambridge, MA: Harvard University Press.

Buskist, W., Sikorski, J., Buckley, T., and Saville, B. K. (2002). Elements of master teaching. In S. F. Davis and W. Buskist (eds.), *The teaching of psychology: Essays in honor of Wilbert J. McKeachie and Charles L. Brewer* (pp. 27–39). Mahwah, NJ: Lawrence Erlbaum Associates, Inc.

Carey, B. (2014). *How we learn: The surprising truth about when, where, and why it happens.* New York: Random House.

Chickering, A. W. and Gamson, Z. F. (1987). Seven principles of good practice in undergraduate education. *AAHE Bulletin*, 39(7), 3–7.

Credé, M. and Kuncel, N. R. (2008). Study habits, skills, and attitudes: The third pillar supporting collegiate academic performance. *Perspectives on Psychological Science*, 3, 425–453.

Dewey, J. (1983). The child and the curriculum. In J. A. Boydston (ed.), *John Dewey: The middle works, 1899–1924: Vol. 2. 1902–1903* (pp. 273–291). Carbondale, IL: Southern Illinois University Press.

Dinham, S. M. (1996). What college teachers need to know. In R. J. Menges, M. Weimer, and Associates (eds.), *Teaching on solid ground: Using scholarship to improve practice* (pp. 297–314). San Francisco, CA: Jossey-Bass.

Donald, J. G. (2002). *Learning to think: Disciplinary perspectives.* San Francisco, CA: Jossey-Bass.

Dunlosky, J., Rawson, K. A., Marsh, E. J., Nathan, M. J., and Willingham, D. T. (2013). Improving students' learning with effective learning techniques: Promising directions from cognitive and educational psychology. *Psychological Science in the Public Interest*, 14, 4–58.

Grossman, P. L., Wilson, S. M., and Shulman, L. S. (1989). Teachers of substance: Subject matter knowledge for teaching. In M. C. Reynolds (ed.), *Knowledge base for the beginning teacher* (pp. 23–34). New York: Pergamon.

Gurung, R. A. R. (2015). Three investigations of the utility of textbook teaching supplements. *Psychology of Learning and Teaching*, 1, 48–59.

Gurung, R. A. R. and Schwartz, E. (2009). *Optimizing teaching and learning: Pedagogical research in practice.* Malden, MA: Blackwell.

Gurung, R. A. R. and Schwartz, B. M. (2010). Riding the third wave of SoTL. *International Journal for the Scholarship of Teaching and Learning*, 4(2). Retrieved from http://digitalcommons.georgiasouthern.edu/ij-sotl.

Gurung, R. A. R., Haynie, A., and Chick, N. (eds.) (2009). *Signature pedagogies across the disciplines.* Arlington, VA: Stylus.

Hattie, J. (2015). The applicability of visible learning to higher education. *Scholarship of Teaching and Learning in Psychology*, 1, 79–91.

Haynie, A., Chick, N., and Gurung, R. A. R. (2012). Signature pedagogies in the liberal arts and beyond. In N. Chick, A. Haynie, and R. A. R. Gurung (eds.), *Exploring more signature pedagogies* (pp. 1–11). Sterling, VA: Stylus.

Karpicke, J. D. (2009). Metacognitive control and strategy selection: Deciding to practice retrieval during learning. *Journal of Experimental Psychology: General*, 138, 469–486.

King, P. M. and Kitchener, K. S. (1994). *Developing reflective judgment: Understanding and promoting intellectual growth and critical thinking in adolescents and adults.* San Francisco, CA: Jossey-Bass.

Knowles, M. (1973). *The adult learner: A neglected species.* Houston, TX: Gulf.

Knowles, M. S. (1980). *The modern practice of adult education.* New York: Cambridge.

Komarraju, M. and Nadler, D. (2013). Self-efficacy and academic achievement: Why do implicit beliefs, goals, and effort regulation matter? *Learning and Individual Differences,* 25, 67–72.

Komarraju, M., Ramsey, A., and Rinella, V. (2013). Cognitive and non-cognitive predictors of college readiness and performance: Role of academic discipline. *Learning and Individual Differences,* 24, 103–109.

Krathwohl, D. R. (2002). A revision of Bloom's Taxonomy: An overview. *Theory Into Practice,* 41, 212–218.

Littleford, L. N., Buskist, W., Frantz, S. M., Galvan, D. B., Hendersen, R. W., McCarthy, M. A., Page, M. C., and Puente, A. E. (2010). Psychology students today and tomorrow. In D. F. Halpern (ed.), *Undergraduate education in psychology: A blueprint for the future of the discipline* (pp. 63–79). Washington, DC: American Psychological Association.

Magolda, M. B. B. (1992). *Knowing and reasoning in college: Gender-related patterns in students' intellectual development.* San Francisco, CA: Jossey-Bass.

McElroy, H. K. and Prentice-Dunn, S. (2005). Graduate students' perceptions of a teaching of psychology course. *Teaching of Psychology,* 32, 123–125.

Meyer, J. and Land, R. (2005). Threshold concepts and troublesome knowledge: Epistemological considerations and a conceptual framework for teaching and learning. *Higher Education,* 49, 373–388.

Millis, K., Baker, S., Owen, J. E., Blakemore, O., Connington, F., Harper, Y. Y., Hung, W.-C., Kohn, A., and Stowell, J. (2010). Teaching and learning in the digital world. In D. F. Halpern (ed.), *Undergraduate education in psychology: A blueprint for the future of the discipline* (pp. 113–128). Washington, DC: American Psychological Association.

National Research Council (2000). *How people learn: Brain, mind, experience and school.* Washington, DC: National Academy Press.

Pace, D. and Middendorf, J. (2004). *Decoding the disciplines: Helping students learn disciplinary ways of thinking.* San Francisco, CA: Jossey-Bass.

Palmer, P. (1998). *The courage to teach: Exploring the inner landscape of a teacher's life.* New York: John Wiley & Sons.

Parini, J. (2005). *The art of teaching.* New York: Oxford University Press.

Pashler, H., McDaniel, M., Rohrer, D., and Bjork, R. (2008). Learning styles: Concepts and evidence. *Psychological Science in the Public Interest,* 9(3), 105–119.

Perry, W. G. (1970). *Forms of intellectual development in the college years.* New York: Holt.

Prieto, L. R. and Meyers, S. A. (1999). Effects of training and supervision on the self-efficacy of psychology graduate teaching assistants. *Teaching of Psychology,* 26, 264–266.

Prieto, L. R. and Scheel, K. R. (2008). Teaching assistant training in counseling psychology. *Counseling Psychology Quarterly,* 21, 49–59.

Rawson, K. A., O'Neil, R., and Dunlosky, J. (2011). Accurate monitoring leads to effective control and greater learning of patient education materials. *Journal of Experimental Psychology: Applied,* 17, 288–302.

Richmond, A. S., Boysen, G. A., Gurung, R. A. R., Tazeau, Y. N., Meyers, S. A., and Sciutto, M. J. (2014). Aspirational Model Teaching Criteria for psychology. *Teaching of Psychology,* 41, 281–295.

Robbins, S., Lauver, K., Le, H., Davis, D., Langley, R., and Carlstrom, A. (2004). Do psychological and study skill factors predict college outcome? A meta-analysis. *Psychological Bulletin*, 130, 261–288.

Schwartz, E. and Gurung, R. A. R. (2012). *Evidence-based teaching in higher education.* Washington, DC: American Psychological Association.

Shell, D. F., Brooks, D. W., Trainin, G., Wilson, K. M., Kauffman, D. F., and Herr, L. M. (2010). *The unified learning model: How motivational, cognitive, and neurobiological sciences inform best teaching practices.* New York: Springer.

Shulman, L. S. (1987). Knowledge and teaching: foundations of the new reform. *Harvard Educational Review*, 57, 1–22.

Shulman, L. S. (2005). Signature pedagogies in the professions. *Daedalus*, 134, 52–59.

Soderstrom, N. C. and Bjork, R. A. (2015). Learning versus performance: An integrative review. *Perspectives on Psychological Science*, 10, 176–199.

Tweed, R. G. and Lehman, D. R. (2002). Learning considered within a cultural context: Confucian and Socratic approaches. *American Psychologist*, 57, 89–99.

Weimer, M. (2010). *Inspired college teaching: A career-long resource for professional growth.* San Francisco, CA: Jossey-Bass.

Weimer, M. (2013). *Learner-centered teaching: Five key changes to practice.* San Francisco, CA: Jossey-Bass.

Wilson, S. G. (2013). The flipped class: A method to address the challenges of an undergraduate statistics course. *Teaching of Psychology*, 40, 193–199.

Wissman, K. T. (2012). How and when do students use flashcards? *Memory*, 20, 568–579.

Worrell, F. C., Casad, B. J., Daniel, D. B., McDaniel, M., Messer, W. S., Miller, H. J., Prohaska, V., and Zlokovich, M. S. (2010). Promising principles for translating psychological science into teaching and learning. In D. F. Halpern (ed.), *Undergraduate education in psychology: A blueprint for the future of the discipline* (pp. 129–144). Washington, DC: American Psychological Association.

4

WHAT INSTRUCTIONAL METHODS DO MODEL TEACHERS USE?

Thousands of studies have been conducted on assessing the efficacy of instructional methods in higher education. Great attention and debate has been given to this issue and to this point specifically: there is no agreement as to what constitutes the *best instructional method*. As such, model instructional methods are elusive and difficult to pin down. Case in point—the three of us have demonstrated effective teaching, but use varied instructional methods. Aaron approaches teaching by using the kitchen-sink method (e.g., sometimes he uses active learning instruction, other times direct instruction, and other times the Socratic method), whereas, Guy typically uses the methods of collaborative learning, the specific technique of interteaching, and direct instruction. Regan uses an extremely conversational style to teach, inviting students into the discussion at every step along the way. Likely, the immutable truth is that there is no silver-bullet teaching method, but model teaching does share some common features. The evidence suggests that these features can be divided into two model criteria: (1) the effective use of broad and varied pedagogical approaches (e.g., collaborative learning, active learning, interteaching), and (2) the ability to demonstrate excellence in specific teaching skills and behaviors (e.g., listening, caring, engagement, rapport).

Before jumping into the nuts-and-bolts of instructional method research and best practices, as practitioners of science we need to establish a baseline measurement of your perceptions of your instructional methods and teaching skills. Please take a few minutes and reflect back on your past teaching experiences, and then complete the self-assessment in Table 4.1. After completing this self-assessment, keep your results in mind while you read the chapter. We will revisit your self-assessment at the end of the chapter and see what you feel like you are doing well and what you can improve upon.

TABLE 4.1 Self-Assessment of Your Instructional Methods Model Teaching Criteria

Directions: Please indicate on the scale below how often you take part in these efforts/activities to improve your instructional methods.

Scale: 5 = Always, 4 = Often, 3 = Sometimes, 2 = Rarely, 1 = Never

Your score

1. You use more than one instructional method (e.g., active learning) when teaching.	
2. You strive to be a better teacher.	
3. You promote class discussion.	
4. You are enthusiastic when you teach.	
5. You are professional.	
6. You are prepared for class.	
7. You are happy, positive, and humorous.	
8. You provide constructive feedback to students.	
9. You understand your students.	
10. You encourage your students.	
11. You care about your students.	
12. You treat students fairly.	
13. You communicate effectively with your students.	
14. Your students respect you.	
15. You are approachable.	
16. Your students are consistently engaged in class.	
17. You adapt your instructional methods to individual student needs.	
18. You are receptive to your students.	
19. Your class is enjoyable for students.	
20. You are compassionate towards your students.	

Note: This self-assessment is adapted and modified from Richmond et al. (2014), Keeley et al. (2006), Boysen et al. (2015), Wilson and Ryan (2013), and Lammers and Gillaspy (2013).

Now that you have assessed your own instructional methods, let's take a look at an example of what someone else might do in a typical class.

CASE STUDY: PROFESSOR PADMA AMIRI'S MEDICAL ANTHROPOLOGY COURSE

Professor Padma Amiri is a full professor of physical/biological anthropology. She has been teaching for more than 20 years. She typically teaches a lower-division course, introduction to medical anthropology. Her student evaluations for teaching for this course are right at the university average. This class has more than 70 enrolled students, but on average only 50 students attend each class. She strictly follows the course syllabus and evaluates her students using ten quizzes and two exams. Her typical class occurs as follows: Dr. Amiri arrives exactly at the scheduled class time. She opens with the student learning objectives of the chapter she is covering and then uses PowerPoint to lecture on the content. She rarely leaves the podium to move around the class. In her lecture, she uses a lot of pictures from medical cases and has a lot of text on her slides. Next, she presents a medical case and has students discuss the case in small groups for about five minutes. During this time, she looks at her notes and prepares for the next portion of the class. After the small group discussion, she lectures for approximately 25 minutes. She then gives a multiple-choice quiz on the reading for that day. The class wraps up with an additional 15 minutes of summary lecture. Dr. Amiri then promptly leaves in order to make it to her next class.

Now take a moment to answer these questions. We will revisit your answers at the end of the chapter. After reading the chapter, yes, you may change your answers.

1. What teaching method is Padma using?
2. How would you describe her teaching skills?
3. Would you say she engages her students? If so, how?
4. Based on the information, do you think she has good rapport with her students?
5. What can she do to improve her teaching?

More Than One? Yes, Model Teachers Use Varied Instructional Methods

Model teachers embrace varied pedagogical approaches that focus on engaging students in the learning process (Boysen et al., 2015; Handelsman et al., 2005; Richmond et al., 2014). In Boysen and colleagues' (2015) study of Model Teaching Criteria, 75 percent of teachers utilized varied instructional methods—the idea of the straight-lecture or straight-discussion teacher seems to be false. In a recent review of contemporary instructional methods, Slavich and Zimbardo (2012) synthesized the shared assumptions among instructional methods and suggested that when teachers use varied instructional techniques, they actively engage students and have the ability to do so in diverse academic settings. Moreover, several meta-analyses and reviews suggest that active learning, collaborative learning, and problem-based learning are effective instructional methods (Dochy et al., 2003; Freeman et al., 2014; Johnson et al., 1998; Prince, 2004; Springer et al., 1999; Walker and Leary, 2009). So what are the best evidenced-based instructional methods? Well, describing all of the effective instructional strategies is beyond the scope of this chapter, but we would like to summarize some of the most widely researched instructional methods with demonstrated effectiveness in enhancing student learning and skills. These methods include active learning, problem-based learning, and interteaching.

The Go-to: Active Learning Instruction

Think of something that you are really, really good at. Pick something specific. Now, consider how you got to be good at what you picked. Chances are you developed your skill by actively practicing it over and over and over. Learning is not a spectator sport—you have to be actively engaged in the process (for a demonstration of how to use this thought exercise in class see Zakrajsek, 2015). Ever since Bonwell and Eison's (1991) call for active learning techniques to be implemented in higher education, practitioners and researchers have studied the use and efficacy of active learning. It is one of the most studied instructional methods in higher education. Active learning builds upon students' prior experiences and emphasizes students' active involvement with the material (Benjamin, 1991). Active learning also emphasizes deep learning, understanding, and accountability on the part of students (Biggs, 1999; Lea et al., 2003). This can be accomplished through instructional methods such as small group activities, discussions, experiments, debates, one-minute reflection papers, role playing, think-pair-shares, journaling, and hands-on demonstrations. Additionally, active learning puts the onus for learning on the student. The role of teachers is that of an expert facilitator; they create learning opportunities and assist students in the understanding, integration, evaluation, and synthesis of material (e.g., Yoder and Hochevar, 2005).

Instruction using active learning can come in many shapes and sizes. However, there are several things that you should keep in mind when implementing active learning. First, it is important to activate students' thought processes, rather than just having them engage in some active behavior. That is, active learning requires more than just doing an activity. When using one of the active learning techniques (e.g., role playing, demonstrations, following an experimental procedure), make sure that you have students connect their experience with the concept by discussing, reflecting, and debriefing. If they just complete an activity that requires some physical activation, they may not actually learn the underlying concept behind the activity. Rather, active learning strategies need to facilitate and reinforce the learning of specific material. Second, active learning instruction requires time and effort on your part. That is, you will need to research different ways to incorporate active learning within your discipline and see which ones work best in particular situations and types of material. In doing so, you may ask yourself some key questions. Will the active learning technique facilitate learning? How will you introduce the activity? How will you explicitly connect it to course material? What might be some unforeseen consequences to doing the activity? Finally, active learning can sometimes cause students to feel uncomfortable or can have seriously detrimental effects on learning. For example, one of our colleagues teaches courses touching on racism, sexism, homophobia, hate speech, date rape, and other sensitive topics, and it is good that there is an unpredictability when using active learning strategies. However, he has to be careful because using these strategies also heightens the importance of being sympathetic about sensitive material. So, establish rules of civility and conduct when debating sensitive topics, allow students to do alternative tasks, and ask for volunteers.

Does active learning instruction really work? The evidence for its effectiveness, although always open to debate, is fairly strong. Research indicates that active learning techniques promote overall student learning (Hake, 1998; Hoellwarth and Moelter, 2011), learning of higher-level concepts (Lea et al., 2003; Richmond and Kindelberger Hagan, 2011; Yoder and Hochevar, 2005), and improved student evaluations of teaching (Richmond and Kindelberger Hagan, 2011). Furthermore, teachers have effectively implemented active learning into all types of academic disciplines (Johnson et al., 1998). Collaborative learning is even supported by multiple meta-analyses (Freeman et al., 2014; Prince, 2004). Considering all of the research on the efficacy of active learning instruction, we believe it is safe to conclude that developing your ability to incorporate active learning into your classroom will undoubtedly improve your teaching, especially when you use it with other instructional methods.

Problem-based Learning Instruction

Both individually and in groups, problem-based learning provides students an opportunity to tackle complex, real-world, multifaceted, and sometimes ambiguous problems (Slavich and Zimbardo, 2012). Originating in the 1960s in medical education, problem-based learning is designed to create cognitive conflict, be context-specific, build on and challenge prior knowledge, and be inductive in nature. Problem-based instruction empowers students' ability to obtain knowledge and the skills to solve real-life problems. As a product of problem-based learning, students also acquire communication and collaboration skills. Within problem-based learning, teachers are viewed as a facilitator and often referred to as a "tutor." The teacher's responsibility is to provide a framework for students to succeed. Teachers assist in student learning by scaffolding, asking questions, and providing models and exemplars of solutions to similar problems (Savery, 2006). As students progress through problem-based instruction, learning becomes their responsibility, and the teacher gradually decreases the guidance and information needed to solve the problem.

The procedures students follow to solve problems is at the heart of this technique. Nilson (2010) suggests that teachers should structure the problem sequentially. To start, students in teams or groups should review an interesting, authentic problem. Students analyze and define the problem (with teacher input and guidance). Next, they organize and identify what they already know about the problem and identify what they need to know to solve the problem (i.e., "learning issues"). Students then prioritize the learning issues and decide how to find the information needed to solve the problem. They divide and complete the work among the group. During this process, students meet and discuss their findings with the group and at the end they present what they believe to be the best possible solution to the problem.

One of the most important steps to problem-based learning is creating a well-crafted but ill-defined problem. This is a much-discussed issue, and it is generally suggested that well-crafted, ill-defined problems are interesting, open-ended, and complex; they also have multiple solutions, require more information than initially available, do not immediately state whether students have made the correct decision, and are authentic to the discipline (Allen et al., 1996; Gallagher, 1997). To illustrate, one of us teaches a course on psychological measurement. The major project for this course is for students to find a faculty or staff member on campus who needs information that can only be provided through the application of psychological measurements. Students then research and propose a solution for this client. Examples of problems related to other disciplines can be found at the National Center for Case Study Teaching in Science website, which provides a wealth of information about problem-based learning (http://science-cases.lib.buffalo.edu/cs). Active learning techniques are certainly not a refuge for lazy teachers looking to avoid work; crafting a good problem for students can be much more labor-intensive and difficult than crafting a good lecture.

Let us illustrate problem-based instruction through an example. Imagine you're a philosophy teacher and you are discussing hate speech in your course. One of the goals in the course is to reflect on trade-offs of particular values (e.g., harm to others, freedom to speak our mind). Your course readings are built around articulating cases for particular ideas (e.g., types of harm, importance of freedom) and concrete applications. In the spirit of problem-based learning, you might ask students whether the n-word should be used on campus or in the workplace. You could divide the class into two groups: (1) for the use and (2) against the use. Your students would then work independently identifying various models of value (e.g., harm and freedom of speech) to build their case for or against the use of the word in those contexts. Next, you would have students present their findings to one another. You would then end by providing feedback to the students.

Much like active learning, problem-based learning has been widely studied in higher education. A few meta-analyses suggest that problem-based learning is effective at promoting student learning (Albanese and Mitchell, 1993; Dochy et al., 2003). Additionally, problem-based learning is enjoyed by students (Albanese and Mitchell, 1993), and, compared to direct instruction, it leads to better problem-solving skills (Edens, 2000), critical thinking (Tiwari et al., 2006), long-term retention of course content (Dochy et al., 2003), and skill development (Prince, 2004). Furthermore, problem-based learning can improve a whole host of other student skills and abilities including teamwork, conceptual understanding, research skills, self-direction, and emotional intelligence (Nilson, 2010). However, Prince (2004) found that in short-term retention of information, problem-based instruction could be detrimental to learning. Regardless, depending on your learning goal (e.g., critically thinking about course content) and in conjunction with other instructional methods, problem-based learning can be a useful and effective instructional method that is adaptable to many different content domains.

Interteaching: What a Novel Idea!

Interteaching was originally proposed by Boyce and Hineline (2002), then further advanced by Saville and colleagues (2005, 2006, 2011). Unlike the previously discussed instructional methods, interteaching is a behavioral approach to instruction that attempts to optimize student learning by changing the classroom environment so that it reinforces early preparation, collaboration, and engagement with the material. Interteaching follows a straightforward sequence of learning activities (Saville et al., 2011). It begins outside of class; the instructor designs a preparation (prep) guide that typically includes 10–15 questions designed to guide the students through an assigned reading. Questions can vary in difficulty and cognitive level (see Chapter 6 for a discussion of Bloom's Taxonomy). Students start their work outside of class as well; they complete the prep guide and come to class prepared to share their answers.

When students come to class, they form pairs and have a guided discussion based on the prep guide (Saville et al., 2011). While students are discussing the prep guide, the teacher and/or teaching assistant moves from dyad to dyad to answer questions and keep students on track. The majority of class time (two-thirds is recommended) is spent engaged in discussion. Upon completion of their discussion, students fill out a record sheet for the teacher that identifies difficult topics they would like reviewed (see Chapter 8 for an example). Based on this feedback, the teacher provides a brief lecture, typically at the start of the next class period, that covers the specific topics students identified as difficult or particularly interesting.

You might be asking yourself, why would students be motivated to do all of this work inside and outside of class? Saville and colleagues (2005, 2011) suggest that interteaching is most effective when teachers assign participation points for each discussion (approximately 10 percent of course grade is recommended). Furthermore, in order to reinforce students for completing the prep guides and using discussion to enhance their learning, it is essential that tests and quizzes include items that are closely based on prep guide questions (Boyce and Hineline, 2002).

There is a growing body of research that demonstrates the efficacy of interteaching to increase student learning of course material (Arntzen and Hoium, 2010; Saville et al. 2005, 2011, 2014; Scoboria and Pascual-Leone, 2009). In one of the first empirical lab-based studies of interteaching, Saville and colleagues (2005) found that students taught using interteaching, as compared to lectures and simply reading the chapter, had significantly higher recall of course content. Saville and colleagues (2006) replicated this study in a classroom-based experiment and found that students taught using interteaching had almost 10 percent higher scores on exams than students taught using direct instruction (e.g., lecture). Finally, one might worry that interteaching would only work with highly motivated and intelligent students, but research has also demonstrated its effectiveness with low- to moderate-achieving students (Saville et al., 2012). If you are interested in creating a classroom environment that embodies active engagement through student-led discussions, interteaching may be the method for you.

We have just covered a few of the most widely researched instructional methods with strong evidence of effectiveness. One instructional method that has yet to be discussed is pure lecture. There is little evidence to suggest that a teacher who solely lectures to their students is a highly effective (model) teacher. Between us, the authors have read thousands of articles and books on pedagogy, and we have yet to encounter a single study showing the superiority of straight lecture over some competing technique being used in a college classroom. This is not to say that model teachers cannot lecture, but they are likely to use several other, more active, instructional methods interwoven with some lecturing.

Interteaching, active learning, and problem-based learning are not the only effective methods of instruction. So, if you are looking for more instructional methods and want to know how to use these methods, in Table 4.2 you will find a summary of several additional instructional methods including their definitions, classroom examples, and sources to further investigate and implement into your teaching.

Model Teachers Use Effective Teaching Skills and Behaviors

Thus far, we have made model instructional practices look as simple as following a recipe—learn an empirically supported teaching technique, add students, stir to combine! As you would expect, there is more to model teaching than selecting a high-quality general method of instruction; model teaching involves the application of a number of specific teaching skills. The importance of specific teaching skills is supported by a great deal of research (Buskist et al., 2002; Epting et al., 2004; Keeley et al., 2006, 2010; Marsh, 1984; Svinicki and McKeachie, 2011). So what are these basic teaching skills? Generally speaking, model teachers exhibit behaviors that are caring and supportive (Keeley et al., 2006); consequently, they have good rapport with students (Wilson et al., 2010). Model teachers are also professional and have strong communication skills (Keeley et al., 2006). They exhibit ethical and principled behaviors (Bain, 2004; Hill and Zinsmeister, 2012). Finally, model teachers create opportunities to engage students (Miller and Butler, 2011). Below we will describe these skills in more detail and outline ways to use them in your classroom.

As discussed in Chapter 2, good teachers—rather, great teachers—exhibit similar model (or master) teaching qualities and behaviors. As Buskist and colleagues put it, model teachers are particularly able to:

TABLE 4.2 Instructional Methods, Definitions, Classroom Examples, and Sources

Method and definition	Classroom examples	Must-reads
Active learning, student-centered and collaborative learning: Forms of instruction which teachers seek to adapt instruction based on students' needs and abilities in a peer or group format.	Guided or active reading, jigsaw, group roundtables, number heads, think-pair-share, learning logs, three-step interview, muddiest point, research teams, etc.	Barkley et al. (2005) Love et al. (2014) Mills (2012) O'Donnell et al. (2006) Weimer (2002)
Problem-based learning: To learn about a subject, students (in groups or individually) are given an open-ended problem to solve through a specific series of steps.	Give students a problem, have them identify what they know about it, determine what other information they need, evaluate possible solutions, solve the problem, and report their findings.	Amador et al. (2006) Duch et al. (2001) Evensen and Hmelo–Silver (2000) Savin–Baden (2000)
Interteaching: A behavioral technique that requires students to prepare for class by engaging in material before class instruction and uses incentives to motivate students.	Before class, students complete a "prep-guide" on assigned reading. In class, student form pairs and have a guided discussion based on the prep guide then identify difficult topics they would like reviewed.	Arntzen and Hoium, 2010 Boyce and Hineline (2002) Saville et al. (2005, 2006, 2011, 2014)
Just-in-time teaching: Pre-class assessments focus students' attention on the current content in the course, maximize classroom discussion, and structure out-of-class learning.	Web-based questions or exercises delivered before class that are meant to identify gaps in student learning	Astin (1993) Novak et al. (1999) Higdon and Topaz (2009) Simkins and Maier (2010)
Experiential, discovery and inquiry-based learning: Students solve problems using prior knowledge to discover new information by exploring and manipulating their environment.	Labs, experiments, hands-on activities, have students engage in the scientific method, discussion boards, blogging, reflective journals, simulations, student presentations, service learning projects	Aditomo et al. (2013) Beard and Wilson (2006) Moon (2004) Nilson (2010)

(continued)

TABLE 4.2 (cont.)

Method and definition	Classroom examples	Must-reads
Socratic teaching: A form of discussion between teachers and students in which the teacher challenges the beliefs of their students by having students defend their position.	Socratic circles, elaborative interrogation, self-questioning, probing questions, expansive questions, be a devil's advocate, seminars.	Biel (1992) Gose (2009) Jarvis (2006) Mangrum (2010)
Situated learning: Learning that is situated within culture, contexts, and an authentic activity that requires social interaction and collaboration.	Solve real-world problems, cognitive apprenticeships, case studies, group work that is authentic to the discipline, fishbowl, triad, pose ambiguous questions.	Brown et al. (1998) Lave and Wenger (1991) McLellan (1996) Young (1993)

Note: Some information in this table is adapted and modified from Slavich and Zimbardo (2012).

(a) instill in their students a desire to learn, (b) help their students actually learn something about the subject matter, (c) help their students discover that what they are learning is interesting, and (d) demonstrate to their students that learning in and of itself is enjoyable.

(Buskist et al., 2002, p. 32)

But how do they do this? Many researchers have attempted to answer this question by investigating the behaviors that help master teachers accomplish these tasks (Buskist et al., 2002; Epting et al., 2004; Keeley et al., 2006; Schaeffer et al., 2003). To study model teaching behaviors, Keeley and colleagues (2006) constructed and validated the 28-item Teacher Behavior Checklist and found that behaviors fall into two categories: (1) caring and supportive behaviors (e.g., is the teacher flexible, open-minded, creative, etc.) and (2) professional competency and communication skills (e.g., whether the teacher is an effective communicator, authoritative, punctual, etc.).

The question then becomes, how does one improve these behaviors? Luckily, both Buskist and colleagues (2002, pp. 34–35) and Keeley and colleagues (2006) have provided a list of model teaching qualities and corresponding examples of behaviors (see Table 2.2 in Chapter 2). Efforts at improvement can begin with an honest self-assessment of your consistency with the behaviors. Alternatively, you could allow students to report their perceptions of your behaviors. Then you can work on developing the behaviors that you or your students identify as relative weaknesses.

Is working on these behaviors worth your time and effort? Actually, there is good evidence that students notice and appreciate model teaching behaviors. For instance, Keeley, Furr and Buskist (2010) found that when students from two separate universities rated their best teacher, their worst teacher, and the teacher of whatever class they had most recently, all three teachers received significantly different ratings with the best teacher being highest and worst teacher being lowest. Similarly, Epting and colleagues (2004) found that students rated "ideal teachers" as more accessible, personable, and flexible. One of the more convincing studies of model teaching behaviors comes from Landrum and Stowell (2013). They had more than 700 students view video clips of teachers demonstrating eight of the model teaching behaviors. The results showed that students were consistent in their agreement about what constituted model teaching (significant correlations ranging from 0.25 to 0.71). Furthermore, Komarraju, Musulkin, and Bhattacharya (2010) found that the model teaching behaviors of approachability, accessibility, respect, and caring could lead to students having higher intrinsic motivation and academic self-concept (e.g., beliefs about academic abilities).

There is also some cross-cultural support for the efficacy of model teaching behaviors. Lammers, Savina, Skotko, and Churlyaeva (2010) found that both US and Russian samples had similar beliefs regarding the model teaching behaviors. Additionally, Keeley, Christopher, and Buskist (2012) found evidence of the same model teaching behaviors in Japanese universities. However, Japanese students tended to emphasize the model teaching behaviors of knowledgeable, effective communication, approachable/personable, and enthusiasm more than American students.

Take a moment and reflect on how your behaviors match up with those listed in Table 2.2. Which behaviors do you need to improve upon? If you have room to grow, do not be frustrated. As Buskist (2004) has suggested, to develop into a model teacher, we need to constantly work on improving these skills so we can ensure that our students get the best possible learning experience.

On the Importance of Teacher and Student Rapport and Teacher Immediacy

If you think about the best teacher you ever had, what characteristics did he or she possess? What drew you to him or her? Research suggests that the teacher likely had great rapport with you. But, what does that mean for you as a teacher? Does it mean that you are popular with students? Does it mean that you are perceived as affable and fun-loving? Does it mean that you are perceived as trustworthy? Rapport has been widely studied and can include all of these attributes, but it is generally defined "as a relationship of mutual trust and liking" (Wilson et al., 2010, pp. 247–248) and "a personal connection and an enjoyable interaction" with students (Gremler and Gwinner, 2000). Wilson and Ryan (2013) state that rapport includes perceptions of the teacher (e.g., enthusiastic, receptive, reliable, caring) and elements of student engagement (e.g., likability, enjoyment, immediacy, and encouragement).

Logically then, how can you increase rapport with students? Wilson and Ryan (2012, p. 86) suggest that we should create "positive student–teacher interactions" by:

- "treating students respectfully;
- offering out-of-class communications such as holding office hours, using email, and using Facebook [or other social media];
- welcoming students to the class via e-mail before the term begins;
- being kind and positive on the first day of class to set up positive student expectations;
- being competent and conscientious;
- avoiding threatening students (e.g., with poor grades); and
- not making a habit of discussing student problems with others."

(Wilson and Ryan, 2012, pp. 86–87)

Furthermore, Meyers (2009) suggests that to increase rapport, you need to care. Specifically, you need to let your students know you care by making eye-contact, using humor, diffusing power by using the personal pronouns of "we" and "our," offering accurate and substantial praise, and talking to students before and after class.

Why do all of this work to improve your rapport with students? Because, evidence suggests that if you improve your rapport with students, their academic performance will improve (Frisby and Martin, 2010; Lammers and Gillaspy, 2013; Wilson et al., 2010; Wilson and Ryan, 2013). Building rapport is associated with increases in variables such as attendance, attention, motivation, participation, and study time (Benson et al., 2005; Buskist and Saville, 2004; Frisby and Martin, 2010; Wilson et al., 2010). Furthermore, strong rapport develops a positive working alliance between faculty and students, which benefits learning (Rogers, 2015). Finally, there is a growing body of research that suggests high rapport with students positively increases students' perceptions of teaching effectiveness (Lammers and Gillaspy, 2013; Richmond et al., 2015; Wilson et al., 2010).

If you recall your favorite teacher again, research suggests that she or he exhibited immediacy with you. What does it mean to be immediate with students? Synonyms of immediacy include proximity, nearness, closeness, and vicinity. So, does this mean model teachers are close with their students both physically and psychologically? Not exactly, as the answer is more complex than that. Teacher immediacy can be operationalized by the degree to which "people are drawn toward persons and things they like, evaluate highly, and prefer: and they avoid or move away from things they dislike, evaluate negatively, or do not prefer" (Mehrabian, 1971, p. 1). In other words, teacher immediacy involves both psychological and physical availability. As such, teacher immediacy is divided into verbal and non-verbal behaviors. For example, non-verbal behaviors include smiling and gesturing naturally. Examples of verbal immediacy include calling students by name and conversing informally with them (Gorham and Christophel, 1990).

To develop your teaching immediacy skills, Richmond, Gorham, and McCroskey (1987), Gorham (1988), and Meyers (2009) suggest that teachers should:

- have a relaxed body posture;
- smile a lot (even digital smiles may help ☺);
- use a dynamic and engaging voice (i.e., avoid a monotone voice);
- move around the classroom (do not solely stand behind a desk or podium/ lectern);
- gesture when talking; and
- make eye-contact.

Additionally, Gorham (1988) and Meyers (2009) suggested teachers who want to show verbal immediacy should:

- have students address you by name and address them by their name;
- ask questions that require students to reflect on their own personal experiences (not rhetorical questions);

- stay positive (avoid publicly criticizing students);
- use volunteers in class (avoid calling out students);
- use appropriate humor; and
- use personal examples.

It is important to improve your teacher immediacy because evidence suggests that it can have a profound effect on student learning and how students perceive you as a teacher. For instance, increased teaching immediacy is associated with student attendance, motivation, affective learning, and academic performance (Frymier, 1994; Pogue and AhYun, 2006; Rocca, 2004; Titsworth, 2001). Exhibiting immediacy also positively affects students' perceptions of teachers' responsiveness, assertiveness (Thomas et al., 1994), and general effectiveness (Moore et al., 1996).

So what was your response to questions 11–14 in Table 4.1? Are you caring? Do you offer encouragement? These are just a few of the things that you can do to increase your rapport and immediacy with students. As the evidence suggests, you should strive to improve these skills to become a model teacher.

The Skill of Ethical Teaching

When you think of the great teachers, does the word ethical come to mind? Some readers might reply, "yes, absolutely!", but we would guess that "no" is actually the most frequent response. We wouldn't have used "ethical teaching" as an adjective to describe great teaching before conducting the research for this book. But regardless of whether you labeled your great teachers as ethical or not, you may have used adjectives such as "fair," "respectful," "honest," and "caring." In these terms, your great teachers were probably highly ethical.

It is an unfortunate fact that ethical teaching skills are typically not part of the conversation about great teachers (Landrum and McCarthy, 2012). Yet, if you think about it, we, as teachers, face ethical teaching dilemmas on a daily basis. For instance, what if (and yes this is a not-so-hypothetical situation) a student came to class woefully underprepared? Do you let the student slide or administer punishment? Your class is full but several students have petitioned to be let in. Do you let any extra students in and how do you decide who deserves the spot if they all have good reasons for needing the class? What if a student tried to pay you to replace a poor grade on an essay? OK, that one has an easy answer. Bribery is a clear violation of academic integrity, and you would follow the required process to report this violation. But what if a student came to you and asked you to redo an essay because a family member died the week the essay was due? This, on the other hand, is not so easy. How can you fairly let one student redo an essay and not offer this opportunity to all students? As you can see, ethics and teaching go hand-in-hand; teachers frequently confront ethical quandaries, some with easy answers and some with no answers at all.

So what does an ethical teacher look like? Hill and Zinsmeister (2012, p. 125) suggest that "A teacher's fundamental responsibilities include constructing courses and classroom environments that encourage learning, evaluating learning fairly and treating students respectfully. Ethical teaching means engaging in behaviors that meet these responsibilities in ways expected by students." Several scholars have addressed this topic (see Landrum and McCarthy's 2012 book title *Teaching ethically: Challenges and opportunities*), but Hill and Zinsmeister (2012) and Svinicki and McKeachie (2011) provide the following specific strategies that you can use to become an ethical teacher.

First, *ethical teachers have disciplinary competence* and *provide balanced content* (Hill and Zinsmeister, 2012). As discussed in Chapter 3, model teachers have superb content knowledge, so where is the ethical dilemma? Well, imagine that your chairperson asks you to teach a course out of your content specialty. In this scenario, as an ethical teacher, it is your duty to be well-prepared and understand the content, so that you can provide current, balanced, and accurate course information to students. To help prepare for this course, you would need to increase your content knowledge by reading advanced textbooks and finding other resources (e.g., ask a colleague who has taught it before) on how to teach this specific topic. Of course, if a topic is too far afield, the ethical choice may simply be to not teach the course.

In addition to knowing course content, the ethical teacher must also provide multiple theoretical perspectives (when they legitimately exist) and allow students to think critically and make their own conclusions about course content. This is opposed to pressuring students to adopt a specific perspective. When you model balanced perspective taking in your teaching, students recognize this, feel more freedom, and are open to discussing alternative viewpoints. Overall, when teachers have strong content knowledge and deliver content in an unbiased manner, they are more effective and promote student learning (Svinicki and McKeachie, 2011).

Second, *ethical teachers protect their students' confidentiality* (Hill and Zinsmeister, 2012; Svinicki and McKeachie, 2011). Teaching ethically can be directly tied to the Family Educational Rights and Privacy Act (FERPA). For example, without student permission, you cannot share personally identifying information or student grades with anyone but university officials who have a legitimate need for the information. As an ethical teacher, it is your responsibility to keep students' academic performance, personal communications, and behaviors confidential. However, student confidentiality can extend beyond obvious confidentiality dilemmas; there are nuanced confidentiality dilemmas as well. Have you overheard a colleague say something along the lines of, "Have you had Chadd Harris in your class? He always bursts out with inappropriate questions and derails the class. What should I do?" Although the purpose of the discussion may be to improve student learning, which is admirable, such discussions can violate student confidentiality. When you violate this right, often students lose respect for you as a teacher, and it can have legal ramifications (Hill and Zinsmeister, 2012). Instead, try to speak in hypothetical situations that leave out student names. In summary, maintaining all aspects of student confidentiality will make you a more effective teacher.

Third, *ethical teachers respect students* (Hill and Zinsmeister, 2012; Svinicki and McKeachie, 2011). Demonstrating respect for students can come in many forms. One form is to respect individual needs of students (this is also a tenet of student-centered/learning-centered approaches to teaching). Whether students have documented special needs (e.g., extra time on exams, a note-taker) or have unique cultural or physical needs, teachers should consult with the appropriate student-services office on campus and take reasonable action to accommodate their needs. Similarly, just as you have a life outside of teaching and scholarship, students have a life outside of your classroom, so respect their personal experiences and history. For example, if a student must misses a test because of some unavoidable life event (e.g., jury duty, grad school interview), respect this responsibility and do not penalize students. In essence, be fair in your treatment of students.

Another form of respect for students is to understand how course content can be particularly discomforting or embarrassing to individual students (Hill and Zinsmeister, 2012). For instance, discussion of politics, sex, prejudice, and other controversial topics can cause you to lose the respect of your students if the issues are not related to course content or if you present them in an unprofessional, biased fashion (e.g., Boysen et al., 2009). This does not mean you should avoid discussing these issues in your class. Rather, you should forewarn students, clarify fact versus opinion, and offer time out of class for students who need to further discuss the topics (Svinicki and McKeachie, 2011). Student sensitivity to emotion-laden course topics is an issue of growing concern on college campuses (Essig, 2014). Personally, we believe that it is ethical to ask students to tackle even the most sensitive and emotionally charged topics as long as the topics are legitimately connected to course learning objectives and the teacher maintains a professional atmosphere.

Finally, it may not have occurred to you that your pedagogical methods can be inherently disrespectful to students and cause students to not only lose their respect for you, but also their trust. All three authors sometimes use experiential learning as an arrow in our instructional method quiver. Yet, Svinicki and McKeachie (2011) suggest that some experiential learning activities require students to disclose information they may not wish to share (e.g., journaling, small group discussion, or a classroom demonstration that is intentionally designed to have students do poorly). This can inadvertently humiliate and demean students. Although these can be extremely powerful learning experiences, teachers should prevent harmful effects by allowing students to complete alternative activities, asking for volunteers, and discussing the true purpose of the activity (i.e., debriefing). As demonstrated in the research on student–professor rapport and teaching behaviors, when model teachers gain the respect of their students, this can lead to more effective student learning and higher student ratings and evaluations of teaching (Keeley et al., 2006; Wilson et al., 2010).

Fourth, *ethical teachers foster academic integrity through course transparency and use objective and fair assessments* (Hill and Zinsmeister, 2012; Svinicki and McKeachie, 2011). One area in which teachers must be completely transparent is their policy regarding academic dishonesty (see Chapter 7 for best practices on how to create these policies in your syllabus). It is incumbent upon ethical teachers to provide clear and concise policies to students that explicitly state the consequences of academic dishonesty and what constitutes unethical behavior. Especially in introductory courses, students are commonly unaware what it means to be academically dishonest. Often, these policies vary from one institution to another, but ethical teachers should follow these policies and educate students about academic integrity to ensure fairness and equality.

In addition to course policies on academic dishonesty, ethical teachers demonstrate academic integrity by developing objective and fair assessments. We find this to be one of the most important and yet ambiguous components of ethical teaching. For a thorough outline of how to evaluate student learning see Chapter 6, and for an outline of how to describe evaluation policies in the syllabus see Chapter 7. In the context of ethical teaching, it is important that teachers assess students objectively and give each student a way to demonstrate their abilities. For example, Hill and Zinsmeister (2012, p. 129) state, "ethical teachers assess content objectives, critical thinking or writing objectives that are specifically stated or emphasized in the course objectives." One of the best ways to be consistent and objective is to develop grading rubrics for all written assignments. By having a standard rubric that clearly states the expectations for the assignment, students are able to predict and understand how they will be graded.

Now, where fairness becomes ambiguous is its conflict with respecting students' individual needs. Often students conflate fairness with equality. Equality is treating everyone the same (in regards to assessment). Fairness is giving students what they need, regardless of what other students receive. For example, one author recently assigned an incomplete grade to a student who had a medical emergency and ended up staying in the hospital long-term. Does this student need to take the exact same quizzes as the other students? How should discussion points be assigned for discussions the person did not and cannot attend? What is the correct balance of fairness and equity? This is a very difficult question to answer and there are varied and staunch opinions on the matter. Like Svinicki and McKeachie (2011), we offer guiding questions rather than answers. Is it a case where all students need to be assessed in the exact same manner (e.g., written versus oral test)? Is it a situation where it is more important to be equal than fair? What situation warrants flexibility in methods of assessment (e.g., special needs)? These are just some of the many questions that model teachers should consider when assessing students.

Finally, *ethical teachers model ethical behavior* (Komarraju and Handelsman, 2012; Svinicki and McKeachie, 2011). How do teachers model ethical behavior? Ethical teaching can be modeled in everything that teachers do, from writing the syllabus, to the choice and implementation of instructional methods, to the way teachers interact with students. Moreover, ethical teaching can be categorized by a given set of behaviors that includes respecting autonomy, non-maleficence, beneficence, justice, fidelity, and caring. As demonstrated in Table 4.3, model teachers employ numerous classroom practices to model ethical teaching. In sum, Svinicki and McKeachie (2011, p. 321) said it best: "We teach not only what we know, but what we are." So if you strive to be an ethical teacher—don't just talk the talk, walk the walk.

Teaching Skills to Engage Students

So your favorite teacher likely had great rapport and was ethical, but was he or she engaging? Almost certainly, yes! Using instructional methods to engage students can have a profound positive impact on both student learning and student evaluations of teaching (Miller and Butler, 2011), and as such, it is an important skill to have in your quiver of instructional methods. But first, what is student engagement? According to Miller (2011, p. 2), student engagement is their "willingness to actively participate in the learning process and persist despite obstacles and challenges." Furthermore, Handelsman and colleagues (2005) demonstrated that student engagement is comprised of several factors. First, student engagement includes the use of academic skills. That is, students who are engaged put forth effort, actively use various learning strategies in the course, and organize their academic efforts. Second, engagement is also based on student emotion. In other words, engaged students are intrinsically motivated to learn or otherwise find ways to invest themselves emotionally in content (e.g., making course content personally relevant). Third, student participation is part of engagement. For instance, engaged students have fun in class, ask questions, participate in discussions, and/or seek out the instructor outside of class to discuss course content. Finally, performance engagement is when students' behaviors are extrinsically motivated. This occurs when students are focused on grading and performance goals and the means to achieve them (Handelsman et al., 2005).

If engaging students is such an important skill to have as a teacher, how do you develop it? We will offer five suggestions on how to be an engaging teacher. First, evidence suggests that you should infuse diversity into the course by using diverse examples and discussing diversity issues (Guenther and Miller, 2011). When you do so, students will be more engaged, critical thinkers (e.g., Pascarella et al., 2001). Second, allow students freedom to make choices about how to achieve their desired course goals (Zepke and Leach, 2010). For instance, allow students to choose among various assignments. You could also have students set learning goals within the course and have them set high, but achievable, expectations for themselves (Guenther and Miller, 2011).

TABLE 4.3 Ethical Teaching Behaviors and Corresponding Classroom Practices

Behavior	Classroom practices
Respect autonomy (right to make independent decisions and respect others)	• Provide students opportunities to choose (e.g., choice between assignments or dropping X number of assessments) • Explicitly distinguish between your opinion and facts • Encourage students to express their beliefs and opinions regardless if they differ from yours • Create a class culture of respect for autonomy (e.g., provide all assignments at the beginning of the semester so that they may turn them in early or on time)
Non-maleficence (above all, do no harm)	• Be prepared for class • When using humor, do not make fun of students • Thoroughly describe the purpose of assignments and exams • Be patient with all students • Acknowledge and respect student opinion
Beneficence (promote student health and welfare)	• Use effective pedagogy to increase student learning • Be an enthusiastic teacher • Use cooperative learning techniques • Teach students how to study (e.g., learning strategies) • Assist students with special needs (e.g., universal design for learning)
Justice (fairness, equality, unbiased)	• Clearly state classroom policies (late work, grading, missing class, etc.) that are fair and equitable in the syllabus • Avoid biased, pejorative, and stereotypical language • Be balanced when discussing divisive or potentially controversial or sensitive topics • Create activities that encourage all students to participate

(continued)

TABLE 4.3 *(cont.)*

Behavior	Classroom practices
Fidelity (trustworthy and honest)	• Promptly respond to student questions and requests • Provide prompt feedback on all assessments • Follow your course syllabus and calendar • Be very accessible to students (e.g., meet them before, after and outside of office hours) • Be consistent and do what you say you are going to do (e.g., practice what you preach!)
Caring	• Show genuine interest in students' personal lives • Allow students to share personal stories that are germane to class discussion • Share your personal stories that relate to class content • When appropriate, demonstrate empathy for students (e.g., if a student is struggling in their personal life, pull them aside and see how you can help)

Third, increasing teacher and student interaction is paramount. This is consistent with the research on student–professor rapport. Not only do you need to increase formal interaction with students (e.g., academic advising, discussing course content), but you should also increase informal interactions (e.g., discussing nonacademic topics). Informal faculty interactions are associated with increased problem-solving skills and elevated intellectual goals (Endo and Harpel, 1982). Fourth, create an active learning culture in your class (Guenther and Miller, 2011; Zepke and Leach, 2010). Learning is not a spectator sport. Engage students in debates, discussions, demonstrations, and whatever other activities professionals in your field do.

Finally, be attentive and adapt to student expectations. This is a more difficult skill to learn because we often get set in our ways in what we think students see as engaging. Times change, and to engage students you will need to change as well. No matter how "cool" you still feel, your students will eventually see you as woefully out of date. For instance, as an attention-grabber you may say "Anyone, anyone, Bueller, Bueller." However, there may not be a single student in class who has seen the 1980s classic *Ferris Bueller's Day Off*! (Yes, this happened to Aaron.) One way to adapt to changing student expectations, however, is to put the responsibility on students to produce the cutting-edge examples and hip references—this results in both active and engaged learning. In the end, it is extremely important that you engage your students, so please develop these skills.

OK, OK, you know the definition of student engagement, you now know how to promote it in your teaching, but do you know the benefits of using these teaching skills? Research suggests that there are wide-ranging positive effects associated with student engagement. In a study of psychology and mathematics students, Handelsman and colleagues (2005) found that student engagement predicted performance on homework assignments and midterm and final exams. Svanum and Bigatti (2009) conducted a longitudinal study to assess how student engagement affected graduation rates, cumulative GPA, and the speed at which students completed their degree. After controlling for various individual difference variables (e.g., college entrance exams, enrollment status), they found that when students were highly engaged, they were 1.5 times more likely to graduate, were faster at completing their degree, and had higher cumulative GPAs. These results have been consistent across multiple studies (Miller and Butler, 2011). There is a growing body of evidence that suggests that increasing student engagement can also improve student evaluations of teaching. In a study of more than 300 general education students, Richmond and colleagues (2015) found that emotional engagement and performance engagement were positively correlated and predicted student evaluations.

How did you score on items 15–18 in Table 4.1? Do you consider yourself an engaging teacher? If so, great! If not, working on ways to increase your engagement is integral to becoming a model teacher. Try out a few of our suggestions and see what works.

CASE STUDY REEXAMINED: PROFESSOR PADMA AMIRI'S MEDICAL ANTHROPOLOGY COURSE

After reading this chapter, what do you now think about Dr. Padma Amiri and how she teaches? Below you will find what we believe she was doing well and needed to work on.

1. *What teaching methods is Padma using?* It is likely that she was using direct instruction/lecture mixed with case-based instruction. As we have discussed in this chapter, she should vary her instructional methods even more. She could incorporate problem-based instruction or collaborative learning.

2. *How would you describe her teaching skills?* She seems to be prepared, professional, authoritative, confident, eloquent, knowledgeable about the subject, punctual, and respectful. But it appears that she should work on building rapport, providing more constructive feedback, listening skills, flexibility, and creativity.

3. *Would you say she engages her students? If so, how?* This is a little difficult to assess, but it is likely that she is engaging students when they are completing the case-based instruction part of her lesson. However, she can do better. She should try to be more active, use humor, express genuine interest in students by asking them to relate course material to their personal lives, or encourage diverse learning experiences.

4. *Based on the information, do you think she has good rapport with her students?* It is unlikely that she has good rapport because she is not making eye-contact, does not make herself available to students before or after class, stands behind the podium, and does not use personal examples.

5. *What can she do to improve her teaching?* As mentioned previously, even the best teachers can always improve their teaching. In Padma's case, she could vary her instructional methods, increase her rapport with students, and be more engaging to better keep and sustain her students' attention.

A Reflection on Your Self-Assessment

So how do you think you performed on the questions in Table 4.1? What areas do you think that you are doing well? What areas do you think you need to improve upon? In truth, all three authors, as teachers, have strengths, but we are not great in all aspects of model instructional methods and teaching skills. For instance, Aaron struggles with effectively implementing the Socratic method; Regan struggles with developing rubrics for his assignments; and Guy, as an introvert who prefers silent reflection to informal chit-chat, and has to slowly build rapport with students rather than taking. In the end, them in immediately with a bubbly and gregarious demeanor there is always room for improvement for all of us.

Summary of Best Practices

As has been discussed throughout this chapter, developing model instructional methods is no easy feat. It is complex, takes time and effort, and requires you to take risks and experiment with what works best. We hope that you are considering using some of the things we have discussed in your classroom. Below you will find a brief summary of what we believe are the key points to creating and implementing model instructional methods.

- *Vary your instructional methods.* Be prepared to incorporate active learning, problem-based learning, interteaching, and a host of other evidence-based instructional methods to serve all students in your class.
- *Develop master/model teaching behaviors.* To develop these behaviors, remember to be confident, creative, punctual, constructive, enthusiastic, prepared, professional, understanding, patient, encouraging, supportive, and clear and open in your communication. And above all, strive to be a better teacher.
- *Develop teacher–student rapport and teacher immediacy.* To do so, treat students respectfully, be competent and conscientious, avoid threatening students with punitive actions, use appropriate humor, use personal examples to demonstrate class content, and be approachable and available to all students.
- *Your students lose out if you are not an ethical teacher.* Strive to be ethical by allowing your students to make independent decisions and encouraging them to respect others. Be fair, unbiased, trustworthy, honest, and caring.
- *Engage, engage, engage your students.* As research has demonstrated, when you engage your students they will pay more attention to what you have to say and learn more from you.

The Very Busy People Book Club: Your Top Five Must-Reads

Oh, there are so many things to read on this subject. We don't think there are nightstands big enough to handle our suggested list for model instructional methods, but here is our best shot at it. Hopefully, your nightstand can handle the heavy weight—or just get a Kindle!

Groccia, J. E., Alsudairi, M. A. T., and Buskist, W. (eds.) (2012). *Handbook of college and university teaching: A global perspective.* Los Angeles, CA: Sage.

Hattie, J. (2012). *Visible learning for teachers: Maximizing impact on learning.* New York: Routledge.

Landrum, R. E. and McCarthy, M. A. (eds.) (2012). *Teaching ethically: Challenges and opportunities.* Washington, DC: American Psychological Association.

Nilson, L. B. (2010). *Teaching at its best: A research-based resource for college instructors*. San Francisco, CA: John Wiley & Sons.

Rotenberg, R. (2010). *The art and craft of college teaching: A guide for new professors and graduate students*. Walnut Creek, CA: Left Coast Press.

References

Aditomo, A., Goodyear, P., Bliuc, A. M., and Ellis, R. A. (2013). Inquiry-based learning in higher education: principal forms, educational objectives, and disciplinary variations. *Studies in Higher Education*, 38(9), 1239–1258.

Albanese, M. A. and Mitchell, S. (1993). Problem-based learning: A review of literature on its outcomes and implementation issues. *Academic Medicine*, 68, 52–81.

Allen, D. E., Duch, B. J., and Groh, S. E. (1996). The power of problem-based learning in teaching introductory science courses. In L. Wilkerson and W. H. Gijselaers (eds.), *Bringing problem-based learning to higher education: Theory and practice* (pp. 43–52). San Francisco, CA: Jossey-Bass.

Amador, J. A., Miles, L., and Peters, C. B. (2006). *The practice of problem-based learning: A guide to implementing PBL in the college classroom*. San Francisco, CA: Jossey Bass.

Arntzen, E. and Hoium, K. (2010). On the effectiveness of interteaching. *The Behavior Analyst Today*, 11, 155–159.

Astin, A. W. (1993). *What matters in college. Four critical years revisited*. San Francisco, CA: Jossey-Bass.

Bain, K. (2004). *What the best college teachers do*. Cambridge, MA: Harvard University Press.

Barkley, E. F., Cross, K. P., and Major, C. H. (2005). *Collaborative learning techniques: A handbook for college faculty*. San Francisco, CA: Jossey-Bass.

Beard, C. and Wilson, J. P. (2006). *Experiential learning: A best practice handbook for trainers and educators* (2nd edn). London: Kogan Page.

Benjamin, L. (1991). Personalization and active learning in the large introductory psychology class. *Teaching of Psychology*, 18, 68–74.

Benson, T. A., Cohen, A. L., and Buskist, W. (2005). Rapport: Its relation to student attitudes and behaviors toward teachers. *Teaching of Psychology*, 32, 237–239.

Biel, J. (1992). Teaching in the shadow of Socrates. *Teaching Philosophy*, 17(4), 345–350.

Biggs, J. B. (1999). *Teaching for quality learning at university*. Buckingham: Open University Press.

Bonwell, C. C. and Eison, J. A. (1991). *Active learning: Creating excitement in the classroom* (ASHE-ERIC Higher Education Rep. No. 1). Washington, DC: George Washington University, School of Education and Human Development.

Boyce, T. E. and Hineline, P. N. (2002). Interteaching: A strategy for enhancing the user-friendliness of behavioral arrangements in the college classroom. *The Behavior Analyst*, 25(2), 215–226.

Boysen, G. A., Vogel, D. L., Cope, M. A., and Hubbard, A. (2009). Incidents of bias in the classroom: Teacher and student perceptions. *Journal of Diversity in Higher Education*, 4, 219–231.

Boysen, G. A., Richmond, A. S., and Gurung, R. A. R. (2015). Model Teaching Criteria for psychology: Initial documentation of teachers' self-reported competency. *The Scholarship of Teaching and Learning in Psychology*, 1, 45–89.

Brown, J. S., Collins, A., and Duguid, P. (1998). *Situated cognition and the culture of learning*. *Educational Researcher*, 18(1), 32–42.

Buskist, W. (2004). Ways of the master teacher. *APS Observer*, 17(9), 23–26.

Buskist, W. and Saville, B. K. (2004). Rapport building: Creating positive emotional contexts for enhancing teaching and learning. In B. Perlman, L. I. McCann, and S. H. McFadden (eds.), *Lessons learned: Practical advice for the teaching of psychology* (Vol. 2, pp. 149–155). Washington, DC: American Psychological Society.

Buskist, W., Sikorski, J., Buckley, T., and Saville, B. K. (2002). Elements of master teaching. In S. F. Davis and W. Buskist (eds.), *The teaching of psychology: Essays in honor of Wilbert J. McKeachie and Charles L. Brewer* (pp. 27–39). Mahwah, NJ: Lawrence Erlbaum.

Dochy, F., Segers, M., Van den Bossche, P., and Gijbels, D. (2003). Effects of problem-based learning: A meta-analysis. *Learning and Instruction*, 13, 533–568.

Duch, B. J., Groh, S. E., and Allen, D. E. (2001). *The power of problem-based learning: a practical "how to" for teaching undergraduate courses in any discipline*. Sterling, VA: Stylus Publishing.

Edens, K. M. (2000). Preparing problem solvers for the 21st century through problem-based learning. *College Teaching*, 48(2), 55–60.

Endo, J. J. and Harpel, R. L. (1982). The effect of student-faculty interaction on students' educational outcomes. *Research in Higher Education*, 19, 115–135.

Epting, L., Zinn, T. E., Buskist, C., and Buskist, W. (2004). Student perspectives on the distinction between ideal and typical teachers. *Teaching of Psychology*, 31, 181–183.

Essig, L. (2014). *Trigger warnings trigger me*. Retrieved from http://chronicle.com/blogs/conversation/2014/03/10/trigger-warnings-trigger-me.

Evensen, D. H. and Hmelo-Silver, C. E. (2000). *Problem-based learning: A research perspective on learning interactions*. New York: Routledge.

Freeman, S., Eddy, S. L., McDonough, M., Smith, M. K., Okorafor, N., Jordt, H., and Wenderoth, M. P. (2014). Active learning increases student performance in science, engineering, and mathematics. *Proceedings of the National Academy of Sciences*, 111(23), 8410–8415.

Frisby, B. N. and Martin, M. M. (2010). Instructor–student and student–student rapport in the classroom. *Communication Education*, 59(2), 146–164.

Frymier, A. B. (1994). A model of immediacy in the classroom. *Communication Quarterly*, 42, 133–144.

Gallagher, S. A. (1997). Problem-based learning: Where did it come from, what does it do, and where is it going? *Journal for the Education of the Gifted*, 20(4), 332–362.

Gorham, J. (1988). The relationship between verbal teacher immediacy behaviors and student learning. *Communication Education*, 37(1), 40–53.

Gorham, J. and Christophel, D. M. (1990). The relationship of teachers' use of humor in the classroom to immediacy and student learning. *Communication Education*, 39, 46–62.

Gose, M. (2009). When Socratic dialogue is flagging: Questions and strategies for engaging students. *College Teaching*, 57(1), 45–50.

Gremler, D. D. and Gwinner, K. P. (2000). Customer–employee rapport in service relationships. *Journal of Service Research*, 3, 82–104.

Guenther, C. and Miller, R. L. (2011). Factors that promote engagement. In R. L. Miller, E. Amsel, B. Marsteller Kowalewski, B. C. Beins, K. D. Keith and B. F. Peden (eds.), *Promoting student engagement. Volume 1: Programs, techniques, and opportunities*. Retrieved from http://teachpsych.org/Resources/Documents/ebooks/pse2011vol1.pdf.

Hake, R. R. (1998). Interactive-engagement versus traditional methods: A six-thousand-student survey of mechanics test data for introductory physics courses. *American Journal of Physics*, 66(1), 64–74.

Handelsman, M. M., Briggs, W. L., Sullivan, N., and Towler, A. (2005). A measure of college student course engagement. *The Journal of Educational Research*, 98(3), 184–192.

Higdon, J. and Topaz, C. (2009). Blogs and wikis as instructional tools: A social software adaptation of just-in-time teaching. *College Teaching*, 57(2), 105–110.

Hill, G. W. and Zinsmeister, D. D. (2012). Becoming an ethical teacher. In W. Buskist and V. A. Benassi (eds.), *Effective college and university teaching: Strategies and tactics for the new professoriate* (pp. 125–137). Thousand Oaks, CA: Sage.

Hoellwarth, C. and Moelter, M. J. (2011). The implications of a robust curriculum in introductory mechanics. *American Journal of Physics*, 79(5), 540–545.

Jarvis, P. (2006). *The Socratic method: The theory* (2nd edn). London: Routledge.

Johnson, D. R., Johnson, R. T., and Smith, K. A. (1998). Cooperative learning returns to college: What evidence is there that it works? *Change: The Magazine of Higher Learning*, 30, 26–35.

Keeley, J., Furr, R. M., and Buskist, W. (2010). Differentiating psychology students' perceptions of teachers using the Teacher Behavior Checklist. *Teaching of Psychology*, 37, 16–20.

Keeley, J., Christopher, A. N., and Buskist, W. (2012). Emerging evidence for excellent teaching across borders. In J. E. Groccia, M. Al-Sudairy, and W. Buskist (eds.), *Handbook of college and university teaching: Global perspectives* (pp. 374–390). Thousand Oaks, CA: Sage.

Keeley, J., Smith, D., and Buskist, W. (2006). The Teacher Behavior Checklist: Factor analysis of its utility for evaluating teaching. *Teaching of Psychology*, 33, 84–91.

Komarraju, M. and Handelsman, M. M. (2012). Preparing to teach: Becoming part of an ethical culture. In R. E. Landrum and M. A. McCarthy (eds.), *Teaching ethically: Challenges and opportunities* (pp. 191–201). Washington, DC: American Psychological Association.

Komarraju, M., Musulkin, S., and Bhattacharya, G. (2010). Role of student–faculty interactions in developing college students' academic self-concept, motivation, and achievement. *Journal of College Student Development*, 51(3), 332–342.

Lammers, W. J. and Gillaspy Jr., J. A. (2013). Brief measure of student–instructor rapport predicts student success in online courses. *International Journal for the Scholarship of Teaching and Learning*, 7(2), 16.

Lammers, W. J., Savina, E., Skotko, D., and Churlyaeva, M. (2010). Faculty and student perceptions of outstanding university teachers in the USA and Russia. *Educational Psychology*, 30(7), 803–815.

Landrum, R. E. and McCarthy, M. A. (eds.) (2012). *Teaching ethically: Challenges and opportunities*. Washington, DC: American Psychological Association.

Landrum, R. E. and Stowell, J. R. (2013). The reliability of student ratings of master teacher behaviors. *Teaching of Psychology*, 40, 300–303.

Lave, J. and Wenger, E. (1991). *Situated learning: Legitimate peripheral participation*. Cambridge: Cambridge University Press.

Lea, S. J., Stephenson, D., and Troy, J. (2003). Higher education students' attitudes to student-centered learning: Beyond "educational bulimia"? *Studies in Higher Education*, 28(3), 321–334.

Love, A. G., Dietrich, A., Fitzgerald, J., and Gordon, D. (2014). Integrating collaborative learning inside and outside of the classroom. *Journal on Excellence in College Teaching*, 25(3&4), 177–196.

McLellan, H. (ed.) (1996). *Situated learning perspectives*. Englewood Cliffs, NJ: Educational Technology Publications.

Mangrum, J. R. (2010). Sharing practice through Socratic seminars. *Phi Delta Kappan*, 91(7), 40–43.

Marsh, H. W. (1984). Students' evaluations of university teaching: Dimensionality, reliability, validity, potential biases, and utility. *Journal of Educational Psychology*, 76, 707–754.

Mehrabian, A. (1971). *Silent messages*. Belmont, CA: Wadsworth Publishing Company.

Meyers, S. A. (2009). Do your students care whether you care about them? *College Teaching*, 57(4), 205–210.

Miller, R. L. (2011). Introduction. In R. L. Miller, E. Amsel, B. Marsteller Kowalewski, B. C. Beins, K. D. Keith and B. F. Peden (eds.), *Promoting student engagement. Volume 1: Programs, techniques, and opportunities*. Retrieved from http://teachpsych.org/Resources/Documents/ebooks/pse2011vol1.pdf.

Miller, R. L. and Butler, J. M. (2011). Outcomes associated with student engagement. In R. L. Miller, E. Amsel, B. Marsteller Kowalewski, B. C. Beins, K. D. Keith and B. F. Peden (eds.), *Promoting student engagement. Volume 1: Programs, techniques, and opportunities*. Retrieved from http://teachpsych.org/Resources/Documents/ebooks/pse2011vol1.pdf.

Mills, B. (2012). *Active Learning Strategies in Face-to-Face Courses*. IDEA Paper #53. Retrieved from http://ideaedu.org/wp-content/uploads/2014/11/paperidea_53.pdf.

Moon, J. A. (2004). *A handbook of reflective and experiential learning: Theory and practice*. New York: Routledge.

Moore, A., Masterson, J. T., Christophel, D. M., and Shea, K.A. (1996). College teacher immediacy and student ratings of instruction. *Communication Education*, 45, 29–39.

Nilson, L. B. (2010). *Teaching at its best: A research-based resource for college instructors*. San Francisco, CA: John Wiley & Sons.

Novak, G. N., Patterson, E. T., Gavrin, A, and Christian, W. (1999). *Just-in-time teaching: Blending active learning and web technology*. Saddle River, NJ: Prentice Hall.

O'Donnell, A. M., Hmelo-Silver, C. E., and Erkens, G. (eds.) (2006). *Collaborative learning, reasoning, and technology*. Mahway, NJ: Lawrence Erlbaum Associates.

Pascarella, E. T., Palmer, B., Moye, M., and Pierson, C. T. (2001). Do diversity experiences influence the development of critical thinking? *Journal of College Student Development*, 42, 257–271.

Pogue, L. and AhYun, K. (2006). The effect of teacher nonverbal immediacy and credibility on student motivation and affective learning. *Communication Education*, 55, 331–344.

Prince, M. (2004). Does active learning work? A review of the research. *Journal of Engineering Research*, 93, 223–232.

Richmond, A. S. and Kindelberger Hagan, L. (2011). Promoting higher level thinking in psychology: Is active learning the answer? *Teaching of Psychology*, 38, 102–105.

Richmond, A. S., Boysen, G. A., Gurung, R. A. R., Tazeau, Y. N., Meyers, S. A., and Sciutto, M. J. (2014). Aspirational Model Teaching Criteria for psychology. *Teaching of Psychology*, 41, 281–295.

Richmond, A. S., Berglund, M. B., Epelbaum, V. B., and Klein, E. M. (2015). a + (b1) professor – student rapport + (b2) humor + (b3) student engagement = ($\hat{Y}$) student ratings of instructors. *Teaching of Psychology*, 42, 119–124.

Richmond, V. P., Gorham, J. S., and McCroskey, J. C. (1987). The relationship between selected immediacy behaviors and cognitive learning. *Communication Yearbook*, 10, 574–590.

Rocca, K. A. (2004). College student attendance: Impact of instructor immediacy and verbal aggression. *Communication Education*, 53, 185–195.

Rogers, D. T. (2015). Further validation of the Learning Alliance Inventory: The roles of working alliance, rapport, and immediacy in student learning. *Teaching of Psychology*, 42, 19–25.

Savery, J. (2006). Overview of problem-based learning: Definitions and distinctions. *The Interdisciplinary Journal of Problem-Based Learning*, 1(1), 12–16.

Saville, B. K., Zinn, T. E., and Elliott, M. P. (2005). Interteaching versus traditional methods of instruction: A preliminary analysis. *Teaching of Psychology*, 32, 161–163.

Saville, B. K., Zinn, T. E., Neef, N. A., Norman, R. V., and Ferreri, S. J. (2006). A comparison of interteaching and lecture in the college classroom. *Journal of Applied Behavior Analysis*, 39, 49–61.

Saville, B. K., Lambert, T., and Robertson, S. (2011). Interteaching: Bringing behavioral education into the 21st century. *The Psychological Record*, 61(1), 153–166.

Saville, B. K., Pope, D., Truelove, J., and Williams, J. (2012). The relation between GPA and exam performance during interteaching and lecture. *The Behavior Analyst Today*, 13(3–4), 27–31.

Saville, B. K., Bureau, A., Eckenrode, C., Fullerton, A., Herbert, R., Maley, M., Porter, A., and Zombakis, J. (2014). Interteaching and lecture: A comparison of long-term recognition memory. *Teaching of Psychology*, 41, 325–329.

Savin-Baden, M. (2000). *Problem-based learning in higher education: Untold stories*. Buckingham: Open University Press.

Schaeffer, G., Epting, K., Zinn, T., and Buskist, W. (2003). Student and faculty perceptions of effective teaching: A successful replication. *Teaching of Psychology*, 30, 133–136.

Scoboria, A. and Pascual-Leone, A. (2009). An "interteaching" informed approach to instructing large undergraduate classes. *Journal of the Scholarship of Teaching and Learning*, 9, 29–37.

Simkins, S. P. and Maier, M. H. (eds.) (2010). *Just-in-time teaching: Across the disciplines, across the academy*. Sterling, VA: Stylus Publishing.

Slavich, G. M. and Zimbardo, P. G. (2012). Transformational teaching: Theoretical underpinnings, basic principles, and core methods. *Educational Psychology Review*, 24, 569–608.

Springer, L., Stanne, M., and Donovan, S. S. (1999). Effects of small-group learning on undergraduates in science, mathematics, engineering, and technology: A meta-analysis. *Review of Educational Research*, 69, 21–51.

Svanum, S. and Bigatti, S. M. (2009). Academic course engagement during one semester forecasts college success: Engaged students are more likely to earn a degree, do it faster, and do it better. *Journal of College Student Development*, 50(1), 120–132.

Svinicki, M. and McKeachie, W. J. (2011). *McKeachie's teaching tips: Strategies, research, and theory for college and university teachers* (13th edn). Belmont, CA: Wadsworth.

Thomas, C. E., Richmond, V. P., and McCroskey, J. C. (1994). The association between immediacy and socio-communicative style. *Communication Research Reports*, 11, 107–115.

Titsworth, B. S. (2001). The effects of teacher immediacy, use of organizational lecture cues, and students' note-taking on cognitive learning. *Communication Education*, 50, 283–297.

Tiwari, A., Lai, P., So, M., and Yuen, K. (2006). A comparison of the effects of problem-based learning and lecturing on the development of students' critical thinking. *Medical Education*, 40(6), 547–554.

Walker, A. and Leary, H. (2009). A problem-based learning meta-analysis: Differences across problem types, implementation types, disciplines, and assessment levels. *Interdisciplinary Journal of Problem-Based Learning*, 3, 6–28.

Weimer, M. (2002). *Learner-centered teaching: Five key changes to practice*. San Francisco, CA: Jossey-Bass.

Wilson, J. H. and Ryan, R. G. (2012). Developing student–teacher rapport in the undergraduate classroom. In W. Buskist and V. A. Benassi (eds.), *Effective college and university teaching: Strategies and tactics for the new professoriate*. Thousand Oaks, CA: Sage.

Wilson, J. H. and Ryan, R. G. (2013). Professor–student rapport scale six items predict student outcomes. *Teaching of Psychology*, 40, 130–133.

Wilson, J. H., Ryan, R. G., and Pugh, J. L. (2010). Professor–student rapport scale predicts student outcomes. *Teaching of Psychology*, 37, 246–251.

Yoder, J. and Hochevar, C. (2005). Encouraging active learning can improve students' performance on examinations. *Teaching of Psychology*, 32, 91–95.

Young, M. F. (1993). Instructional design for situated learning. *Education Technology Research and Development*, 41, 43–58.

Zakrajsek, T. (2015). *How students learn: Strategies for teaching from the psychology of learning*. Retrieved from www.youtube.com/watch?v=niJvQjL9UDE.

Zepke, N. and Leach, L. (2010). Improving student engagement: Ten proposals for action. *Active learning in Higher Education*, 11, 167–177.

5

WHAT DO STUDENTS LEARN IN MODEL TEACHERS' COURSES?

One of the many benefits of being on a search committee is that it provides fascinating insights into how different people treat content knowledge coverage. We have all served on many search committees and noted how candidates respond to the question "Which courses would you be able to teach?" Savvy candidates always demonstrate confidence and willingness to teach the courses required in the job advertisement, but sometimes they do so with no evidence of expertise in the area whatsoever. Teach American History though your degree is British Literature? Sure. Develop a course on organic chemistry although inorganic is where you have published all your work? Sure. OK. There is a lot of variance in how knowledgeable faculty are to teach some of their courses. But how hard can it be? Adopt a textbook for the class, read the chapters before the students do, develop lectures based on the chapters, and you are set, right? Well, no. It is not that simple. What should you be covering in a particular class? Do you need to go beyond disciplinary content? Is there content applicable across the board that every college student should be schooled in? In this chapter we address a little-discussed element of good college teaching: content.

Self-Assessment Time!

Before we dive into the wonders of deciding on content, it is a good time to get a sense of where you stand on this criterion. Think about a class that you feel most confident about and one that you feel the least confident about. Take a few minutes and complete the model content self-assessment in Table 5.1. Perhaps you can then consider all the courses you teach.

TABLE 5.1 Self-Assessment of Your Course Content and Student Learning Model Teaching Criteria

Directions: Please indicate on the scale below how often you incorporate these efforts / activities to improve your course content.

Scale: 5 = Always, 4 = Often, 3 = Sometimes, 2 = Rarely, 1 = Never   *Your score*

1. Your course learning goals reflect the breadth of content in your discipline.	_____
2. You foster the development of student written communication skills.	_____
3. You foster the development of student critical thinking skills.	_____
4. You foster the development of student information literacy skills.	_____
5. You foster the development of student ability to work effectively and collaborate with others.	_____
6. You foster the development of student oral communication skills.	_____
7. You infuse ethical issues throughout your teaching.	_____
8. You infuse diversity issues throughout your teaching.	_____

Note: This self-assessment is adapted and modified from Boysen et al. (2015) and Richmond et al. (2014).

Now that you have assessed your course content status, let's take a look at an example of another prototypical junior faculty member. Consider this case study:

CASE STUDY: ASSISTANT PROFESSOR OF HUBRIS

Jamie was excited about his new job. He had just graduated with a PhD in political science from the same large university where he received his BA and MA. His job was as at a small liberal arts college—there were only three faculty in his department—located in a large urban center. Midway through his first semester, a department colleague asked him to lunch. After some easygoing chit-chat, the colleague, who had been the chair of Jamie's search committee, pointedly asked, "Are you ready to teach American Urban Politics in the spring?" This was a sore topic for Jamie. Desperate to land a job, he had been forced to exaggerate his ability to teach the course during his interview. The truth was that all he had done up until now was pick a textbook (based on it having the most positive reviews on Amazon—he looked forward to reading it).

Feeling cornered, Jamie bluffed yet again. He mentioned the textbook and cited his intended focus on topics gleaned from chapter titles: party machines, reform, city/suburban divides, city government, and so on. "Hmm," his colleague said, "What's the format going to be?" The truth was that Jamie taught his classes the same way he had seen all of his professors teach. He chose a textbook, he spent several classes lecturing on the chapters sequentially using the publisher's PowerPoint slides (he typically skipped the last several chapters as he ran out of time), and he gave four multiple-choice tests using the publisher's test bank. Jamie blithely outlined all this to his lunch companion, who he sensed was growing ill at ease. "Surely you are going discuss the recent protests in the city about policing in the black communities?" his colleague said. "We have quite a few recent immigrants studying here, the issues they have faced with voting..." Changing topics, the colleague said "These students need to be able to write a basic lit review by the time they get to the methods course you know." Jamie did not.

Returning to his office, Jamie curiously picked up the textbook he had chosen. Going to the publisher's website he realized that the niche textbook topic meant there were no ancillary materials available—no slides, no test bank, no crutches at all. He began to think, "You know, I have to start teaching that methods course next year." Then, he began to worry.

Consider your answers to the following questions. We will return to this case at the end of the chapter and discuss our own approach to Jamie's case.

1. How could Jamie's approach to content selection be improved?
2. Aside from facts and figures from a textbook, what other content does Jamie need to consider?
3. Jamie's courses seem to focus on developing students' skill of remembering facts on multiple-choice tests. How could he expand the types of skills students learn in his courses?

Jamie is not alone. Each of us (Aaron, Guy, and Regan) has had to develop a new course during our careers. And it is not just a task for new faculty. Regan had been teaching for 16 years when he was asked to develop a brand new course. In just the last school year, Guy developed a new course in order to fill a gap being left by a retiring colleague. Some teachers have to develop courses much more often that they would like. For small schools with just a handful of faculty per department, it is commonplace for teachers to have to cover large swaths of the curriculum.

Disciplines vary substantially in content, and instructors bring a wide variety of backgrounds and perspectives to the classroom. As such, the specific content of individual courses is likely to resist standardization. Your choice of what to include in a course is influenced by your disciplinary training and expertise. Our friends who teach English literature have full control over which novels they adopt and have their students read. In fact, one of our friends is known to change all her course reading material every time she teaches and, not surprisingly, her favorite authors are the ones who feature prominently. Similarly, introduction to psychology instructors who are social psychologists tend to emphasize social psychology (Homa et al., 2013). In history, instructors tend to favor certain milestones more than others (Sipress and Voelker, 2009). Regardless of pet interests, there are more commonalities to course content across disciplines than most faculty realize. For example, almost all disciplines want their students to be critical thinkers, good writers, and proficient speakers (Chick et al., 2012; Gurung et al., 2009).

Despite the diversity of disciplines, model teachers of all backgrounds and teaching specialties infuse some broad educational themes outlined below into their courses. This chapter explores this characteristic and issues surrounding content. We discuss how teachers need to establish learning objectives that both reflect core elements of their discipline, including some of the breadth of disciplinary theories and applications, and broader liberal education outcomes. Model teachers foster liberal arts skills in their courses; they also establish content related to ethics and diversity (American Association of Colleges and Universities, n.d.a.; American Psychological Association, 2013).

Key Content Components: Learning Objectives Reflecting Discipline's Breath of Content

Every discipline, whether sociology, history, communication, or physics, has a core foundation (Gurung et al., 2009). In the natural and social sciences, for example, scientific knowledge is at the core of the undergraduate curriculum (Dunn et al., 2010). Before diving into some specific aspects of this Model Teaching Criteria, it is worth examining some guiding principles on selecting content for a class.

Can Content be Standardized?

Every discipline is broad and we bet it would be very difficult for a group of faculty to get together and agree on what core content should be. What should English classes contain? What historical events should feature in a history class? What sociological theories do students need to know (and which can be left out)? Teachers of the different disciplines bring a wide variety of backgrounds and perspectives to the classroom. As such, the specific content of individual courses is likely to resist standardization even though greater commonality across courses provides a singular message to students and the public about what constitutes a particular field. Also, high commonality across all institutions offers consistency in what majors and students taking the course receive; this is important during a time in which more and more students are transferring between colleges. For example, in business, the Association to Advance Collegiate Schools of Business Standard 11 states: "Programs resulting in the same degree credential are structured and designed to ensure equivalence" (AACSB, n.d.). In psychology, "Internal and external pressures on the discipline ... suggest a need for a common, coherent core curriculum for the undergraduate psychology major" (Dunn et al., 2010, p. 53). This is the case in many disciplines.

There have been many calls for national guidelines and/or a common core. In 2009, the Lumina Foundation for Education initiated a year-long project, Tuning USA, whose aim was "to create a shared understanding among higher education's stakeholders of the subject-specific knowledge and transferable skills that students in six fields (biology, chemistry, education, history, physics, and graphic design) must demonstrate in each course and upon completion of a degree program." (Texas Higher Education Coordinating Board, n.d.). Many disciplinary societies have initiated their own tuning projects. In history, the American Historical Association recently worked to create a history discipline core. Also called the Tuning Project, this effort "aimed to describe the skills, knowledge, and habits of mind that students develop in history courses and degree programs" (American Historical Association, 2013, #1). Committee members used input from faculty of 70 institutions to "articulate the ways history supports an educated workforce and citizenry and demonstrate that its value goes far beyond narrow professional training" (American Historical Association, 2013, #1). There now exists a set of core competencies and examples of specific ways students might demonstrate their competence (American Historical Association, 2013).

Similarly, there exist national guidelines in the field of chemistry. The American Chemical Society (2009) released a set of guidelines for chemistry in two-year programs. Together with guidelines for the institutional environment, faculty and staff, infrastructure, student mentoring, student development, and more, the document includes an outline of the chemistry curriculum. Specifically, the guidelines present recommendations for what should be covered in general chemistry, chemistry laboratory experiences, and some specialized chemistry courses as well.

The case being made for a common core is particularly strong in our home discipline of psychology. A national meeting of psychology educators concluded: "Given the ubiquitous relevance of psychology to other majors and fields, most jobs, and the world in general, as well as the many contributions an understanding of psychology can have to personal growth and development, all students need to receive a common core of content" (Dunn et al., 2010, p. 59). Similar to the American Chemical Society guidelines for chemistry, a lot of the focus in psychology has turned to the introductory courses and perhaps the foundation courses are most in need of common cores across the disciplines. In fact, most introductory courses serve similar purposes. Take a look at what Wolfle (1942, p. 687) suggested Introductory Psychology should have 70 years ago. You will see the five goals: (1) teach facts and principles of psychology, (2) develop scientific method or habits of critical thoughts, (3) provide better ability in making personal adjustments, (4) prepare students for later courses, or interest them in psychology, and (5) teach what psychology is and is not, or eliminate popular superstitions, can relatively easily be modified to extend to different disciplines. No such attempts to standardize other higher-level courses exist, but the discipline of psychology also created guidelines for the entire undergraduate curriculum (American Psychological Association, 2007, 2013) similar to what historians just completed.

Why bother with consistency? There is a compelling reason to have greater conceptual consistency. Consistency aids in efforts to improve accountability and student outcomes through the process of assessment. Assessment, whether across instructors or across time, at the department level or across institutions, necessitates a similar, if not a standardized experience. Fields such as physics have common content assessments such as the *Force Concept Inventory* (Hestenes et al., 1992). Other disciplines such as philosophy have recommended 'core readings' (American Philosophical Association, n.d.a.). Chemistry, through the American Chemical Society's Division of Chemical Education Examination Institute, also has examinations used by campuses nationally (American Chemical Society, n.d.). Teacher educators have their students complete the Pre-Professional Skills Test (the Praxis) and the National Education Association has developed several methods to help teachers assist student success on the Praxis (e.g., Phelps and Ryan, 1995). Having some level of consistency in curricula is hard to argue against and is a direction most disciplines are moving in.

Our point in this section is not to put a limit on academic freedom or to take away the delight of teaching college courses that relate to one's expertise. Rather, we want to emphasize that teachers do not choose course content in a bubble; their courses fit into broader schemes at the program, college, and professional levels. As such, model teachers select course content that is fundamental to the placement of their course into broader educational frameworks.

Content Fundamentals 101

Unlike teaching in high school or in college professional programs (e.g., nursing, education) where state boards, accreditations bodies, or national disciplinary bodies have clear content guidelines (e.g., Nursing and Social Work proficiency requirements for accreditation, the American Psychological Association's national standards for high school psychology), most college faculty have a lot of flexibility in terms of what content to include in their classes. This flexibility may vary based on factors such as how many different instructors teach the course, the level of the course, and whether or not the course meets departmental or university requirements. If you are teaching a general education course you often have to include university general education outcomes. If your course is a prerequisite for later courses, you often have to include some previously agreed on material. Correspondingly, the first step in selecting content is to make sure you know what purpose the course plays in the department and in the university curriculum.

Most departments have mission statements and department-level learning outcomes (more on student learning outcomes in Chapter 6 on assessment). These learning outcomes are normally based on the learning outcomes for the discipline. For example, at the University of Wisconsin-Green Bay, the psychology department's learning outcomes directly map on to the American Psychological

Association's *Guidelines for the undergraduate psychology major* (American Psychological Association, 2013). The fit of courses into a set curriculum tends to be especially important in professional programs such as business. For example, most accounting programs structure their curricula to align with the material addressed on the CPA exam, and the American Institute of CPAs has identified content and skills included on this exam (AICPA, 2015). Specifically, "content refers to CPA Examination questions—multiple-choice, written communication and task-based simulations—reflecting the subject matter eligible to be tested" (AICPA, n.d.). Any accounting faculty members can get easy access to what they have to cover. For example, at the time of writing, content for 2016 were available on the AICPA website for easy reference and course planning (AICPA, 2015).

As another business example, the Association to Advance Collegiate Schools of Business (AACSB, 2013), the accrediting body for business programs worldwide, has accreditation standards that relate to students developing specific knowledge (e.g., financial theories, information systems). The AACSB, like many other disciplinary and professional organizations, allows for some flexibility in content selection but urges faculty to constantly monitor content with an eye to changing specific topics, theories, or facts as times change. It states: "Curricula address general content areas—skills and knowledge—that would normally be included in the type of degree program under consideration. While most skill areas are likely to remain consistently important over time, knowledge areas are likely to be more dynamic as theory and practice of business and management changes over time" (AACSB, n.d.). Overall, the main point is that no matter what course or area they specialize in, model teachers cover content that is consistent with the learning outcomes required by their disciplinary curriculum.

Perhaps the courses you teach have no stipulations about required content. There is no consensus on standard content for some disciplines and some specific courses. Extremely specialized courses pose a similar issue. For example, special topic seminars are created by individual faculty members. Regan teaches a seminar titled "Gods, ghosts, and goblins: The psychology of belief," and curates an interdisciplinary set of readings for his students. In cases such as this, the pressure is on you to select learning objectives (see Chapter 6 on assessment for more on writing your own learning objectives). A great place to start is the class textbook. Most textbooks are written using student learning outcomes as a framework. Reviewing different textbooks for the class provides you with potential learning outcomes and a feel for the content covered by the course. Warning: Do not be swayed by just one textbook; consider more than one whenever possible. Textbook representatives are always trying to tempt you to use their product and will happily drop off copies for your consideration.

Textbooks can also be supplemented with content from primary sources. If you are not doing research on the content area of your course and correspondingly are not up-to-date on the literature for the course, it is time well-spent to look over the table of contents of relevant journals in the area. A quick note on keeping up-to-date on content is in order. If you have a heavy teaching load, six to eight courses a year or more, you may not have looked at a journal outside of your specialty area in some time. One way to make the content of your class come to life is for you to know what is being published in that area. Making time to do this is important. One trick is use technology and sign up to receive the table of contents of course-related journals via email. Every time a new issue is published, you automatically get notified. Another technique is to set up Google Scholar (http://scholar.google.com) alerts that will send you an email each time research fitting specific keywords is published. Regardless of the tools used to do it, model teachers keep the content of their courses fresh and up-to-date.

Surveying department learning outcomes, textbooks, and journals will help you decide what you want to accomplish in your one class, but remember to think beyond the semester. In one of our favorite textbooks on research methods, the author starts each chapter by stating what the student should be able to do in a year from that point (Morling, 2015). This is a great way to think about content. What would you want students to remember from the course a year away? Five years? Imagine running into a past student of the course when she is a business professional or a politician. What would you want her to have remembered from the course?

Once you have a sense of what you want students to know, you now have to face the challenge of making sure it is not too much. Especially in our early years of teaching, the three of us squeezed too much into our courses. Sometimes, we still have the tendency to pack too much in when we are excited about new developments, or when we want students to think we are smart. Out excitement about content is not unique, because many disciplines have traditionally used pedagogical styles that heavily emphasize content. For example, historians traditionally use a "coverage" model emphasizing "the transmission of knowledge from professor to student" (Sipress and Voelker, 2009, p. 19). More recently, historians such as Calder (2002) have proposed a model of "uncoverage," a "deliberate attempt to lay bare for students the central assumptions, forms of inquiry and cognitive habits that transform data into knowledge for practitioners of our discipline" (p. 44). Very often survey courses in biology, physics, chemistry, and psychology likewise tend to include large amounts of information that may not be the best way to foster long-term learning (Landrum and Gurung, 2013). Perhaps more disciplines should consider an uncoverage approach giving students cognitive insights and skills, building critical thinking, and correspondingly increasing their understanding of content knowledge (Nelson, 1999). This will probably entail being willing to cut down on content coverage.

Davis (2009) gives us some good reminders on managing content. She suggests first listing everything you feel is important to cover and then paring down the topics you have listed. If you cannot just cut off topics, divide what you have into high-priority and low-priority items or essential and optional material. You may want to draw a concept map to determine important concepts,

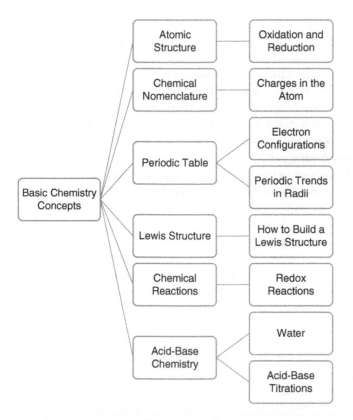

FIGURE 5.1   An example of a concept map for content organization in an introductory chemistry course.

charting out central, major, and minor concepts and the relationship between them (Amundsen et al., 2004). Concepts are usually enclosed in circles or boxes and relationships between concepts are shown by a connecting line between two concepts. Concepts are represented in a hierarchical fashion, with the most comprehensive concepts at the top of the map and the more detailed specific concepts at the deeper level. Concept maps help teachers to actively monitor their mental frameworks for teaching (Salmon and Kelly, 2015). For example, an introductory chemistry teacher may want to organize their class by visualizing the major concepts using a concept map (see Figure 5.1). Concept maps do require planning and initial learning on how to construct them. If you want a good overview, see Figure 5.2 for a concept map *of a concept map*.

Another way to think of content selection is to compare secondary content to what we subjugate to footnotes when writing an article with a page limit. If you have to write a 30-page paper and your draft weighs in at 35 pages, the first thing you can do is select material that would go in footnotes. Once you take time away from the piece and go back to it, you may notice that you can live without

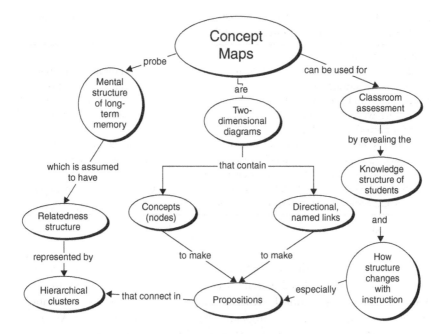

FIGURE 5.2 A concept map for concept maps. Source: www.flaguide.org/cat/conmap/conmap1.php.

the footnotes. Trust us, in most classes, students can live without our content footnotes. And they will probably thank you for it.

Key Content Components: Basic Liberal Arts Skills

Regan went to a small liberal arts college, Carleton College in Northfield Minnesota. Many of his good friends pooh-poohed his choice and instead went for larger schools renowned for specific topics such as engineering, physics, and medicine. Years later, Regan is very happy with his choice. A liberal arts education depends on more than the type of college that you attend, however. Any college and any teacher can emphasize the set of skills typically defined as part of the liberal arts. To oversimplify a bit, students who have received a liberal arts education should be able to communicate clearly, think critically, and collaborate with others. It is this type of diversity in knowledge and skills that Regan developed as part of his liberal education, and it has served him well. Your students can benefit from a liberal arts education too, but this requires you to incorporate liberal arts skills into your course content.

Liberal arts skills have gained some recent national attention because of the efforts of some organizations to reform and improve higher education. Today, large universities and small colleges alike are ensuring that their students get a liberal

TABLE 5.2 The Association of American Colleges and Universities' Liberal Education and America's Promise (LEAP) Essential Learning Outcomes

Students will have:
1. Knowledge of human culture and the physical and natural world through the study of science, mathematics, social sciences, humanities, histories, languages, and the arts.
2. Intellectual and practical skills including inquiry and analysis, critical and creative thinking, written and oral communication, quantitative literacy, information literacy, and teamwork and problem solving.
3. Developed personal and social responsibility including civic knowledge and local and global engagement, intercultural knowledge and competence, ethical reasoning and action, and foundations and skills for lifelong learning.
4. Developed integrative and applied learning including synthesis and advanced accomplishment across general and specialized studies.

Source: AAC&U (n.d.a.).

arts education. In fact, the Association of American Colleges and Universities (AAC&U) champions liberal education (and has done for a century). In 2005, AAC&U launched a "national advocacy, campus action, and research initiative" to advance liberal education, a program called Liberal Education and America's Promise (LEAP, AAC&U, n.d.a.). AAC&U's LEAP initiative advocates that we providing a liberal education to all students regardless of school type or discipline, with the belief that a liberally educated student is better for the nation. When thinking about the content of your course, consider how you can incorporate LEAP outcomes (see Table 5.2).

As you look over the list, you can see why most faculty can agree that the LEAP outcomes should be part of every teacher's goals. No matter what a student majors in, it is important to have a breadth of education (Outcome 1), be a critical thinker and communicate well (Outcome 2), and be aware of cultural diversity (Outcome 3). Most jobs today involve collaborative work. Even when students master subject-specific content, the curriculum should also train them more broadly to communicate effectively, work collaboratively, and think critically.

The LEAP framework is not the only recent effort to improve college education that has emphasized liberal arts skills. A joint effort by the Lumina Foundation, the Institute for Evidence-Based Change, and the National Institute for Learning Outcomes Assessment resulted in a set of common undergraduate learning goals designed to cut across disciplines and institutions (Lumina Foundation, 2014). These goals, collectively referred to as the Degree Qualifications Profile (DQP), provide descriptions of what college graduates should be able to do upon completion of their program of study. The DQP provides a near-comprehensive tour of the liberal arts. For example, the broad goal of "communication fluency" includes sub-goals for students to convey intellectual arguments orally and in writing (Lumina Foundation, 2014). "Intellectual skills" in the DQP include analytical thinking habits such as "consideration of... competing views" and "evaluat[ing] competing perspectives" (Lumina Foundation, 2014, p. 16). Furthermore, according to the DQP, students' work does not occur in a social vacuum; rather, a student should be able to "negotiate... a strategy for group research or performance" and "collaborate... with others in developing and implementing an approach to a civic issue" (Lumina Foundation, 2014, pp. 16, 18). The terminology used across these goals may be unique to the DQP, but the underlying message is familiar: Students must be able to communicate, think critically, and collaborate with others.

Many disciplines, not surprisingly, are explicit in their endorsement of liberal arts skills. For example, the study of history is not just memorizing facts and dates—it involves synthesis of ideas, extensive practice at writing, and working with other scholars and their ideas, (History Major and Liberal Education, 2009). As another example, the American Philosophical Association's *Statement on the teaching of philosophy* explicitly discusses the importance of strong writing skills and the ability to think critically, articulate and examine ideas, and present arguments (American Philosophical Association, n.d.b.). The AACSB has accreditation standards that relate to students developing the skills of written communication and reflective thinking. The American Psychological Association (2007, 2013) undergraduate major goals explicitly outline these liberal arts goals and the revisions of the guidelines were written explicitly to "continue to focus on the broad liberal arts preparation achievable at the undergraduate level" in a way that readies them for the broad swath of postgraduate placements that are typical among psychology majors (American Psychological Association, 2013, p. 10).

The reach of goals for the development of liberal arts also extends to academic programs at individual colleges. For example, American University in Washington, DC, has students in biology "demonstrate informational literacy by having the ability and skills to effectively and legitimately use various sources of information required for functioning in a global, information society" (American University College of Arts and Sciences, n.d.). Similarly, the University of North Carolina in Wilmington has students majoring in physics be able to "demonstrate basic communication skills by working in groups on laboratory experiments and the thoughtful discussion and interpretation of data" (University of North Carolina Wilmington, n.d.). If you do not know the learning goals associated with the department that you are teaching in—first of all, read Chapter 6 to see why this is a bad idea—check them out. We are willing to bet that liberal arts skills are part of those goals, and thus, part of your responsibilities as an educator.

Although the role of liberal arts skills in the undergraduate curriculum is important, their practical benefits are noteworthy as well. Most of our students will need to go out and find a job once they leave the comfy confines of college. What will their potential employers be looking for? You guessed it, liberal arts skills. Employers report that written communication skills and teamwork skills are, respectively, the number one (tied with leadership) and two most important things they are looking for in job candidates (National Association of College and Employers, 2014). Heck, these skills rate higher than work ethic! That's right, the absence of writing skills might hurt the job prospects of graduates more than laziness. Although they are slightly further down the list, it is important to note that analytical skills and verbal communication skills also rank highly. Such results clearly illustrate that a liberal education is not a luxury or waste of time, it is an investment. As such, model teachers incorporate liberal arts skills as learning goals in their courses. They also provide students with opportunities to practice these skills through such activities as written assignments, discussion, public speaking, and collaborative work.

A Focus on Diversity and Ethical Issues

Diversity and ethics are among the core values of many disciplines and higher education in general as well. The AAC&U states: "As we move forward in an increasingly contentious global century and face a civic learning gap nationally, the United States must make civic and democratic learning for all students a top national priority" (AAC&U, n.d.b.). A large part of "civil" learning is working in multicultural groups and living ethically. These two components of educational content, which also feature in the LEAP outcomes discussed above, bear greater scrutiny. See Chapter 4 for what it means to be an ethical teacher.

Fostering Cultural Literacy

Our cultural background is one of the most fascinating aspects of who we are. Modern-day workplaces are populated with individuals from multiple cultures, and it is important to have an understanding of the differences and know how to work well with potential variance in attitudes and behaviors. Correspondingly, many disciplines draw attention to the need to educate students about cultural diversity. Culture is broadly defined and is much more than race or ethnicity, two commonly misused synonyms for culture. Whereas our predominantly white students often begin by thinking their culture is circumscribed to being "American" or "white" or "Christian" —that is if they perceive themselves as having a culture or race at all (Sue, 2006)—it is a mind-expanding experience for them to also consider their own socioeconomic status, geographical location, sexual orientation, gender identity, or sex. These are just *some* of the many other components of culture. Comparisons between different groups illustrate both the diversity of human life as well as highlighting important commonalities.

The importance of diversity-related learning in higher education is illustrated by how strongly it is represented across the undergraduate learning goals set forth in the DQP. One of the major goals of the DQP is "global learning," and "engaging diverse perspectives" is one of the specific intellectual skills students are expected to develop (Lumina Foundation, 2014). Global learning includes goals such as being able to "explain… diverse positions, including those representing different cultural, economic and geographic interests" (Lumina Foundation, 2014, p. 19). Engaging diverse perspectives includes the ability to complete a project "expressing an alternate cultural, political or technological vision and explain[ing] how this vision differs from current realities" (Lumina Foundation, 2014, p. 17). As you can see, these are lofty goals, but they do not specify what types of diversity are most relevant or how diverse perspectives are best evaluated and implemented—those lessons must occur within specific disciplines.

Many disciplines make recognizing cultural diversity a specific learning outcome. For example, the Association to Advance Collegiate Schools of Business accreditation standards explicitly list as an outcome the ability to work well in multicultural work environments (AACSB, n.d.). The American Psychological Association's (2007) guidelines for the undergraduate major include the ability to "recognize and respect human diversity" (p. 17). Of course, teachers should foster respect for and recognition of diversity for several reasons beyond disciplinary prescriptions. With the increasingly diverse North American population, teachers have a responsibility to address the diversity of their students and to prepare them to function in a diverse world. Model teachers infuse learning goals related to diversity into their courses and strong programs ensure diversity goals are taught across the curriculum (Littleford et al., 2010; Trimble et al., 2003). To facilitate this, many disciplines provide special resources to aid teaching about diversity. For example, the American Philosophical Association has a number of resources on diversity and inclusiveness, including a collection of syllabi that demonstrate the inclusion of diversity into courses (American Philosophical Association, n.d.c.). Although many of the syllabi are for courses specifically devoted to issues of diversity such as world philosophies and feminist philosophy, the syllabi also reflect the fact that philosophers have incorporated diversity issues into courses such as bioethics, philosophy of science, and philosophy of art that would be easy to fill with content unrelated to diversity. This illustrates that model teachers of all teaching specialties address diversity content in their courses.

We have heard colleagues in some disciplines agree that diversity is important but feel so pressured to cover content (e.g., all the chapters in a textbook or all major events in history) that they report not having time for diversity. We want to stress that covering diversity and fostering cultural literacy is not just about covering the achievements of non-white individuals, but can also be aided by the use of examples in class and on exams that use non-white names. Guy has friends in mathematics who use diverse groups of people and diversity-related issues when constructing math problems as a way of introducing diversity even when the topic itself is not about diversity. Teachers in chemistry, physics, and biology disciplines with large amounts of factual and technical information, can do the same. It may be a little easier in the humanities. Regan has friends in English who make sure they pick works by non-white authors to give students a feel for different styles, approaches, and worldviews. In general, programs can infuse issues of diversity throughout the curriculum using a wide variety of methods (Gurung and Prieto, 2009).

Given the existing and ever-increasing importance of diversity, model teachers incorporate issues of diversity into their teaching. We would argue that diversity content is wide-ranging in both its scope and its effects. In terms of its scope, all disciplines involve ideas or practices that are embedded within a specific culture; thus, model teachers must prepare students to function within the diversity of ideas and people in that culture. In terms of its effects, exposure to diversity in higher education does more than just make students more appreciative of diversity: it can also improve students' ability to think critically (Loes et al., 2012). After all, critical thinking is largely a process of considering alternative perspectives. Furthermore, the ability to work with others, one of the key liberal arts skills outlined above, is at least partially dependent on an appreciation of diverse people and perspectives. Thus, model teachers incorporate diversity issues into their teaching for both the direct and indirect benefits.

Fostering Ethical Literacy

All academics are bound to implicit or explicit ethical codes of conduct whether in regard to teaching (e.g., do not show favoritism), writing (e.g., be mindful of plagiarism), or scholarship (e.g., collect evidence in a respectful way and do no harm). Behaving ethically is a central value to education. Good citizens are ethical in all that they do whether at home or work. The connection between ethics and some college courses is obvious. Students might take entire courses devoted to the philosophical or religious underpinnings of ethics principles. However, ethics is also important in areas of study sometimes perceived as value-free. For example, ethical training is essential for students in the sciences and engineering (Hollander et al., 2013). These students will need to make ethical decisions about how they conduct research, the ownership of ideas produced by research, and the application of scientific principles in the real world. In reality, no field of study is value-free, and model teachers recognize this fact.

Once again, the DQP illustrates the importance of ethical learning goals in undergraduate education. "Ethical reasoning" is one of the main intellectual skills outlined in the DQP. Furthermore, application of knowledge to civic and global problems is a theme that runs throughout the DQP. For example, one specific goal is for students to be able to identify the "key ethical issues present in at least one prominent social or cultural problem... and defend... an approach to address the ethical issue productively" (Lumina Foundation, 2014, p. 17). At a narrower level, specific ethical behaviors are represented as well, such as the requirement that a student "properly cites multiple information resources" (Lumina Foundation, 2014, p. 16). Although these goals provide some guidance, just as with diversity goals, individual disciplines must determine how they are best implemented.

Many disciplines include educating about ethical behavior as a learning outcome for students in addition to prescribing guidelines for professional ethics. The Association of American Educators (n.d.) developed a *Code of ethics for educators* highlighting the role of ethics and many disciplines have professional guidelines featuring ethics. The Modern Language Association (n.d.), for example, has a statement of professional ethics governing ethical conduct in teaching and learning, service, and scholarship. Similarly, the American Mathematical Society (n.d.) adopted a set of ethical guidelines in 2005 that cover research and its presentation and the "social responsibility of mathematicians."

In business, the Association to Advance Collegiate Schools of Business accreditation standards prominently feature ethical understanding and reasoning. For example, one of the general skill areas they identify is for students to be "able to identify ethical issues and address the issues in a socially responsible manner." They also identify the "social responsibility" of fostering sustainability and ethical management practices as part of their core knowledge base (Standard 9, AACSB, n.d.). The American Psychological Association's learning outcome for the undergraduate major is to "Recognize the necessity of ethical behavior in all aspects of the science and practice of psychology" (American Psychological Association, 2007, p. 17). More specifically, students should have a basic grasp of ethics codes and should follow the American Psychological Association ethics code when conducting research. Just as with diversity, programs should infuse ethics throughout the curriculum (Dunn et al., 2007).

Model teachers infuse ethical issues throughout their courses. Of course, the centrality of ethics will vary based on the specific topic being taught, but ethics even plays a role in subjects that might seem on the surface to be value-free. The education students receive is incomplete if they leave college without the tools needed for ethical judgments and behavior. To teach students the facts of your discipline without also building an ethical foundation on which to make judgments about how to use those facts will result in the production of graduates who are intellectual "bricklayers rather than architects" (Stuhlfaut and Farrell, 2009, p. 173).

Unanswered Questions in the Scholarship of Teaching and Learning on Content

We have made a number of recommendations about course content. To be honest, formulating recommendations related to content presented us with an interesting quandary. Content is clearly a big part of teaching, but there are few applicable research articles directly testing courses varying in content or the results of changing content. The majority of content suggestions are based on the wisdom of experience, commentary from expert teachers often written up in teaching tips books, without empirical basis. Even when tips are accompanied by a citation, looking up the cited reference and reading it (yes, we did that a lot), does not reveal longitudinal, experimental, or even correlational research but case studies (e.g., Amundsen et al., 2004) or essays (e.g., Wankat and Oreovicz, 1998). This is not surprising or necessarily a slam on the tipsters, as research on content is difficult to do.

Would students remember more if they learned one set of facts versus another set? This is hard to test. Would students remember more if they learned fewer facts and worked on deeper processing instead? Faced with covering a whole introductory biology textbook in his classes, Nelson (1999) decided to cut back on content and instead focus on building critical thinking skills. He gave students more examples, and had them interact with the content more. He found that not only did students remember material better, but he did not end up cutting out as much content across the semester as expected. He covered less in class but students could handle more content on their own outside of class. He argues the trade-off between teaching less content and more critical thinking is illusory (Nelson, 1999).

Unfortunately, there are not too many more studies on content. Research on how people learn (Bransford et al., 2000) suggests we should not tax students with too much content, but few studies exist that test this. We have taken the best advice available, sifted and winnowed through it, and presented you with guidelines most consistent with the available research. For example, research on how students study (Gurung and McCann, 2012) and hence interact with the content can help shape how we select and present content. That said, there is a wealth of opportunity and benefits to varying content in the classroom. We can easily see that fostering scientific literacy, liberal arts skills, and ethical and diversity values is a good thing. Now we need more scholarship of teaching and learning done on the best ways to do it and perhaps the benefits of incorporating this content into our classes. Once teachers have a better knowledge base in regard to content, they will be better equipped to make intentional and systematic changes to their curricula in order to best help students learn.

CASE STUDY REEXAMINED: ASSISTANT PROFESSOR OF HUBRIS

Let's get back to Jamie fretting about prepping a new class. We trust that by the time he gets to this part of the chapter, he will feel armed with some key things he can do to get ready.

1. *How could Jamie's approach to content selection be improved?* Jamie seems to rely exclusively on the content deemed important by textbook

authors and publishers. Textbooks are an extremely useful place to start the content-selection process, but he needs to go further. To begin, rather than relying on just one textbook, he should consider several of them to determine the common themes. Also, he should examine recent journals and other publications that are related to course topics. Jamie seems to have a problem with trying to cover too much content because he constantly runs out of time. He should attempt to reduce the content he covers to the most essential topics he wants students to remember after they graduate. Going beyond course-specific content, Jamie needs to check with his department and college to determine if the course is designed to fill any specific program needs.

2. *Aside from facts and figures from a textbook, what other content does Jamie need to consider?* Jamie appears to see little connection between the events in the world, the students in his class, and the content of his course. Diversity issues are a part of our world and a part of our classrooms. Students need to be exposed to content that will prepare them for the cross-cultural experiences they face in their careers and personal lives. It appears that Jamie has an excellent opportunity to tie local diversity issues directly to the content of his class. Jamie probably has not considered the inherent ethical issues related to politics either, and he should try to connect that content to his course as well.

3. *Jamie's courses seem to focus on developing students' skill of remembering facts on multiple-choice tests. How could he expand the types of skills students learn in his courses?* Although it is certainly possible to develop some liberal arts skills in a course that only includes multiple-choice tests, there are more direct ways to foster those skills. Given the expectations that students be able to write and do research in a later course, Jamie needs to start introducing these skills in his courses. Arguably, being able to think critically and communicate clearly are the only learning outcomes that students will use throughout their lives no matter what path they follow after college; as such, development of those skills needs to be infused into all courses. Jamie may decide that he cannot teach students how to write well, speak clearly, do research, think critically, and collaborate with others in every single one of his courses, but he should consider including at least a few of these skills that are most appropriate to each of his courses.

A Reflection on Your Self-Assessment

Let's go back to your self-assessment of your course content. Are there areas you found yourself particularly strong on? Are there areas you realize you just do not touch on? If you rated two courses side-by-side (your strongest and weakest perhaps), how much variance was there between them?

We trust that we touched on at least some issues in this chapter that you may not have given as much thought to. There are many aspects of course content going beyond just how many chapters students read or facts they have to memorize. You will note that many of the questions in Table 5.1 focused on liberal education outcomes. Do you feel you give each of them their fair share of attention? We are guessing that your course goals reflect the breadth of content in your discipline but given what you have read, it may be prudent to check with department and disciplinary learning outcomes. Are your course goals consistent? In regard to written and oral communication, are there ways to foster the development of these two elements? If you feel you do not have time, based on how much content you have to cover, we hope our section on trimming content and content selection gives you some ideas on how to make place for critical thinking skill development and advancing communication. In our experience, faculty often feel they discuss ethical issues and diversity issues as much as they should. Our study of psychology faculty showed 36 percent of the sample could not document infusing psychological values (ethical and diversity issues) in their class (Boysen et al., 2015). Given these values are an explicit part of the American Psychological Association's learning outcomes for undergraduate education, this is a high percentage. We agree that it is not always easy to both cover content knowledge and foster the variety of skills we discuss, but the reality is that both these types of content (facts and skills) make for model courses. Whereas our chapter on training can help you with pragmatic ways to enhance your content coverage and skill development, we hope the content of this chapter provided you with some good food for course planning-related thought.

Summary of Best Practices

To be honest, this was one of the most difficult chapters of the book to write. On one hand, college faculty enjoy the academic freedom to pick what content to include in a class. On the other hand, departments and disciplines often have strong suggestions for what courses should cover (even stronger mandates for professional programs). In this chapter we have pointed to the main places for you to look to ensure you are covering the content that you need to. Enjoy your (academic) freedoms, but make sure your students are getting the content, skills, and values that the discipline expects them to get. In addition to content knowledge, we also highlight the importance of covering the basic elements of a liberal education. When we busy ourselves with covering a lot of material, we may forget about discussing issues such as ethics and diversity that are critical to a well-rounded education. When it comes to course content, it is critical to be abreast of developments in your discipline and the learning outcomes of your department and university (e.g., general education).

The Very Busy People Book Club: Your Top Five Must-Reads

As we didn't include every journal article, book, or book chapter in the main portion of this chapter, we wanted to direct you to some other great sources for suggestions on how to select content. For your pleasure reading, refer to the following list.

Bean, J. C. (2011). *Engaging ideas: The professor's guide to integrating writing, critical thinking, and active learning in the classroom.* San Francisco, CA: John Wiley & Sons.

Bransford, J. D., Brown, A. L., and Cocking, R. R. (2000). *How people learn: Brain, mind, experience, and school.* Washington, DC: National Academy Press.

Davis, B. G. (2009). *Tools for teaching* (2nd edn). San Francisco, CA: Jossey-Bass.

Lumina Foundation (2014). *The Degree Qualifications Profile: A learning-centered framework for what college graduates should know and behavior to do to earn the associate, Bachelor's or Master's degree.* Retrieved from http://degreeprofile.org/press_four/wp-content/uploads/2014/09/DQP-web-download.pdf.

Svinicki, M. and McKeachie, W. J. (2013). *McKeachie's teaching tips* (14th edn). Belmont, CA: Wadsworth.

References

AACSB (n.d.). *Learning and teaching standards.* Retrieved from www.aacsb.edu/accreditation/standards/2013-business/learning-and-teaching.

AACSB (2013). *2013 business accreditation standards.* Retrieved from www.aacsb.edu/accreditation/standards/2013-business/learning-and-teaching/standard9.aspx.

AAC&U (n.d.a). *About AAC&U.* Retrieved from www.aacu.org/leap.

AAC&U (n.d.b.). *Civic learning and democratic engagement.* Retrieved from www.aacu.org/clde.

AICPA (n.d.). *CPA examination content.* Retrieved from www.aicpa.org/BecomeACPA/CPAExam/ExaminationContent/Pages/default.aspx.

AICPA (2015). *Content and skill specifications for the uniform CPA examination.* Retrieved from www.aicpa.org/BecomeACPA/CPAExam/ExaminationContent/ContentAndSkills/DownloadableDocuments/CSOs-SSOs-Effective-Jan-2015.pdf.

American Chemical Society (n.d.). *American Chemical Society: Division of chemical education examinations institute.* Retrieved from http://chemexams.chem.iastate.edu/about-us.

American Chemical Society (2009). *ACS guidelines for chemistry in two-year college programs.* Retrieved from www.acs.org/content/acs/en/education/policies/twoyearcollege.html.

American Historical Association (2013). *AHA history turning project: History discipline core.* Retrieved from www.historians.org/teaching-and-learning/current-projects/tuning/history-discipline-core.

American Mathematical Society (n.d.). *Ethical guidelines.* Retrieved from www.ams.org/about-us/governance/policy-statements/sec-ethics.

American Philosophical Association (n.d.a.). *Teaching resources.* Retrieved from http://www.apaonline.org/?page=teaching_resources.

American Philosophical Association (n.d.b.). *Statement on the teaching of philosophy.* Retrieved from www.apaonline.org/?teaching.

American Philosophical Association (n.d.c.). *Resources on diversity and inclusiveness.* Retrieved from www.apaonline.org/?page=diversity_resources.

American Psychological Association (2007). *APA guidelines for the undergraduate psychology major.* Washington, DC: American Psychological Association. Retrieved from www.apa.org/ed/resources.html.

American Psychological Association (2013). *APA Guidelines for the undergraduate psychology major 2.0.* Washington, DC: American Psychological Association. Retrieved from www.apa.org/ed/resources.html.

American University College of Arts and Sciences (n.d.). *Biology learning outcomes.* Retrieved from www.american.edu/cas/biology/learning-outcomes.cfm.

Amundsen, C., Saroyan, A., and Donald, J. (2004). Analysis of course content. In A. Saroyan and C. Amundsen (eds.), *Rethinking teaching in higher education: From a course design workshop to a faculty development framework.* Sterling, VA: Stylus.

Association of American Educators (n.d.). *Code of ethics for educators.* Retrieved from www.aaeteachers.org/index.php/about-us/aae-code-of-ethics.

Boysen, G. A., Richmond, A. S., and Gurung, R. A. R. (2015). Model Teaching Criteria for psychology: Initial documentation of teachers' self-reported competency. *Scholarship of Teaching and Learning in Psychology*, 1, 48–59.

Bransford, J. D., Brown, A. L., and Cocking, R. R. (2000). *How people learn: Brain, mind, experience, and school.* Washington, DC: National Academy Press.

Calder, L. (2002). Looking for learning in the history survey. *Perspectives: The newsmagazine of the American Historical Association*, 40(3), 43–45.

Chick, N., Haynie, A., and Gurung, R. A. R. (eds.) (2012). *Exploring more signature pedagogies.* Sterling, VA: Stylus.

Davis, B. G. (2009). *Tools for teaching* (2nd edn). San Francisco, CA: Jossey-Bass.

Dunn, D. S., McCarthy, M. A., Baker, S., Halonen, J. S., and Hill, G. I. (2007). Quality benchmarks in undergraduate psychology programs. *American Psychologist*, 62, 650–670.

Dunn, D. S., Brewer, C. L., Cautin, R. L., Gurung, R. R., Keith, K. D, McGregor, L. N., Nida, S. A., Puccio, P., and Voigt, M. J. (2010). The undergraduate psychology curriculum: Call for a core. In D. F. Halpern (ed.), *Undergraduate education in psychology: A blueprint for the future of the discipline* (pp. 47–61). Washington, DC: American Psychological Association.

Gurung, R. A. R. and McCann, L. (2012). Study techniques and teaching. In B. Schwartz and R. A. R. Gurung (eds.), *Evidence-based teaching in higher education* (pp. 99–116). Washington, DC: American Psychological Association.

Gurung, R. A. R. and Prieto, L. (eds.) (2009). *Getting culture: Incorporating diversity across the curriculum.* Arlington, VA: Stylus.

Gurung, R. A. R., Haynie, A., and Chick, N. (eds.) (2009). *Signature pedagogies across the disciplines.* Arlington, VA: Stylus.

Hestenes, D., Wells, M., and Swackhamer, G. (1992). Force Concept Inventory. *The Physics Teacher*, 30, 141–158.

History Major and Liberal Education (2009). *Liberal Education*, 95(2), 40–47.

Hollander, R. D., Fletcher, C. H., and Benya, F. F. (eds.) (2013). *Practical guidance on science and engineering ethics education for instructors and administrators: Papers and summary from a workshop, December 12, 2012.* Washington, DC: National Academies Press.

Homa, N., Hackathorn, J., Brown, C., Garczynski, A., Solomon, E., Tennial, R., Sanborn, U., and Gurung, R. A. R. (2013). How consistent are introductory psychology course syllabi? Examining objectives and content. *Teaching of Psychology*, 40, 169–174.

Landrum, R. E. and Gurung, R. A. R. (2013). The memorability of introductory psychology revisited. *Teaching of Psychology*, 40, 222–227.

Littleford, L. N., Buskist, W., Frantz, S. M., Galvan, D. B., Henderson, R. W., McCarthy, M. A., Page, M. C., and Puente, A. E. (2010). Psychology students today and tomorrow. In D. F. Halpern (ed.), *Undergraduate education in psychology: A blueprint for the future of the discipline* (pp. 63–79). Washington, DC: American Psychological Association.

Loes, C., Pascarella, E. T., and Umbach, P. D. (2012). Effects of diversity experiences on critical thinking skills: Who benefits? *The Journal of Higher Education*, 83, 1–24.

Lumina Foundation (2014). *The Degree Qualifications Profile: A learning-centered framework for what college graduates should know and behavior to do to earn the associate, Bachelor's or Master's degree*. Retrieved from http://degreeprofile.org/press_four/wp-content/uploads/2014/09/DQP-web-download.pdf.

Modern Language Association (n.d.). *Statement of professional ethics*. Retrieved from http://www.mla.org/repview_profethics.

Morling, B. (2015). *Research methods in psychology: Evaluating a world of information*. New York: Norton.

National Association of College and Employers (2014). *Job outlook: The candidate skills/qualities employers want, the influence of attributes*. Retrieved from www.naceweb.org/s11122014/job-outlook-skills-qualities-employers-want.aspx?terms=job%20skills.

Nelson, C. E. (1999). On the persistence of unicorns: The trade-off between content and critical thinking revisited. In B. Pescosolido and R. Aminzade (eds.), *The social world of higher education: Handbook for teaching in a new century*. Thousand Oaks, CA: Pine Forge Press.

Phelps, P. H. and Ryan, P. M. (1995). Synthesizing theory and practice: Praxis for professors. *The NEA Higher Education Journal*, 121–128.

Richmond, A. S., Boysen, G. A., Gurung, R. A. R., Tazeau, Y. N., Meyers, S. A., and Sciutto, M. J. (2014). Aspirational Model Teaching Criteria for psychology. *Teaching of Psychology*, 41, 281–295.

Salmon, D. and Kelly, M. (2015). *Using concept mapping to foster adaptive expertise: Enhancing teacher metacognitive learning to improve student academic performance*. New York: Peter Lamb.

Sipress, J. M. and Voelker, D. J. (2009). From learning history to doing history: Beyond the coverage model. In R. A. R. Gurung, N. L. Chick, and A. Haynie (eds.), *Exploring signature pedagogies: Approaches to disciplinary habits of mind* (pp. 19–35). Sterling, VA: Stylus.

Stuhlfaut, M. W. and Farrell, M. (2009). Pedagogic cacophony: The teaching of ethical, legal, and societal issues in advertising education. *Journalism & Mass Communication Educator*, 64, 173–190.

Sue, D. W. (2006) The invisible whiteness of being: Whiteness, white supremacy, white privilege, and racism. In D. W. Sue and M. G. Constantine (eds.), *Addressing racism: Facilitating cultural competence in mental health and educational settings* (pp. 15–30). Hoboken, NJ: John Wiley & Sons.

Texas Higher Education Coordinating Board (n.d.). *Texas tuning project*. Retrieved from www.thecb.state.tx.us/Texas_Tuning_Project.

Trimble, J. E., Stevenson, M. R., and Worell, J. (2003). Toward an inclusive psychology: Infusing the introductory psychology textbook with diversity content. Retrieved from www.apa.org/pi/oema/programs/recruitment/inclusive-textbooks.pdf.

University of North Carolina Wilmington (n.d.). *Student learning outcomes and sample syllabi*. Retrieved from http://uncw.edu/phy/about/slos.html.

Wankat, P. and Oreovicz, F. (1998). Content tyranny. *Prism*, 8, 15. Retrieved from www.asee.org/prism/october/html/october_teaching.htm.

Wolfle, D. (1942). The first course in psychology. *Psychological Bulletin*, 39, 685–713.

6

HOW DO MODEL TEACHERS ASSESS STUDENT LEARNING?

Recently, a colleague in student affairs, who is employed as the assessment director at a large university, was giving a lecture on current assessment practices in
higher education; an instructor in the audience said that he "gave this assessment
fad just a few more years"—to which the assessment director replied "I'm not
worried about *my* job security." The reply suggested a truth in higher education: assessment isn't going away. The academy is sometimes beset by administrative pushes or teaching fads that, if ignored, will eventually fade into the
background (remember MOOCs?). In contrast, the systematic collection and
utilization of data regarding student learning appears to be growing in importance
rather than fading.

If assessment is a fad, then it is a fad in the same sense that rap is a fad. Both
emerged out of the 1970s, grew to popular acceptance in the 1980s, and have
only increased in mainstream acceptance with each passing decade. It is funny that
something older than the students sitting in most of our classes can be dismissed as
a fad in higher education—what a glacial pace for change we have in the academy.
Also like rap, assessment was the center of extreme controversy in its early days
that has continued in the following years, albeit with less fervor; both have also
been frequently dismissed or ignored. Rap isn't going away either.

Early objections about assessment centered on the supposed ineffability of
college outcomes, the implementation of business-based practices in a college
setting, and the assumption that college success is accurately measured by gains
in test scores (Ewell, 2002). As the assessment process became more entrenched,
concerns arose about its use in accreditation and the potential for encroachment
on academic freedom (Cain, 2014; Halpern, 2013). It does not take much time
on a college campus to hear faculty dismissing assessment as "for the administrators," "just a hoop," or "a waste of time." Model teachers, in contrast, take charge

Set learning goals

Make revisions

Facilitate learning

Assess outcomes

FIGURE 6.1   The assessment process.

of their own assessment practices, perform meaningful assessments, and seamlessly integrate assessment, teaching, and scholarship. Assessment, like rap, can be truly great in the hands of the right person (see Snoop Dogg).

"But I already do assessment! I assign grades to every single student!" This is a common faculty lament, but it is based on confusion over terminology. Educational jargon often inhibits clear communication across disciplines. For example, the term "assessment" means something different to elementary school teachers, educational psychologists, psychometricians, and curriculum specialists in higher education. As such, it is important to clearly establish the terminology of this chapter.

Assessment refers to a process (Suskie, 2009; Walvoord, 2010). The assessment process begins by determining what students should achieve after a learning experience; these are the learning goals, objectives, or outcomes. Although these terms are used inconsistently in the literature, we use *goals* to refer to plans for learning that are broad and cut across programs or universities, we use *objectives* to refer to narrow, course-specific plans for learning, and we use *outcomes* to refer to the actual learning exhibited by students. Once learning goals are set, the assessment process continues with the design of learning experiences to achieve those goals. Next, data are collected in order to determine if the learning has occurred as planned. This step typically includes *evaluations*, which are one-time judgments about the quality of student performance (e.g., rubric scores, test results). Finally, outcomes data is utilized to make improvements to the entire process; this is often referred to as "closing the loop" (see Figure 6.1). Engaging in assessment is an essential part of an evidence-based approach to teaching, and this chapter offers an overview of the key components of the process (for more detailed treatments of assessment see the "must-read" list). How many of these key components do you already engage in? Take the self-assessment in Table 6.1 to see how your current practices match up to the Model Teaching Criteria.

TABLE 6.1 Self-Assessment of the Model Assessment Teaching Criteria

Directions: Please indicate on the scale below how often you incorporate these elements/activities to improve your assessment practices. *Scale: 5 = Always, 4 = Often, 3 = Sometimes, 2 = Rarely, 1 = Never*	*Your score*
1. You articulate specific, measurable learning objectives in your syllabi or other course documents (e.g., sample lesson plans, a list of course objectives).	
2. You change course syllabi, material, lesson plans, or teaching methods based on formal and informal assessment.	
3. You align class activities, lectures, and reading assignments with learning objectives.	
4. You provide constructive feedback to students that is related to their achievement of learning objectives (e.g., use of rubrics).	
5. You publically disseminate information about teaching innovations and outcomes (e.g., publications and presentations).	

Note: This self-assessment is adapted and modified from Richmond et al. (2014) and Boysen et al. (2015).

Assessment? Who Cares? (Everyone!)

There are a number of reasons to care about assessment, but a basic place to start is the fact that college teachers have little choice but to care—assessment is universal in higher education. At the individual college level, you would be hard-pressed to find a college that did not tout its dedication to assessment of student learning—find an exception to this rule, and you have found, for reasons that will soon become immediately clear, a college to avoid at all costs. In terms of higher education organizations, dozens of them have teamed together to endorse a statement outlining their commitment to the use of assessment in order to increase the quality and quantity of college graduates (New Leadership Alliance for Student Learning and Accountability, 2012). So fundamental is agreement about the value of assessment that all regional accrediting bodies require colleges to have learning goals, evidence of student learning, and evidence of assessment-based improvement (Provezis, 2010). So, why avoid a college that does not concern itself with assessment? It may not be a college for long, that's why.

As indicated by accreditation requirements, learning goals are an especially important and ubiquitous aspect of assessment. Research indicates that 84 percent of college provosts report having institution-wide learning goals (Kuh et al., 2013). Similarly, 88 percent of department heads report having program learning goals or being in the process of developing them (Ewell et al., 2011). Are you teaching at a college? Are you teaching in an academic department? A "yes" to either one of these questions virtually guarantees that you are responsible for moving students toward specific learning goals.

Wait, isn't assessment the responsibility of some specific committee on campus? In fact, teachers are the individuals most directly involved with the central question of assessment—"Are students learning?" As such, the consensus best practice is to place responsibility for assessment onto faculty (Cain, 2014; Halpern, 2013; Hutchings, 2010; Provezis, 2010). After all, assessment results are largely based on data from individual courses, and the impact of assessments is likely to feed back into individual courses and programs (Kuh et al., 2013). To that end, department heads report that the most common reasons for assessment are program and instructional improvement (Ewell et al., 2011).

Although it is tempting to pawn off assessment onto others, would you really want someone else assessing learning in your course? Academic freedom is certainly more secure if individual faculty, rather than committees or administrators, take charge of assessment in the classroom (Cain, 2014). An awkward moment one of us witnessed during a departmental meeting illustrates these points well. An English-scholar-cum-dean told a room full of empirically minded cognitive psychologists "You guys must all love Dr. Phil! Psychology is basically a healthcare profession." Polite grinding of teeth ensued. Did those cognitive psychologists want an English scholar dictating assessment in their courses? Of course not. English professors know best how to assess English objectives, and cognitive scientists know best how to assess cognitive science objectives.

Faculty should also care about assessment for the same reasons that they got into teaching in the first place: passion for a subject, desire to answer interesting questions, and dedication to students. Assessment is a chance for teachers to focus even more deeply on the discipline that they love (Hutchings, 2010). Teachers who care about seeing the spark of insight on students' faces or who want students to be engaged in their discipline should be motivated to ensure that these desired outcomes occur. Perhaps a different sales pitch is needed for the more world-weary group of teachers who resent students for their indifference, lack of preparation, and surliness. Assessment is for the curmudgeonly set as well. Stop complaining and use assessment to determine why students act that way and what pedagogy will change their behaviors.

A final reason to care about assessment is because of its status as the ultimate evidence-based practice. Following the assessment process is like having a research program on your own pedagogy. The overarching research question is "How do students best learn this material?" Each teaching method constitutes a manipulated variable in your grand teaching experiment, and student learning outcomes are the dependent variables. Going further with the metaphor, making changes to a learning experience is based on the hypothesis that the new method will lead to better outcomes than the old method. Of course, such a hypothesis cannot be supported without gathering evidence. When model teachers engage in assessment, they have evidence—empirical data in fact—to support their hypothesized teaching effectiveness.

Our Work is Never Done: Assessment as a Process

Model teachers engage in the assessment process as part of their normal pedagogical practices. Systematic planning and evaluation of course outcomes is part of the learning-centered approach to education (Blumberg, 2009; Harden et al., 1999; Huba and Freed, 2000). A teaching-centered approach to education tends to focus on what the teacher does, but a learning-centered approach focuses on what students learn; this distinction is also commonly referred to as the "sage on the stage" versus the "guide on the side" approach. The difference was clearly illustrated by a recent faculty essay in *The Chronicle of Higher Education*. The author bemoaned the current "fad" of active learning because he had tried it and students informed him that what they really wanted was to hear an expert explain what they needed to know. From a learning-centered standpoint, the author's argument is totally beside the point. The real question is which approach allows more students to achieve important learning goals—evaluation of pedagogy should center on student learning. Knowing that learning outcomes should drive education, model teachers' classroom assessment procedures mimic the larger assessment process; they set learning objectives, assess learning outcomes, and utilize outcomes information to improve teaching and learning (Walvoord, 2010).

CASE STUDY: SOMEONE CALL 911! DR. MEAD HAS AN ASSESSMENT CRISIS

Dr. Mead just taught Advanced Sociological Methods for the first time. He was finishing up his dissertation over the summer and, other than selecting a textbook and writing a bare-bones syllabus, he did not have time to do much in terms of course preparation before the course began. Basically, the course consisted of textbook reading assignments and classroom lectures. Dr. Mead stayed one chapter ahead of the class while planning his lectures. There were four multiple-choice tests spread throughout the semester and one "research paper" on a sociological topic of students' choosing. His tests consisted of a random selection of test-bank questions and a few items that he wrote based on lecture material. The paper assignment simply asked students to "review the research literature related to a specific sociology topic using at least 15 sources" with a suggested length of 15 to 20 pages.

The end of the semester led to several crises for Dr. Mead. The most practical and pressing problem was the department chair's request for his "general education assessment data." Unbeknown to Dr. Mead, Advanced Sociological Methods was part of the general education program and had learning goals do develop students' "discipline-specific writing proficiency," "ethical decision-making," and "problem-solving skills." Dr. Mead had no data to support student outcomes related to these goals.

The second crisis stemmed from his frustration with students' apparent inability to think critically. He had expected papers to contain the type of insightful research analysis that he had been modeling in his lectures all semester long. Rather, students' papers consisted of summaries of 15 sources without evaluation, synthesis, or, apparently, any thought at all. Dr. Mead wondered what was wrong with students.

Now take a moment to answer these questions. We will revisit your answer at the end of the section. And, yes, after reading the section you may change your answers.

1. What should Dr. Mead do with his class in terms of learning objectives?
2. How would learning objectives affect student learning in Dr. Mead's class?
3. Does Dr. Mead know if students learned anything in his classes? Why or why not?

Students Can't Hit the Mark Without a Target: The Importance of Learning Objectives

Having specific learning objectives can make all the difference in education. One of us once had a German history course with three required books on the Weimar Republic alone—that should have been a clear sign of trouble. The reading assignments were massive, and the only teaching technique consisted of sitting in a circle and discussing the thick German-history tomes that we were wading through. To clarify, the goal was to have discussion, but mostly we stared blankly at the books as the professor tossed out question after question we had no idea how to answer. Everyone, including the professor, was lost. All of the students were frustrated and, looking back, it seems likely that the professor was equally frustrated by our inability to pick up on what were obvious, to a historian at least, themes in the readings. What was the missing ingredient? Students desperately wanted some sort of direction for what we were supposed to be learning from the hundreds and hundreds of pages of reading, and the teacher wanted us to grasp some basic historical points. The class desperately needed clear learning objectives.

Model teachers set specific, measurable learning objectives for their classes. Most teachers have general ideas about what they want students to get out of their classes. "I want them to be critical thinkers." "I want them to be able to communicate clearly." "They should be able to analyze scholarly sources." Broad goals such as these are most appropriate for entire programs or colleges, and they often make their way onto course syllabi as well (Anderson et al., 2005; Harden, 2002; Palomba and Banta, 1999). Being able to analyze scholarly sources is a wonderful educational goal, but it would not have helped students understand what they were supposed to be getting out of those dense books on German history. Thus, model teachers also create learning objectives for each of their courses. Learning objectives are specific, behavioral statements of the intended result of a particular educational experience; they are often formulated as statements of knowledge, skills, or attitudes. "Describe the major factors that led to the end of the Weimar Republic"—that is the type of specific learning objective that can guide reading, classroom activities, and assessment.

Some traditionalists might object at this point—"Students will learn what I teach them. What makes this middle step of defining objectives necessary?" The answer here is simple: Providing students with learning objectives increases learning. Research shows that providing people with specific, challenging goals leads to better performance than if they have no goals or even if they have specific goals that are easy (Locke et al., 1981). A series of studies on this topic in the 1970s showed that more learning occurred when students had objectives than when they simply reviewed material without objectives (Duchastel and Brown, 1974; Duell, 1974; Gagné and Rothkopf, 1975; Kaplan, 1976; Kaplan and Simmons, 1974; Rothkopf and Kaplan, 1972; Royer, 1977). Other interesting effects emerged as well. Specific objectives resulted in more learning than general objectives (Kaplan, 1976; Rothkopf and Kaplan, 1972), use of objectives increased learning without significantly increasing studying time (Duchastel and Brown, 1974), and the objectives were effective for information presented in written or lecture format (Royer, 1977). Overall, there is a strong, empirical rationale for taking the time and effort to write learning objectives.

Keeping with the evidence-based theme, we would also argue that learning objectives and scientific hypotheses function in much the same way. Hypotheses are testable predictions used in research, and learning objectives are testable predictions of what will occur in students' minds after a learning experience. Good scientists commit themselves to a hypothesis before conducting an experiment so that they can clearly determine their success, and good teachers set learning objectives to determine the success of their pedagogy.

The initial process of writing useful learning objectives for classes occurs in three steps: determining the learning content, writing measurable learning objective statements, and evaluating how well the resultant learning objectives meet desired educational goals (Huba and Freed, 2000). Instructors should begin the process by asking the following question: What should students be able to do after this learning experience? Answers to this question can come from formal and informal sources (see Table 6.2). Formal sources include systematic statements made by organizations about what students need to learn—many of these sources are discussed in Chapter 5 on course content.

Two formal sources of objectives stand above all others: the academic department and the college. When planning learning objectives, it is useful to first consult with the academic department through which a course is being offered. Well-run departments will not only have learning goals, but they will have maps of the curriculum stipulating what courses are responsible for contributing to what goals. Department heads are great sources for such information. College-level learning goals are another important source. When one of us switched colleges a few

TABLE 6.2 Sources of Content for Learning Experiences

Formal sources
- College or university mission and learning goals
- Department mission and learning goals
- Accreditation or licensure standards
- Professional organizations
- Admission requirements for postgraduate programs

Informal sources
- Personal experience in the subject
- Examination of textbooks
- Examination of similar syllabi
- Discussion with peers
- Surveys of employers

Note: Adapted from Boysen (2013) and Suskie (2009).

years ago, a new general-education learning goal—exhibiting personal and social responsibility—came with the teaching responsibilities. Contributing to students' general education meant figuring out the intention behind that goal and how faculty were expected to help students achieve it. In fact, the goal primarily relates to service learning and community engagement, which translated into a new course objective to "execute educational projects that increase scientific literacy in the general public." The lesson here is that model teachers put in special effort to ensure that their courses facilitate goals identified as essential by their departments and colleges.

Although they are valuable, formal sources of content for learning experiences will only go so far, and teachers also need to explore informal sources. Formal and informal sources differ in degree of official approval and recognition; informal sources may have little or no official recognition. The advice of colleagues and mentors who have taught the same course is a prime example of an informal source. Previous teachers will have textbooks and syllabi that can be utilized for inspiration (but do not steal without permission!). As scary as this may seem at times, you are the ultimate and definitive source of objectives. Even the strictest of accreditation standards do not dictate everything to be learned in a course. What do you want students to know by the end of the semester? Better yet, what do you want them to remember five years from now? These are the things that should be rendered into learning objectives.

Learning objectives can be formulated in many ways, but the ABCD format is comprehensive and easy to remember (D'Andrea, 1999; Osborne and Wagor, 2004; Smaldino et al., 2005). Using this format, objective statements include audience (A), behavior (B), condition (C), and degree (D). Starting with audience (A), it simply refers to the people who will be doing the learning. Practically speaking, the audience statement needs to be made only once: "Students in this course will…" The point to emphasize, however, is that each course is an audience unto itself; thus, every single course needs its own list of objectives.

TABLE 6.3 Examples of Learning Objectives Organized According to Cognitive Level

Cognitive skill	Behavior term	Example learning objectives from AP psychology, biology, and physics	Additional behavior terms
Knowledge	Recognize Identify State	Recognize the strengths and limitations of applying theories to explain behavior. Identify essential properties of shared, core life processes that provide insights into the history of life on earth. State the general relation between force and potential energy.	Label List Match Name Order Reproduce Select
Comprehension	Discuss Describe Explain	Discuss the effect of the endocrine system on behavior. Describe specific examples of conserved core biological processes and features shared by all domains or within one domain of life. Explain how linear momentum conservation follows as a consequence of Newton's Third Law for an isolated system.	Classify Identify Indicate Locate Paraphrase Restate Translate Summarize
Application	Apply Predict Use	Apply basic descriptive statistical concepts, including interpreting and constructing graphs and calculating simple descriptive statistics. Use data from a real or simulated population(s), based on graphs or models of types of selection, to predict what will happen to the population in the future. Use the equation $v = v_0 + at$ to solve problems involving one-dimensional motion.	Demonstrate Change Illustrate Manipulate Predict Show Relate Use Write

Category	Key Verbs	Learning Objectives	Associated Verbs
Analysis	Differentiate Compare Analyze	Differentiate types of research with regard to purpose, strengths, and weaknesses. Compare and contrast processes by which genetic variation is produced and maintained in organisms from multiple domains. Analyze situations in which an object moves with specified acceleration under the influence of one or more forces so they can determine the magnitude and direction of the net force.	Appraise Break down Calculate Categorize Compare Contrast Discriminate Examine Question Test
Synthesis	Synthesize Create Arrange	Synthesize how biological, cognitive, and cultural factors converge to facilitate development of language. Create representation(s) that depict how cell-to-cell communication occurs by direct contact or from a distance through chemical signaling. Arrange in order of increasing wavelength the following: visible light of various colors, ultraviolet light, infrared light, radio waves, x-rays, and gamma rays.	Compose Combine Develop Formulate Generate Plan Propose Relate Revise Synthesize
Evaluation	Debate Evaluate Determine	Debate the appropriate testing practices, particularly in relation to culture-fair test uses. Evaluate evidence provided by data to qualitatively and quantitatively investigate the role of natural selection in evolution. Determine an appropriate expression for displacement to describe simple harmonic motion.	Argue Choose Defend Discriminate Judge Rate Recommend Support

Note: All learning objectives are adapted from AP course overviews published by the College Board (collegeboard.com).

The most important and labor-intensive part of writing learning objective statements is determining the behavior (B). Remember, one goal is to produce data that can be measured; as such, behavior terms need to correspond to something that students can and will demonstrate on a test, paper, or other classroom assignment. Nothing is more useful in writing learning objectives than Bloom's Taxonomy because it organizes learning into several levels of cognitive complexity that can be translated into specific behavioral terms (see Table 6.3).

Although cognitive objectives receive the most attention, learning related to skills is also important. Writing objectives for skills is straightforward because teachers often have a very clear idea of what they want students to be able to do. Writing the learning objective is as simple as putting words to the goal. For example, skill-based objectives might include the following: "format papers using APA style," "search the JSTOR database," "build set designs," "apply first aid to athletic injuries," and "write a literature review."

Learning objectives can also focus on attitudes and values. Some teachers may be reticent to admit that they intentionally shape students' attitudes and values, but the practice is not as controversial as it may seem at first. For example, would you want to see a doctor whose medical school did not instill value for the Hippocratic Oath? Would you entrust your life savings to an investment banker whose degree came from a school that had no learning goals related to business ethics? Model teachers incorporate attitudes and values into their teaching (see Chapter 5 for discussion of value-related content such as ethics and diversity), but a corollary is that they can and should be upfront about the attitudes and values that they are trying to instill. Specific learning objectives are the best way to accomplish that task.

Learning objectives associated with attitudes and values may be somewhat less concrete than cognitive- and skill-based objectives, but they can still be formulated into measurable statements (Suskie, 2009). "Appreciation for diversity" is a common value-based goal at the college and program level, but an individual teacher might use their class to increase students' ability to: "show respect for diverse faith traditions," "acknowledge the legitimacy of diverse worldviews," or "recognize variations in cultural communication patterns." Another common value-based learning goal is "demonstrating social and ethical responsibility." In relation to this goal, teachers might have objectives that lead students to "engage in service learning," "make ethical decisions," or "support community education." These attitude and value objectives can be assessed, but that assessment is unlikely to be effective using only tests and quizzes: thus, more complex assignments or even attitude surveys may be necessary.

Returning to the ABCD format, once the behavior (B) is set, the condition (C) and degree (D) are optional refinements that a teacher can utilize to make the learning objective even more specific. Adding a condition clarifies the situation in which students will learn and be evaluated. For example, what tools or resources will students be using? Will they use a calculator, a map, a manual, formulas, computer programs, or artistic supplies? The condition may also be specified by providing more details about the learning situation. For example, will they be given a passage to read, raw data to analyze, or a scene to direct?

Degree (D) indicates how much or how well students will learn. It might refer to a certain number of examples, articles, pieces of art, solutions, or theories that students must utilize. Or, degree can set a desired level of accuracy. Papers might need to be written with zero formatting errors. Measurements may need to occur within a thousandth of an inch. Estimates might need to be within a standard deviation. Inclusion of conditions and degrees are not essential to constructing quality behavioral learning objectives, but they add clarity that can be useful to students as they are attempting to meet course expectations and to teachers as they are attempting to determine if instructional activities are having the intended effects.

Evaluation (E) is the third and final step in creating learning objectives statements. Just because a learning objective exists does not mean it is any good. As such, model teachers should ask themselves the following five questions about the objectives they have produced (Huba and Freed, 2000; Smaldino et al., 2005; Suskie, 2009).

1. *Is the learning objective related to important content?* Learning objectives are quite numerous in comparison to broad goals. In fact, a single course could require 100 to 200 objectives (e.g., Nuhfer and Knipp, 2003). To illustrate, one of us takes the following approach in setting up goals and objectives for courses. Each course has about ten broad goals that correspond to departmental and university missions, and they are displayed on the first page of the syllabus so their importance is plainly clear to both students and administrators. In addition to these broad goals, there are typically more than 100 specific learning objectives that correspond to every course reading assignment, lecture, and activity. One downside to this process is that explicitly defining everything that students are supposed to learn can escalate quickly into burying them in content. Imagine that there are 200 learning objectives for your course. One month after the course is over, students might recall 20 percent of the content. What if you cut the number of objectives to 100 and students remembered 50 percent of the content because of the increased time and effort put into teaching and learning those topics? There would still be an increase in learning, even with the content cut in half. Teachers must reflect on what the absolutely essential content is for their course (see Chapter 5 for additional discussion of choosing content).

2. *Is the objective meaningfully related to important content?* The process of translating deep academic topics into measurable objectives has the potential to render them flabby and toothless. For example, translating the broad goal of learning

to think critically into meaningful learning objectives is especially challenging. One strategy is to break critical thinking down into its component parts. Such an approach leaves the teachers with objectives such as "consider multiple viewpoints" and "analyze potential biases in evidence." However, do the combined objectives fail to capture the gestalt of critical thinking? This is just one difficulty of many in making goals measurable and meaningful. Another factor to consider in assessing meaningfulness is the level of Bloom's Taxonomy objectives tend to represent. If teachers have the goal of fostering higher-level thinking skills but all the objectives are at the knowledge or comprehension level, a meaningful relation to intended content is missing. Similarly, if the intention is to have students produce a complex product such as a piece of art or literature review, then some learning objectives must be at the application level or higher.

3. *Is the objective measurable?* Learning objectives often make vague statements that students should "know," "understand," "think critically," or "write well." However, objectives that include terms such as those do not provide enough detail to allow measurement. How will you know if students understand? What will they do to demonstrate knowledge and critical thinking? If reading an objective does not elicit specific ideas for how students can show that they have accomplished the learning, it needs to be revised using more specific, behavioral language.

4. *Does the objective focus on learning outcomes rather than teaching methods?* Imagine that you are telling the story of your most recent vacation. Would you mostly talk about the fun things you did at the vacation spot, or would you focus on the transportation used to get to the spot? It's about the destination, right? The same is true of learning objectives; the point is to define where students should get to, not the methods for getting them there. As such, statements such as "read contemporary fiction," "visit historic sites," or "watch a theater production" are not learning objectives, they are activities teachers use to facilitate learning. Learning objectives must focus on what students should be able to do *after* teaching activities.

5. *Do the objectives need to be revised?* Technically, this question is unlikely to arise until after a teacher has implemented objectives at least once, but it is too important to leave off the list. Assessment is a process, and goals for student learning are open to revision as part of that process. Learning objectives are not written on stone tablets to be passed down to future generations; they should evolve based on formal and informal assessment of student success in the learning process. After conducting their courses, teachers might decide that there are too many objectives, that some of them are unclear, that the objectives are too easy or hard, that too many are at a specific cognitive level, or that intermediate objectives are needed to move students to higher objectives (Suskie, 2009). In these cases and others, learning objectives can and should be revised.

Embedded Assessment Plans: All the Fun of Assessment With a Fraction of the Work!

As the member of campus assessment committees, one of us has had to knock on doors, hat in hand, to ask colleagues for their departmental learning goals. Despite colleagues' unfailing kindness, the task is a dreadful one. Why so sheepish? The reason is that teachers' primary complaint about assessment is all the "extra" work it entails. Asking people to do assessment is perceived as tantamount to assigning them a heavier workload. It does not have to be that way, however. Model teachers engage in embedded assessment, which integrates most of the work of assessing outcomes directly into existing classroom activities.

Making assessment part of regular teaching practices is the key idea behind embedded assessment. Teachers begin the process by determining the learning goals for a course. Then they match course assignments with course learning goals. Assignments become the tools for assessing learning outcomes. Thus, as part of regular evaluation of student performance, teachers are also producing assessment data that can be used to provide objective evidence of student learning.

Certainly, external measures such as the National Survey of Student Engagement and ETS Major Field Tests provide valuable information for educators, but assessment embedded in actual coursework is now considered an essential best practice (Cain, 2014; Cummings et al., 2008; Hutchings, 2010; Richman and Ariovich, 2013; Walvoord, 2010). In addition to using faculty time efficiently, embedded assessment keeps the process close to actual classrooms, which is where the data is needed most. It also allows faculty to focus on evaluating and improving outcomes in the areas where they have the most expertise and passion. Students directly benefit as well. Embedded assessment requires nothing extra on their part; in fact, they will likely have no idea that assignments are serving double duty for purposes of evaluation and assessment. Because students are aware only that their grades depend on the work, their participation level and motivation will be higher than for external tests and surveys. As if these advantages were not enough, planning embedded assessments is not particularly complex or time-consuming.

Creating an embedded assessment plan for a course begins with diagramming a matrix of leaning goals and evaluations (McCarthy et al., 2011). Teachers can begin by listing learning goals in the far left-hand column of a table with each goal receiving its own row (see Table 6.4). Next, consider the various course assignments and how they relate to each of the goals. Each type of assignment can be laid out in an individual column, with columns extending as far to the right as needed. Finally, the cells of the resulting matrix indicate what assignments are designed to assess what learning goals. It is important to note that broad goals are a better fit for embedded course assessment than specific objectives. Courses will have too many learning objectives to efficiently map out, and broad goals will suffice because they should directly correspond to the more specific learning objectives. For example, a broad goal might be for students to

TABLE 6.4 Example of an Embedded Assessment Plan Matrix

Learning goals	Exams	Papers	Homework	Presentations
1. Students will describe basic theories in political science.	X	X	X	
2. Students will apply basic political science theories to current events.	X	X	X	
3. Students will write in a professional style using the American Political Science Association style.		X	X	
4. Students will communicate professionally in an oral format.				X

"communicate professionally in writing," but there may be specific objectives related to formatting, mechanics, use of evidence, and quality of arguments; each of those objectives does not need its own assessment plan because they fit into the larger goal.

The assessment matrix is useful for planning how assessment will occur, but more details are needed to outline a full assessment plan. A full assessment plan can be summarized in a template that stipulates the goal to be assessed each semester a course is taught (Table 6.5). An essential part of assessment is the record of actions taken as a result of learning outcomes. Documenting actions emphasizes the fact that assessment data is for using, not archiving. Thus, the results of assessments can also be briefly summarized in the template, making it a hybrid assessment plan and report. Although detailed records of assessment results are worth keeping so that they can be referenced later or shared with others (Walvoord, 2010), a brief summary is all that is needed for a basic assessment template because it can be referenced quickly and easily by both the teacher and any third parties who are interested in the results (e.g., chairs, tenure committees).

Assessment does not end once actions are taken because those actions need to be evaluated as well. Remember, assessment is a process. Assessment plans ideally schedule opportunities to reassess the same outcomes in fairly short succession (i.e., within a semester or two). If a learning objective is reevaluated, then the teacher has evidence that changes to teaching actually impacted learning (Fulcher et al., 2014). A mechanic would not make repairs to an engine without taking the car out for a test drive to see if it is fixed. Similarly, teachers should not assume that learning has improved simply because they made a change. Course alterations might improve learning, hinder learning, or have no effect at all; but the effect is unknown unless there is a follow-up assessment of outcomes.

It is impossible to know if learning goals are being met without assessment. Model teachers do not take it as a matter of faith that goals are being met. Rather,

TABLE 6.5 Example of an Embedded Assessment Template

Semester	Learning goal	Assessment results	Action taken
Fall	1 & 2	Students performed at the 75th percentile on comprehensive final exam.	Added an optional reading reviewing earlier concepts. Created a review assignment.
Spring	1 & 2	Students performed at the 80th percentile.	Retained optional reading.
Fall	3 & 4	Average scores on the writing and oral communication rubrics were at *below expectations*.	Posted example assignments and revised assignment descriptions.
Spring	3 & 4	Average scores on the rubrics were at *below expectations*.	Required drafts of the assignments.

they take the assessment process into their own hands to provide clear evidence of student learning. By planning out the entire assessment process and embedding assessment practices into their courses, model teachers are able to demonstrate in objective terms what students get out of their courses.

CASE STUDY REEXAMINED: SOMEONE CALL 911! DR. MEAD HAS AN ASSESSMENT CRISIS

1. *What should Dr. Mead do with his class in terms of learning objectives?*
    Dr. Mead set no learning objectives. By planning classes during the semester, he could not articulate specific learning objectives for the course ahead of time. Failure to have preset objectives also caused Dr. Mead to overlook the goals already set up for the course by the general education program. Although Dr. Mead did expect students to learn critical thinking, this goal was not formalized in any way or expressed to students. Dr. Mead should have formally set specific learning objectives before the semester begun.
2. *How would learning objectives affect student learning in Dr. Mead's class?*
    Dr. Mead's students probably learned during the semester, but that learning cannot be said to be related to any set of objectives. Because he was unaware of the general education requirements, Dr. Mead could not intentionally facilitate experiences to help students achieve those important goals. Because his critical thinking objective was not formalized, it is not clear what students should have been learning about critical thinking from his lectures or the paper. Dr. Mead's teaching should have been intentionally designed to move students toward achievement of preset learning objectives.

3. *Does Dr. Mead know if students learned anything in his classes? Why or why not?* Dr. Mead did assign grades for multiple-choice tests and a research paper. However, student performance on those assignments may or may not have been related to important learning objectives. Because there were no objectives for the course, it is unlikely that the assignments fostered the general education goals related to "ethical decision-making" and "problem-solving skills." The paper may have taught "discipline-specific writing proficiency," but assignment of grades alone does not allow for a clear determination of student performance on this goal. Dr. Mead needed to pick assessment tools that directly related to his preset learning objectives. Ideally, these would consist of assignments that are already part of coursework.

Making the Grade: Evaluation of Student Learning

Using the assessment process to determine if students have learned must include measurement of performance on some task. Student performance is often synonymous with evaluation and grading. Evaluations consist of summative judgments of student performance, and assignment grades as part of evaluation is one of the inescapable, and often woeful, requirements of teaching. Experienced teachers know that there is a natural arc to the college semester. Classes begin with excitement and energy. Both teachers and students have high hopes. The honeymoon lasts until the first major grades are assigned and the disappointment of failed expectations—among both students and teachers—enters the classroom. As a wise teacher once said, "I teach for free, it's the grading they have to pay me for." Despite its inescapable pitfalls, there are a number of ways to make evaluations more useful to both students and the assessment process. Evaluating student performance may not be worth doing for free, but it can be done well.

Evaluation is a learning tool that most teachers probably do not adequately consider in their course design. Methods of evaluation can sometimes be an afterthought because teachers are enthralled with course content. However, teachers who are motivated to ensure that students learn content can take advantage of evaluations in systematic ways. There is a great deal of research on the evaluation of students, and their benefits are key to educational endeavors (Black and William, 1998; Crooks, 1988). Evaluations motivate students to study and reflect on learning. They help students learn by focusing their attention on important material and by providing regular, useful feedback on performance. Given these findings, model teachers conduct evaluations directly aligned with learning objectives and provide students with useful feedback on their learning.

CASE STUDY: THE GRADE GRUBBERS

Dr. Zinn teaches a lower-level course in US history. Forty percent of the course grade is based on a midterm exam that requires students to synthesize the major historical themes covered in the first part of the course; the other 60 percent is accounted for by the final exam. In order to prepare students for the midterm, Dr. Zinn gives them a study guide consisting of 30 major events and trends covered in the first part of the course. On the midterm, Dr. Zinn selects four events/trends to be the topic of an essay. Students have two hours to write the essay in class. The instructions read as follows: "Your job is to (1) accurately describe the four events and trends and (2) outline the relation between the events and trends. The purpose of your essay is to show that you have a basic understanding of both the facts of history and their interrelation."

Dr. Zinn takes well over two weeks to grade the essays. The delay is based on the fact that she corrects for both factual information and writing style. Each essay is filled with editorial marks indicating factual errors and writing mistakes. For the essay grade, Dr. Zinn assigns 75 percent of the points based on accuracy of ideas, 20 percent based on writing, and 5 percent based on originality. Rather than bring the midterms back to class, Dr. Zinn holds the essays in her office and requires students to pick them up.

Dr. Zinn is consistently disappointed that only a small fraction of students actually stop by to pick up their essays. She is further disappointed by the fact that students frequently complain about her "unfair" grading system. Students frequently challenge their grades with her and the department chair—she dismisses these students as "grade grubbers."

Now take a moment to answer these questions. We will revisit your answer at the end of the section. After reading the section, yes, you may change your answers.

1. What is problematic about Dr. Zinn's testing strategy?
2. How could Dr. Zinn improve how she evaluates students?
3. How can Dr. Zinn improve the feedback she gives to students?

Evaluation Directness: The Way to Avoid Making Student Enemies

As a novice teacher, one of us made the mistake of trying to do too much with exams. Believing that students must be held accountable for higher-level thinking, essay questions focused on making connections between course topics. For example, a question might read, "We have discussed classical conditioning and operant conditioning. Compare their utility for changing behavior in the real world." That is valid-enough information for students to know, but a student eventually pointed the flaw in such exam questions. In class we spent time covering a set of basic facts, but then exams required students to connect those facts in unexpected ways. The learning objectives were for students to know about classical condition and about operant conditioning, and this was completely clear. However, there was no way for students to know that they were also accountable for integrating those concepts; moreover, no class time was spent on integration. In other words, the evaluation of students did not align with the learning objectives or the teaching practices—a rookie mistake indeed.

Alignment of learning objectives and evaluations is something that model teachers consider long before a course begins. Course design includes three sequential steps: (1) setting learning objectives, (2) designing evaluations of the objectives, (3) planning lessons to foster learning of the objectives and success on the evaluations (Rust, 2002). This planning process may seem backwards to some, and because of that fact, it has been ingeniously named "backward design" (Wiggins and McTighe, 1998). The process does not seem backward, however, when considering the learning-centered approach. The focus of a learning-centered classroom is what students are getting out of their education, not what the teacher puts into it (Huba and Freed, 2000). By planning evaluations side-by-side with objectives, teachers can more successfully engage in the model practice of aligning evaluations with objectives (Nicol and MacFarlane-Dick, 2006; Palomba and Banta, 1999).

Planning evaluations that directly align with learning objectives has a number of advantages. In terms of the overall topic of this chapter, an embedded assessment plan makes little sense if the evaluations in the course do not relate to the learning objectives. Bad alignment renders information gained from embedded assessment meaningless. Evaluations certainly could take place, but they would provide no evidence that the course was fulfilling its intended goals. For example, imagine a course with a goal for students to "apply critical thinking to real-world situations," but the evaluation of students consists only of multiple-choice tests. Can application of critical thinking really be said to occur when all the answers are on the test page? At an even more basic level, what if the class had an objective for students to "communicate clearly"? In both cases, either the objectives or the evaluations need to be revised.

If a more practical reason to worry about evaluation alignment is needed, consider the satisfaction of students. Capricious evaluations can result in a swift student revolt. The teacher whose tests include random details from sidebars in the textbook may have the lofty intention of motivating students to read thoroughly, but students will resent evaluations they perceive as unfair, which can result in reduced motivation and increased dissent (Chory-Assad, 2002; Goodboy, 2011). That being said, students can also resent the evaluation of important learning goals. For example, students are often shocked when their writing is evaluated outside of composition courses. They shouldn't be, however, as long as writing is clearly included in the course objectives. Model teachers align evaluations with learning objectives, and students perceive their grading as fair, predictable, and meaningful.

Evaluation Utility: The Way to Make Lots of Student Friends

Every student has war stories about their teachers who were bad graders. One of the authors still has deep scholarly resentments for an undergraduate professor whose course included just two assignments—a midterm blue book essay and final blue book essay—and whose entire semester feedback to students consisted of a single letter grade written on the top of the midterm essay. What did that red letter B in the blue book mean? What was the grade based on? Was there any way to do better? Did the teacher even read the essay? These questions were never answered, and the evaluation remained useless as a learning tool.

Seeing evaluations for the tools that they are, model teachers conduct them in a way that serves the dual purposes of judging performance and providing feedback. The first point to emphasize is that evaluations provide an essential learning tool for students: feedback on performance. A large body of research has definitively shown that performance is enhanced by feedback (Kluger and DeNisi, 1996). Actually, it can be downright impossible to learn if feedback is absent or meaningless. Imagine trying to perfect the game of golf if you were never allowed to see where your shot went (i.e., the woods). Similarly, imagine trying to master a new academic subject if midterm is the first time you received feedback. Even the traditional approach of three tests and a final exam seems inadequate if the tests are the only way students can determine if they are successfully learning course material. Model teachers provide feedback to students early and often (Nicol and MacFarlane-Dick, 2006).

Useful evaluations have several characteristics (Nicol and MacFarlane-Dick, 2006; Rust, 2002). As outlined previously, they stem directly from clearly stated learning objectives. Students must know the standards that they are being held to. Useful feedback references learning objectives and provides students with guidance on how to better reach those objectives. A single letter grade does not tell a student how to improve. Comments should explain the grade, elicit student reflection, and offer specific suggestions for improvement.

Feedback from evaluations should also be prompt. Quick feedback allows for quick adjustment in efforts at learning. Once again, imagine learning how to play golf, except rather than being blindfolded you cannot see where your shot went until the next day. Improvement would be next to impossible with such delayed feedback. In one of the author's recent introductory courses, a student failed the first quiz in the second week of class and then never got another grade below B+. The student later said that the first quiz was important because he "realized that you have to actually study." If the first evaluation in that class had occurred at midterm, not only would the student have been likely to waste half of a semester's worth of learning opportunities, but his grade might have been unsalvageable.

Rubrics: Teachers' (and Students') Little Helper

In John Bean's (2011) excellent book *Engaging ideas: The professor's guide to integrating writing, critical thinking, and active learning in the classroom,* he relates the results of a study in which 53 teachers from different fields graded 300 essays using a nine-point quality scale. Amazingly, 94 percent of the essays received seven or more different ratings from the teachers. One third of the essays received all nine possible scores. Let's agree right now not to tell our students about this study. Actually, there was some good news in the apparent grading chaos. It turns out that the variation in scores resulted from the teachers weighting different factors—grammar, quality of ideas, creativity—in the grading process. The solution to grading chaos is to make the evaluation criteria more explicit, and there exists no better tool for outlining expectations than rubrics.

The term "rubric" can refer to a number of different grading schemes, but this section will focus on the rubrics referred to as "descriptive" or "analytic" because they provide the most detailed and useful feedback to students (Huba and Freed, 2000; Suskie, 2009). Continuing with the theme of backward design, construction of a useful rubric begins with selecting learning goals for an assignment; then the assignment is designed so that it will lead students toward achievement of those goals. Once an assignment is designed, construction of the rubric proper begins by breaking down the components of the assignment that are key to its quality. For example, an extremely basic rubric for a paper might have two key components of quality: content and writing. However, content might be further broken down into separate sections regarding the thesis, sources, and arguments. Writing could be broken down into mechanics, organization, and formatting. Each essential component of quality becomes a row in the rubric (see Figures 6.2, 6.3, 6.4).

Once the key components of the assignment are arranged into rows, the levels of performance can be described. Levels of performance start with three to four descriptive labels that indicate, in general terms, how a particular piece of work relates to accepted standards; they are represented in the columns of the rubric using labels in the first row. Many label variations exist, but Huba and Freed (2000) suggest the following variations:

- Sophisticated, Competent, Not yet competent
- Exemplary, Proficient, Marginal, Unacceptable
- Advanced, Intermediate high, Intermediate low, Novice
- Exceeds expectations, Meets expectations, Below expectations
- Accomplished, Average, Developing, Beginning.

Teachers are left to decide what labels best match the standards being applied. Labels provide the general picture of performance levels, but the true utility of rubrics lies in the detailed descriptions of what the assignment components look

Assignment component	Level of performance			
	Advanced	**High intermediate**	**Low intermediate**	**Beginning**
Scholarly sources (Score ___)	4	3	2	1
	Claims are fully supported with sources. All sources are scholarly and primary. Multiple sources are synthesized.	Claims are fully supported with sources. All sources are scholarly and primary. Multiple sources are cited to support claims but they are not synthesized.	Claims are mostly supported with sources. Sources are scholarly but are not primary (i.e., do not present original data or theory).	Claims are unsupported. Sources are not scholarly (e.g., Wikipedia, magazines).
Thesis (Score ___)	4	3	2	1
	The thesis represents a clear statement that can be supported with evidence and is meaningful.	The thesis is somewhat unclear or would be somewhat difficult to support with evidence but it is meaningful.	The thesis is unclear, would be difficult to support with evidence, or lacks meaning.	No thesis is identifiable, or it cannot be understood.
Arguments (Score ___)	4	3	2	1
	A student-generated, original thesis or hypothesis is supported by multiple valid arguments. Arguments are supported by original empirical or qualitative research.	A thesis or hypothesis is supported by multiple valid arguments. Arguments are supported by multiple references to research.	Ideas accurately apply psychological theory or research. Ideas are not based on references to the research literature.	Ideas are not connected to research or cannot be supported with evidence.

Total score _____

FIGURE 6.2 An example analytic rubric for a research-based writing assignment.

Assignment component	Level of performance		
	Advanced	**Intermediate**	**Beginning**
Understanding	10 9	8 7 6 5 4	3 2 1
	The solution is complete and accurate. It demonstrates full understanding of the mathematical components.	The solution is partially complete. Some understanding of the mathematical components is present.	No solution is found for the problem. The related mathematical components are not represented.
Reasoning and strategies	5	4 3 2	1 0
	The strategies and reasoning are sophisticated and efficient. The solution is correct and verified.	The strategies and reasoning are sound. Procedures lead to a correct answer.	There is no evidence of mathematical strategies or reasoning.
Communication	5	4 3 2	1 0
	Solutions are clearly explained in steps. Mathematical symbols are used as a means of communicating reasoning and solutions.	Solutions are clearly explained. Mathematical symbols are used correctly.	Solutions are not explained. Mathematical symbols are misused.
Comments: Total score: ___			

FIGURE 6.3 An example analytic rubric for a math assignment adapted from www.exemplars.com/assets/files/Classic3LevelRubric.pdf.

like at each specific performance level. For example, what are the characteristics of a thesis at the *Exemplary* level versus the *Proficient* level?

With the basic structure of the rubric defined, the next step is to fill in the individual cells with performance descriptions. Filling in the rubric descriptions is a highly individual process because it depends on both the nature of the assignment and the standards of the teacher. A general rule of thumb is to start by describing the ideal performance on the assignment; it becomes the highest level of performance. Then, think about the types of mistakes, omissions, or developmental problems that might emerge on the assignment. Incrementally introduce those issues into the descriptions at each level until the description represents the

Characteristic	Excellent 3	Developing 2	Incomplete 1	Score
Frequency	Posts on over 75% of threads.	Posts on 50–75% of threads.	Posts on less than 50% of threads.	
Substance	All posts are substantive and knowledgeable.	The majority of posts are substantive and knowledgeable.	The majority of posts are superficial or illustrate lack of knowledge.	
Responsiveness	Posts demonstrate that the preceding posts have been read closely.	Posts demonstrate that the majority of the preceding posts have been read.	Posts demonstrate that the majority of previous posts have not been read.	
Constructiveness	Comments are consistently insightful and clearly move the discussion forward.	Comments show occasional insight and generally move discussion forward.	Comments are superficial and/ or hold discussion back.	
Professionalism	All posts are constructive, civil, and professionally written.	All posts are constructive and civil, but some unprofessional content is present.	One or more posts are not constructive or not civil. Most posts are unprofessional.	
			Total: ___	

FIGURE 6.4   An example analytic rubric for an online discussion forum.

work of beginners; that becomes the description of the lowest level of performance. Be sure that the descriptions are clear, objective, and non-overlapping. If possible, try piloting the rubric on previous work before implementing it in real evaluations. Also, do not forget that rubrics are not written in stone. If a rubric is flawed or not useful, revise it. If an assignment evolves, the rubric should evolve with it (Suskie, 2009).

If this whole process seems daunting, there are numerous rubric resources on the Internet to assist you. A quick search will produce hundreds of example rubrics and even websites with software to assist in rubric construction. In addition, course management software now includes programs for constructing online rubrics that attach directly to assignments. One specific place to start looking for rubric exemplars, especially for educational topics that cut across disciplines, is the American Association of Colleges and Universities Valid Assessment of Learning in Undergraduate Education (VALUE) Rubric Project. Fully-developed rubrics for 16 common learning goals are available for downloading on the VALUE Rubric Project website (www.aacu.org/value/rubrics), and teachers are free to implement them in their own courses.

An important fact to keep in mind with rubrics is that they are a communication tool. Faculty's first question about rubrics is often "Is it appropriate to share these with students?" Let's imagine that, after their creation, rubrics had to be kept secret from students—they are on lockdown with answer keys for tests and the copy of the school charter that actually does contain the rule that students get all As if their roommate dies. Think about all of the communication opportunities that would be lost. Discipline-specific standards for quality work would not be as clear. Criteria for grading and the reasoning behind assigned grades would be obscured. Students would not have as clear an idea of how they can improve their work. For these reasons and more, rubrics should be shared with students (Huba and Freed, 2000). In fact, set aside time for going over rubrics in class when introducing assignments. Provide students with a copy of the rubric and encourage its use as a guide for completing the assignment. Students can even be required to turn in a completed rubric with their assignments or, better yet, rough drafts of their assignments. Overall, rubrics serve many of the same purposes as learning objectives in the learning-centered approach; they communicate standards, set expectations for learning, and clarify evaluation procedures.

Creating useful rubrics requires practice and effort, but there are a number of reasons to undertake such an investment. Students and teachers alike believe that rubrics clarify expectations; in that sense, rubrics represent a specific way to improve teaching (Jonsson and Svingby, 2007; Reddy and Andrade, 2010). Students are able to use rubrics to accurately self-assess their own work, and this highlights the rubric's potential to increase students' awareness of their own learning (Jonsson and Svingby, 2007). Moreover, there is direct experimental evidence that students assigned to use a grading rubric during the writing process subsequently produce papers of significantly higher quality than students who do not use the rubric (Greenberg, 2015). Assessment is also assisted by rubrics. Using a rubric makes documentation of assessment results simple; the teacher only has to report the percentage of students at each level of performance on the rubric. Then the effect of any instructional changes can be evaluated by comparing the new and old performance levels using the same rubric.

Rubrics also alleviate grading stress for teachers in several ways (Suskie, 2009). One stress of grading is how long it takes, and well-written rubrics can make grading easier and more efficient. Another stress is grading disagreements, and this can be largely eliminated with a clear rubric that students have access to ahead of time. Students seem to rarely argue that teachers have applied their own grading rubric incorrectly. Alternatively, it could be that students have less to complain about because rubrics make grading more reliable (Jonsson and Svingby, 2007; Thaler et al., 2009). The reliability of rubrics may never be perfect, but they offer a vast improvement over the anarchy that can occur when teachers use idiosyncratic and inconsistent methods of evaluation. As such, model teachers make frequent use of rubrics when evaluating student work.

Feedback Early and Often: Formative Assessment Techniques

One of the characteristics that makes evaluations useful to students is promptness. Students are in trouble if midterm is the first point at which they realize a basic failure to grasp course concepts. However, the teacher who finds out at midterm that students are not learning is in trouble as well—at least the teacher can set a curve. There is no need for teachers to wait until after the first test, essay, or other major assignment to find out if students are meeting course learning objectives. All teachers use summative evaluations of student performance to assign grades, but model teachers also use formative evaluations to gather informal, unofficial data on student learning. Formative evaluations are often referred to as classroom assessment techniques (CATs), and Angelo and Cross's (1993) handbook of the same name is the standard source on the subject. The easiest way to summarize the main idea of CATs is this: If you want to know what is on the minds of students, ask them.

The various methods for gathering formative data are as varied as teachers themselves, but Angelo and Cross (1993) outline some basic guidelines to follow for all types of CATs. Like so many things in this chapter, CATs begin with learning objectives. Without a clear idea of what students should be learning, there is no assessment question to be answered. Based on what students are expected to learn, teachers can formulate an assessment question that helps them evaluate students' actual level of learning. The inspiration for what specific objective to assess could emerge informally—such as a perception of many more questions about a certain topic in class—or it could come for more formal assessment or evaluation data—such as a high number of students failing a quiz. Based on the identified question, the teacher plans an assessment to gather data. Once the data is gathered, the teacher analyzes the results to find an answer to the initial question. Finally, instructional changes are made based on the data.

Three of the most versatile CATs are minute papers, the muddiest point, and concept maps (Angelo and Cross, 1993). The minute paper is exactly what it sounds like; students have a minute to answer a specific question. For example, the last few minutes of class might be devoted to students providing a written summary of the most important thing that they learned in class that day. The muddiest point is a slight twist on the minute paper. Rather than asking what was learned, the teacher asks students to report "the muddiest point, what was least clear from today's class?" One of the authors used the muddiest point quite frequently in a recent semester because of a course redesign. As is frequently the case when teaching from a new lesson plan, there were often more learning objectives than time to cover them in class. Without the muddiest point CAT, it would have been tempting to simply press on and cover all of the objectives in the next class. However, by asking students to identify what was unclear, it was possible to return only to the objectives students had trouble understanding on their own.

Minute papers and muddiest points are fairly simple assessment techniques for gathering fairly simple information, but concept maps can be used to assess complicated ideas and their relation (Angelo and Cross, 1993). Concept mapping requires students to diagram their knowledge of a subject using nodes and connections between nodes. Maps can be as simple or complex as the underlying concepts require. They are particularly useful in testing students' understanding of the interconnections between topics. For example, concept maps stand out as a perfect way to see if students grasp the big picture of a course. Near the end of the semester, students could be assigned to map the concepts they have learned and the connections between those concepts. Mapping out a whole course would be an excellent way to combine a learning activity and an assessment activity.

CATs and other formative assessments are endlessly modifiable (Kelly, 2008). Concept maps could be constructed in teams or alone; they could be made using scratch paper or specialized software. Minute papers could occur every day or once a semester; students could be identified or anonymous; papers could be written in-class or as homework. As discussed in Chapter 8, CATs can also be used as formative student evaluations of teaching. The key idea is to make the data useful, something that can theoretically lead to better teaching and learning. Teachers should not assess something if they are unwilling to work toward its improvement.

Evaluating students is an inescapable and sometimes difficult process for teachers. However, model teachers take advantage of the evaluation process by making evaluations useful to students and useful to broader efforts at assessment. Grading with rubrics, alignment of evaluation with learning objectives, providing prompt and useful feedback—these are all standard practices for model teachers.

CASE STUDY REEXAMINED: THE GRADE GRUBBERS

This section began with the case of Dr. Zinn, a history professor whose grading of essay exams caused troubles for both her and her students. Let's return to the cause with a discussion of the questions we posed about the case.

1. *What is problematic about Dr. Zinn's testing strategy?* Dr. Zinn is disappointed that students do not appreciate her written feedback on mid-term essays and that they complain about grades; these disappointments stem from her failure to maximize evaluation directness and usefulness. Starting with directness, Dr. Zinn evaluates students' writing without

explicitly stating the expectation that the essay be written according to specific standards. Students, believing that historical knowledge is the only essay requirement, are rightly flummoxed by grades based on unexpected criteria.

2. *How could Dr. Zinn improve how she evaluates students?* One solution to this problem would be for Dr. Zinn to clearly communicate to students these previously hidden expectations; the fact that writing and originality are part of the grade needs to be made completely clear and connected to course learning objectives. However, Dr. Zinn should also consider revising her writing expectations for in-class essays. It is unlikely that an essay constructed over a two-hour span with no opportunity for revision constitutes an accurate evaluation of students' writing capabilities. Writing experts believe that overemphasizing composition quality on essay exams is counterproductive because it diminishes the revision process that is central to good writing (Bean, 2011). A formal paper would be a more direct evaluation of learning goals related to writing.

3. *How can Dr. Zinn improve the feedback she gives to students?* Dr. Zinn's grading procedures do not provide students with useful feedback. Too much time passes between students' performance and their feedback—students have moved on. Along the same lines, earlier feedback on student learning is needed. Waiting until midterm to evaluate students does not provide adequate time for teaching and learning adjustments. Finally, providing extensive writing feedback on an essay exam is not particularly useful if students do not know that writing is being evaluated and are not expected to use the feedback for revision. Dr. Zinn should consider offering earlier and more frequent opportunities for students to receive feedback on learning. The feedback they receive should be prompt and focused on the objectives being evaluated (e.g., knowledge).

Scholarship of Teaching and Learning

Answer quickly: What is the relation between scholarly productivity and teaching effectiveness? University folklore is clear on this matter. Time spent on teaching is time that cannot be spent writing or conducting research. Or, if you are at a small college, research productivity comes at the cost of time spent teaching students. We have encountered belief in the teaching–research dichotomy everywhere that we have been students and teachers. Nonetheless, the fact is that the correlation between scholarly productivity and teaching effectiveness is so small that it is virtually meaningless as a predictor of faculty abilities (Arnold, 2008; Hattie and Marsh, 1996). The perceived conflict between productivity in teaching and scholarship is simply false (in fact, the correlation, although small, is positive). There is nothing that prevents a productive scholar from being a great teacher or, to be fair, a terrible scholar from also being a horrendous teacher. However, model teachers ensure that teaching and scholarship coexist in productive harmony through their use of scholarship of teaching and learning.

CASE STUDY: THE TENURE SURPRISE

Dr. Lee was concerned by students missing key ideas from reading assignments. Some students got so bogged down in details that they missed the larger points. Conversely, some students read only deep enough to get the big picture and grasped none of the important details. Of course, some students did not read at all.

In order to discover ways to address the problem, Dr. Lee examined the research literature on student motivation and learning. Based on the review, Dr. Lee determined that students benefit from direction concerning the most important points in readings. He also found that informal, low-stakes writing is effective at prompting students to engage in critical thinking. Thus, he created new low-stakes writing assignments, due before class, that are entirely administered and graded by course management software. Exam scores increased significantly in courses where he implemented the writing assignment.

Dr. Lee included a description of this project in his application for tenure in the "scholarship" section of his dossier. He was shocked when the tenure committee did not count this project toward the research requirements for tenure. Dr. Lee thinks what he did is no different from other professors who got tenure for researching education in the school systems or for researching learning in the laboratory.

Now take a moment to answer these questions. We will revisit your answer at the end of the section. After reading the section, yes, you may change your answers.

1. What is the relation between assessment and scholarship of teaching?
2. Was Dr. Lee doing research? Why or why not?
3. What could Dr. Lee have done to avoid his tenure surprise?

Confusion still occurs around the term scholarship of teaching. One of us knew a productive researcher who dismissed scholarship of teaching as "an attempt to pass off teaching as scholarship." However, when confronted with the actual definition of scholarship of teaching, the researcher said "Well, that's fine! That's just research!" He was right. Scholarship of teaching and learning applies the principles of research to the craft of teaching. Doing scholarship of teaching and learning is the process of making teaching public so that it can be evaluated by peers and so that knowledge can accumulate (Buskist et al., 2008; McCarthy, 2008; Smith, 2008, 2013). The concept stems from Boyer's call to end the teaching-versus-research conflict, but it is part of the larger trend toward assessment and learning-focused education (Hutchings et al., 2011). In fact, the essential motivations of assessment and scholarship of teaching and learning—desire for evidence, documentation of learning, improving outcomes—are identical. The main difference between assessment and scholarship of teaching and learning is in the use of knowledge produced.

One of the main misconceptions that people have about scholarship of teaching and learning is that it is nothing more than teaching in a scholarly manner. Scholarly teaching begins with a desire to increase learning; this motivates innovation in the classroom, and the teacher assesses the impact of innovation on student success. Scholarly teaching is laudable, but it is not scholarship of teaching. In order to move scholarly teaching into the realm of scholarship of teaching, results must be shared in a public format. Practically speaking, scholarship of teaching and learning can be said to occur any time teaching is integrated with the peer-review process of scholarship; topics could include course design, design of activities, program evaluation, advising, student experiences, learning outcomes, and virtually anything else that might advance pedagogy or be helpful to other teachers (Hutchings et al., 2011).

How can teachers go about conducting studies on the scholarship of teaching and learning? Answering such a question is as complicated as trying to explain how to do scholarship in general. Nonetheless, the approach to conducting empirical research on teaching proceeds using following four steps (Dickson and Treml, 2013).

1. Identify an area in which student learning can be improved.
2. Examine existing scholarship of teaching research related to the identified area.
3. Implement a teaching innovation while simultaneously assessing the outcome.
4. Publish the results.

Most teachers probably engage in steps 1 and 3 all of the time. Course design is never finished, and teachers constantly tweak their syllabi, lesson plans, and assignments based on the informal sense that changes would improve the course. The real trick is to do these modifications systematically. Before making a change, try to determine if someone has already tried it. If there is already research on the subject, heed it in when making modifications. If there is no research on the subject, the topic may be ripe for investigation.

Step 3 consists of conducting an investigation of a teaching innovation, and it follows the normal procedures of educational or social science research. Validity in study design and the measurement of outcomes is just as important as in any other type of research (Bartsch, 2013a). In terms of specific design, most classroom-based investigations will utilize either a between-groups, within-groups, or pre-post design (Bartsch, 2013a). In a between-groups design, the researcher compares students who are exposed to the new technique to a control group of students who are not exposed. For example, a teacher might compare performance on a writing assignment between two sections of a class when one section had access to an online tutorial and another section did not. In a within-subjects design, students serve as their own control group; the researcher measures outcomes when the new technique is being used and when it is not being used. An example would be an investigation of online reading quizzes. The instructor could randomly assign some material to be associated with reading quizzes and then compare exam performance over material covered and not covered by the quizzes. Pre-post designs measure variables of interest twice, once before an intervention and once after an intervention. An instructor with a new method for teaching critical thinking might administer a standardized critical thinking test at the start and end of a course. As evidenced by a glance through any social science textbook or journal, the variations on these designs are numerous, but these basic techniques offer a place to start when planning an investigation.

Scholarship related to classroom instruction leads to a number of practical questions (Bartsch, 2013a, 2013b). Below are some of them with possible answers. For a full discussion of these questions and more we suggest reading Bartsch's (2013a, 2013b) guides on the subject.

What should I measure? Assuming that increased learning is the expected outcome, you should measure learning. Yet another advantage of embedded assessment is that, should a teacher decide to conduct research, evaluations of learning are already in place. Although it may be counterintuitive, asking students about their perceptions of a teaching technique is not essential. Students' enjoyment of a teaching technique and perception of its utility in learning are not good predictors of actual learning (Bartsch, 2013a; Wesp and Miele, 2008).

Can I do research if my class is small? There are indeed some class sizes that make empirical research difficult, but even a class of 15 can yield useful data if a within-subjects design is utilized. When participants serve as their own controls, the number needed for valid comparisons between treatments is cut in half.

Can I do research if I only teach one section of class? The answer to the single-section problem is to simply split the class in half. However, it is important to note that causation can only be assumed when formation of groups within the class is random. Also, remember that patience is rewarded. Each of us has served on the editorial board of journals that publish scholarship of teaching and learning. One of the most frequent reasons for rejecting submissions is that the results are too ambiguous because they only represent one semester's worth of data. Collecting data over several semesters in which teaching techniques are varied is a way around the single-section problem, and it is a way to increase the validity of your study.

Do I need approval from my Institutional Review Board? As with other types of research, the answer to this question depends on both the procedures being used and the idiosyncrasies of the local IRB (Martin, 2013). However, the type of scholarship being discussed here—interventions performed directly on students—meets the standards of human subjects research; it ethically requires IRB approval before the project starts.

Step 4 in conducting scholarship of teaching and learning—publishing the results—is what transforms scholarly teaching into just plain scholarship. It is also the step that is likely to be the most daunting to many teachers. The good news is that there have never been more outlets for the publication of research on teaching. The Kennesaw State University Center for Excellence in Teaching and Learning website lists more than 400 publications related to teaching (www.cetl. kennesaw.edu). This huge number includes general higher education journals and more specific topical journals; in fact, academic disciplines often have multiple journals devoted to teaching. Yet more good news is that publication of research can also come in the form of presentations at conferences. With all the local, regional, national, and international options, a motivated scholar can probably find a conference with teaching-related programming at the time and location of their choosing.

Classroom research projects are just one of the many ways that teachers can engage in scholarship of teaching and learning. Laboratory research is another option. To cite a single example from the current literature, the use of testing to enhance learning started as a program of laboratory research and has since extended to studies of actual classroom learning (Roediger et al., 2011). Laboratory research is especially useful if the researcher wants to exert tighter control over the study than allowed by real-life classrooms. Non-empirical scholarship is valuable as well. Writing a textbook, creating a new course, producing educational standards for a discipline—these are all contributions that can be as, or even more, impactful than an empirical study. Another option is peer review of courses. The Peer Review of Teaching Project (www.courseportfolio.org) offers a forum for structured evaluation of portfolios representing entire courses or specific issues of teaching and learning.

Faculty identifying primarily as teachers or primarily as researchers could reasonably ask how scholarship of teaching and learning can possibly benefit them. For teaching-focused faculty, research may seem beside the point of day-to-day classroom responsibilities. For research-focused faculty, scholarship with a focus on teaching may seem like a distraction from more important areas of scholarly interest. In reality, all types of faculty can benefit from scholarship of teaching (Hutchings et al., 2011; Smith, 2013). To begin, it is scholarship, and faculty tend to be rewarded for scholarly work. Research indicates that about half of academic departments count scholarship of teaching when evaluating faculty for tenure and promotion (Smith, 2013). Furthermore, like all scholarship, becoming an expert in a specific area can lead to a self-perpetuating cycle in which more opportunities arise. Being the well-known teaching guru in a discipline can result in invitations to share expertise at conferences and in publications. Similarly, opportunities for leadership related to education can emerge within teachers' discipline-specific organizations and societies. Campus leadership is also a possible outcome. The transition from faculty to administrator can be facilitated by being a published expert on teaching and learning—of course, this could be a reason to flaunt or hide scholarship of teaching depending on personal opinions about administrative work.

All of these professional benefits miss the point somewhat, however, because they ignore the main idea of scholarship of teaching and learning: improving educational outcomes. Just as with assessment, teachers benefit from scholarship of teaching by finding ways to improve student learning; this is a direct benefit to both teachers and students (Hutchings et al., 2011; Smith, 2013). What evidence is there that scholarship of teaching and learning actually improves outcomes? This is a difficult question to answer, but one way to think about it is that every piece of research that has ever documented student learning because of an intervention is evidence of the positive effect of scholarship of teaching (Hutchings et al., 2011). When considered cumulatively in this way, the impact is huge. Ultimately, what makes scholarship of teaching and learning so special is that these positive effects are made public so that everyone can benefit from the good work being done behind what are, commonly, the closed doors of college classrooms.

Model teachers do not buy into the dichotomy between research and teaching. Rather, they contribute to the accumulation of knowledge about teaching through scholarship of teaching and learning. As with any type of research, scholarship of teaching and learning can be conducted in a number of ways. However, the key idea is that model teachers share their teaching innovations for the benefit of all.

CASE STUDY REEXAMINED: THE TENURE SURPRISE

1. *What is the relation between assessment and scholarship of teaching?* The two activities are intimately related, which is why they are joined in this chapter. Assessment is the process of systematically investigating student learning outcomes and using that information to improve learning experiences. Scholarship of teaching and learning makes the results of assessment public. By publicizing what is learned from assessment, it becomes scholarship due to the potential for peer review and advancement of knowledge.

2. *Was Dr. Lee doing research? Why or why not?* Dr. Lee was not engaged in scholarship of teaching and learning research. He did perform the following steps: (a) identify an area for improvement of learning, (b) review the literature ideas to assess existing knowledge, (c) assess the outcomes of an innovative teaching technique. However, he failed to engage in the final step of sharing the results so that they can be reviewed by peers and so that knowledge can accumulate. This step is what separates scholarly teaching from scholarship of teaching and learning.

3. *What could Dr. Lee have done to avoid his tenure surprise?* To ensure that the project counted as research, Dr. Lee should have sought publication of the results. He also should have checked the promotion and tenure guidelines to determine what types of scholarly activity count toward tenure.

A Reflection on Your Self-Assessment

Now that you have read over the chapter, let's return to your self-assessment. What are the areas that you are particularly strong in? What areas need work? If your answer for most of the areas was "They need work!", then we would encourage you to start looking over selections from the recommendation readings below and resources offered by the National Institute for Learning Outcomes Assessment (www.learningoutcomesassessment.org). In addition, seek out the assessment gurus on your campus; take them out to lunch in exchange for a free consult on your assessment practices. Along the same lines, if scholarship of teaching and learning is daunting to you, seek out our suggested readings and explore resources offered by the International Society for the Scholarship of Teaching and Learning (www.issotl.com). In addition, find someone on campus who is engaged in the process and collaborate; perhaps your first publication on the topic will be the result!

Summary of Best Practices

If someone asked you to prove that you are a good teacher, could you do it? What evidence would you provide? You could offer student evaluations, but we all know teachers whose high marks seem to relate inversely to their use of the Model Teaching Criteria. Student grades could be offered, but they are determined by much more than our own efforts. Peer observations? Often our peers are motivated by kindness rather than honesty. In truth, we would argue that no evidence could be superior to demonstration of learning through direct assessment of student outcomes. Assessment is now a requirement in higher education, and model teachers embrace the process. They engage in practices such as:

- planning the entire assessment process before teaching a course;
- writing detailed, behavioral learning objectives that can be measured;
- assessing student achievement of learning objectives using regular course assignments; and
- documenting assessment by keeping records of objectives, outcomes of assessments, and actions taken because of assessment results.

Model teachers take the related process of evaluation very seriously as well. Knowing that quality evaluation is essential to student satisfaction, learning, and assessment, model teachers engage in practices such as:

- evaluating student learning in a way that directly corresponds to the learning objectives that have been shared with students;
- giving students feedback on their course performance early and often;
- creating grading rubrics for assignments and allowing students to use the rubrics to guide and evaluate their own work; and
- conducting informal evaluations (i.e., CATs) to gather evidence related to the learning not directly assessed by graded evaluations.

Once you have mastered the process of assessment, scholarship of teaching and learning should be easy. Simply translate what you learn from assessment into a research paper or presentation; once it has been peer-reviewed in some way, you are doing research on teaching. Engaging in assessment and scholarship of teaching does not always ensure that students learn, but it does prevent teachers from instructing in the dark, unsure of what is happening around them in students' minds.

The Very Busy People Book Club: Your Top Five Must-Reads

Angelo, T. A. and Cross, K. P. (1993). *Classroom assessment techniques: A handbook for college teachers* (2nd edn). San Francisco, CA: Jossey-Bass.

Bartsch, R. A. (2013a). Designing SoTL studies—part I: Validity. *New Directions for Teaching & Learning*, 2013(136), 17–33.

Bartsch, R. A. (2013b). Designing SoTL studies—part II: Practicality. *New Directions for Teaching & Learning*, 2013(136), 35–48.

Huba, M. E. and J. E. Freed. (2000). *Learner-centered assessment on college campuses: Shifting the focus from teaching to learning.* Boston, MA: Allyn and Bacon.

Suskie, L. (2009). *Assessing student learning: A common sense guide* (2nd edn). San Francisco, CA: Jossey-Bass.

References

Anderson, H. M., Moore, D. L., Anaya, G., and Bird, E. (2005). Student learning outcomes assessment: A component of program assessment. *American Journal of Pharmaceutical Education*, 69, 256–268.

Angelo, T. A. and Cross, K. P. (1993). *Classroom assessment techniques: A handbook for college teachers* (2nd edn). San Francisco, CA: Jossey-Bass.

Arnold, I. M. (2008). Course level and the relationship between research productivity and teaching effectiveness. *Journal of Economic Education*, 39, 307–321.

Bartsch, R. A. (2013a). Designing SoTL studies—part I: Validity. *New Directions for Teaching & Learning*, 2013(136), 17–33.

Bartsch, R. A. (2013b). Designing SoTL studies-part II: Practicality. *New Directions for Teaching & Learning*, 2013(136), 35–48.

Bean, J. C. (2011). *Engaging ideas: The professor's guide to integrating writing, critical thinking, and active learning in the classroom*. San Francisco, CA: Jossey-Bass.

Black, P. J. and William, D. (1998). Assessment and classroom learning. *Assessment in Education: Principles Policy and Practice*, 5, 7–73.

Blumberg, P. (2009). *Developing learner-centered teaching: A practical guide for faculty*. San Francisco, CA: Jossey-Bass.

Boysen, G. A. (2013). *A guide to writing learning objectives for teachers of psychology*. Retrieved from http://teachpsych.org/resources/Documents/otrp/resources/boysen12.pdf.

Boysen, G. A., Richmond, A. S., and Gurung, R. A. R. (2015). Model Teaching Criteria for psychology: Initial documentation of teachers' self-reported competency. *Scholarship of Teaching and Learning in Psychology*, 1, 48–59.

Buskist, W., Carlson, J. R., Christopher, A. N., Prieto, L., and Smith, R. A. (2008). Models and exemplars of scholarship in the teaching of psychology. *Teaching of Psychology*, 35, 267–277.

Cain, T. R. (2014). *Assessment and academic freedom: In concert, not conflict*. Urbana, IL: National Institute for Learning Outcomes Assessment.

Chory-Assad, R. M. (2002). Classroom justice: Perceptions of fairness as a predictor of student motivation, learning, and aggression. *Communication Quarterly*, 50, 58–77.

Crooks, T. J. (1988). The impact of classroom evaluation practices on students. *Review of Educational Research*, 58, 438–481.

Cummings, R., Maddux, C. D., and Richmond, A. (2008). Curriculum-embedded performance assessment in higher education: Maximum efficiency and minimum disruption. *Assessment & Evaluation in Higher Education*, 33, 599–605.

D'Andrea, V. (1999). Organizing teaching and learning: Outcomes-based planning. In H. Fry, S. Ketteridge, and S. Marshall (eds.), *A handbook for teaching and learning in higher education: Enhancing academic practice* (pp. 41–57). London: Kogan Page.

Dickson, K. L. and Treml, M. M. (2013). Using assessment and SoTL to enhance student learning. *New Directions for Teaching & Learning*, 2013(136), 7–16.

Duchastel, P. C. and Brown, B. R. (1974). Incidental and relevant learning with instructional objectives. *Journal of Educational Psychology*, 66, 481–485.

Duell, O. P. (1974). Effect of type of objective, level of test questions, and the judged importance of tested materials upon posttest performance. *Journal of Educational Psychology*, 66, 225–323.

Ewell, P. T. (2002). An emerging scholarship: A brief history of assessment. In T. W. Banta (ed.), *Building a scholarship of assessment* (pp. 3–25). San Francisco, CA. Jossey-Bass.

Ewell, P. T., Paulson, K., and Kinzie, J. (2011). *Down and in: Assessment practices at the program level*. Urbana, IL: National Institute for Learning Outcomes Assessment.

Fulcher, K. H., Good, M. R., Coleman, C. M., and Smith, K. L. (2014). *A simple model for learning improvement: Weigh pig, feed pig, weigh pig*. Urbana, IL: National Institute for Learning Outcomes Assessment.

Gagné, E. D. and Rothkopf, E. Z. (1975). Text organization and learning goals. *Journal of Educational Psychology*, 67, 445–450.

Goodboy, A. K. (2011). Instructional dissent in the college classroom. *Communication Education*, 60, 296–313.

Greenberg, K. P. (2015). Rubric use in formative assessment: A detailed behavioral rubric helps students improve their scientific writing skills. *Teaching of Psychology*, 42, 211–217.

Halpern, D. F. (2013). A is for assessment: The other scarlet letter. *Teaching of Psychology*, 40, 358–362.

Harden, R. M. (2002). Learning outcomes and instructional objectives: Is there a difference? *Medical Teacher*, 24, 151–155.

Harden, R. M., Crosby, J. R. and Davis, M. H. (1999). AMEE Guide No. 14: Outcome-based education: Part 1—an introduction to outcome-based education. *Medical Teacher*, 21, 7–14.

Hattie, J. and Marsh, H. W. (1996). The relationship between research and teaching: A meta-analysis. *Review of Educational Research*, 4, 507–542.

Huba, M. E. and J. E. Freed. (2000). *Learner-centered assessment on college campuses: Shifting the focus from teaching to learning*. Boston, MA: Allyn and Bacon.

Hutchings, P. (2010). *Opening doors to faculty involvement in assessment*. Urbana, IL: National Institute for Learning Outcomes Assessment.

Hutchings, P., Huber, M. T., and Ciccone, A. (2011). *The scholarship of teaching and learning reconsidered: Institutional integration and impact*. San Francisco, CA: Jossey-Bass.

Jonsson, A. and Svingby, G. (2007). The use of scoring rubrics: Reliability, validity and educational consequences. *Educational Research Review*, 2, 130–144.

Kaplan, R. (1976). Effects of grouping and response characteristics of instructional objectives on learning from prose. *Journal of Educational Psychology*, 68, 424–430.

Kaplan, R. and Simmons, F. G. (1974). Effects of instructional objectives used as orienting stimuli or as summary/review upon prose learning. *Journal of Educational Psychology*, 66, 614–622.

Kelly, D. (2008). Evaluating teaching and learning: Enhancing the scholarship of teaching by asking students what they are learning. In R. Murray (ed.), *The scholarship of teaching and learning in higher education* (pp. 80–90). New York: McGraw-Hill.

Kluger, A. N. and DeNisi, A. (1996). The effects of feedback interventions on performance: A historical review, a meta-analysis, and a preliminary feedback intervention theory. *Psychological Bulletin*, 119, 254–284.

Kuh, G. D., Jankowski, N., Ikenberry, S. O., and Kinzie, J. (2013). *Knowing what students know and can do: The current state of student learning outcomes in US colleges and universities*. Urbana, IL: National Institute for Learning Outcomes Assessment.

Locke, E. A., Shaw, K. N., Saari, L. M., and Latham, G. P. (1981). Goal setting and task performance: 1969–1980. *Psychological Bulletin*, 90, 125–152.

Martin, R. C. (2013). Navigating the IRB: The ethics of SoTL. *New Directions for Teaching & Learning*, 2013(136), 59–71.

McCarthy, M. (2008). The scholarship of teaching and learning in higher education: An overview. In R. Murray (ed.), *The scholarship of teaching and learning in higher education* (pp. 6–15). New York: McGraw-Hill.

McCarthy, M. A., Niederjohn, D. M., and Bosack, T. N. (2011). Embedded assessment: A measure of student learning and teaching effectiveness. *Teaching of Psychology*, 38, 78–82.

New Leadership Alliance for Student Learning and Accountability (2012). *Committing to quality: Guidelines for assessment and accountability in higher education*. Washington, DC: New Leadership Alliance for Student Learning and Accountability.

Nicol, D. J. and MacFarlane-Dick, D. (2006). Formative assessment and self-regulated learning: A model and seven principles of good feedback practice. *Studies in Higher Education*, 31, 199–2018.

Nuhfer, E. and Knipp, D. (2003). The knowledge survey: A tool for all reasons. *To Improve the Academy*, 21, 59–78.

Osborne, R. E. and Wagor, W. F. (2004). Course assessment: Developing and assessing assessable objectives by using an integrative assessment model. In D. Dunn, C. Mehrotra, and J. Halonen (eds.), *Measuring up: Educational assessment challenges and practices for psychology* (pp. 11–26). Washington, DC: American Psychological Association.

Palomba, C. A. and Banta, T. W. (1999). *Assessment essentials: Planning, implementing, and improving assessment in higher education*. San Francisco, CA: Jossey-Bass.

Provezis, S. (2010). *Regional accreditation and student learning outcomes: Mapping the territory*. Urbana, IL: National Institute for Learning Outcomes Assessment.

Richman, W. A. and Ariovich, L. (2013). *All-in-one: Combining grading, course, program, and general education outcomes assessment*. Urbana, IL: National Institute for Learning Outcomes Assessment.

Richmond, A. S., Boysen, G. A., Gurung, R. A. R., Tazeau, Y. N., Meyers, S. A., and Sciutto, M. J. (2014). Aspirational Model Teaching Criteria for psychology. *Teaching of Psychology*, 41, 281–295.

Reddy, Y. M. and Andrade, H. (2010). A review of rubric use in higher education. *Assessment & Evaluation in Higher Education*, 35, 435–448.

Roediger, H. L., Putnam, A. L., and Smith, M. A. (2011). Ten benefits of testing and their applications to educational practice. In J. Mestre and B. Ross (eds.), *Psychology of learning and motivation: Cognition in education* (pp. 1–36). Oxford: Elsevier.

Rothkopf, E. Z. and Kaplan, R. (1972). Exploration of the effect of density and specificity of instructional objectives on learning from text. *Journal of Educational Psychology*, 63, 295–302.

Royer, P. N. (1977). Effects of specificity and position of written instructional objectives on learning from lecture. *Journal of Educational Psychology*, 69, 40–45.

Rust, C. (2002). The impact of assessment on student learning: How can the research literature practically help to inform the development of departmental assessment strategies and learning-centered assessment practices? *Active Learning in Higher Education*, 3, 145–158.

Smaldino, S. E., Russell, J. D., Heinich, R., and Molenda, M. (2005). *Instructional technology and media for learning*. Upper Saddle River, NJ: Pearson.

Smith, R. A. (2008). Moving toward the scholarship of teaching and learning: The classroom can be a lab, too! *Teaching of Psychology*, 35, 262–266.

Smith, R. A. (2013). Benefits of using SoTL in picking and choosing pedagogy. In B. M. Schwartz and R. A. R. Gurung (eds.), *Evidence-based teaching for higher education* (pp. 7–22). Washington, DC: American Psychological Association.

Suskie, L. (2009). *Assessing student learning: A common sense guide* (2nd edn). San Francisco, CA: Jossey-Bass.

Thaler, N., Kazemi, E., and Huscher, C. (2009). Developing a rubric to assess student learning outcomes using a class assignment. *Teaching of Psychology*, 36, 113–116.

Walvoord, B. E. (2010). *Assessment clear and simple: A practical guide for institutions, departments, and general education* (2nd edn). San Francisco, CA: Jossey-Bass.

Wesp, R. and Miele, J. (2008). Student opinions of the quality of teaching activities poorly predict pedagogical effectiveness. *Teaching of Psychology*, 35, 360–362.

Wiggins, G. and McTighe, J. (1998). *Understanding by design*. Alexandria, VA: Association for Supervision and Curriculum Development.

7

HOW DO MODEL TEACHERS CONSTRUCT SYLLABI?

Imagine it is the first day of class. What is your typical script for this day? Do you go over the syllabus (i.e., read from it and discuss a few things), do an ice-breaker, and then let students go? Our guess is that, if we survey your students, they would confirm this script. As is often the case, across all academic disciplines and across all types of institutions, the first day of class is dedicated to "introductions" and going over the syllabus. So, if you dedicate an entire class to the syllabus, how much work do you put into constructing it beforehand? Did you use a syllabus given to you by someone else? Did you spend as much time prepping your syllabus as you did your most difficult topic to teach in the class? On the first day, are your students excited and engaged (we hope so) or do they just want to get the syllabus and leave? Some of these questions have answers that are clearly related to Model Teaching Criteria, and we hope this chapter will point you in the right direction in terms of your course syllabi. Specifically, in this chapter we will provide a description of what elements to include in the syllabus, summaries of what research tells us regarding creation and use of the syllabus, and strategies to get your students to use the syllabus. Before we dive in, however, consider the following case.

CASE STUDY: AN OFFER SHE CAN'T REFUSE

It was just weeks prior to the start of the fall semester. After receiving a suspiciously vague meeting request via email, Jocelyn, a third-year doctoral student in chemistry, nervously went to the office of the chair of her department. The chair informed her that Dr. Haber, one of the high-powered researchers in the department, was leaving for the private sector, which meant Chemistry I was without an instructor—the class was

Jocelyn's, should she accept it. Jocelyn was eager to help the department and to get the teaching experience that would land her a job in a few years. However, with just weeks to prepare, she felt overwhelmed before even saying yes. After voicing this concern, the chair said "Relax! Dr. Haber already has a textbook and syllabus set up that you can use." With that, she accepted.

Unfortunately, Jocelyn soon realized that the class was not as complete as the chair made it out to be. Dr. Haber's syllabus was just barely a skeleton. It included a blank spot for her name and contact information, a catalog description of the course, the name of the textbook, a week-by-week schedule of topics, dates for eight quizzes, the grading scale, an ADA policy statement, and an academic integrity policy. Jocelyn thought there surely had to be more to a syllabus than this. Previously, she had loved being a TA and wanted her new students to know that she enjoyed teaching and wanted to help them learn—this syllabus looked like it was written by someone who hated teaching (and it was). More than anything, she wanted students to succeed in her courses; poor student evaluations were a surefire way for a graduate student to never teach again. But what else did this syllabus need to ensure that her students did well? Jocelyn immediately started making a list of all the things she would add to the syllabus, but then she thought "Am I wasting my time? After all, students never think about the syllabus again after the first day of class." With more questions than answers, she sought out advice from her supervisor.

Now take a moment to answer these questions. We will revisit your answers at the end of the chapter. Yes, after reading the chapter you may change your answers.

1. If you were Jocelyn's supervisor, what would you advise her to do?
2. Based on the description of the syllabus, what elements are missing?
3. How would you change the syllabus to reflect your teaching style and expectations?

Self-Assessment Time!

But first, as practitioners of science, we need to establish a baseline measurement of your typical syllabus. So grab what you believe to be your best syllabus and take a few minutes to complete the model syllabi self-assessment in Table 7.1. While reading the rest of the chapter, periodically glimpse back at your results of the self-assessment and connect what you have learned to what you have practiced in the past. We will then revisit your results at the end of the chapter.

TABLE 7.1 Self-Assessment of the Model Syllabus Teaching Criteria

Directions: Please indicate on the scale below how often you incorporate these efforts/activities to improve your syllabus. *Scale: 5 = Always, 4 = Often, 3 = Sometimes, 2 = Rarely, 1 = Never*	*Your score*
1. Your syllabus reflects an intentional link of course goals to class activities.	
2. Your syllabus reflects an intentional link of course goals to evaluation methods.	
3. Your syllabus reflects an intentional link of course goals to course assignments.	
4. Your syllabus has an attractive and readable layout.	
5. Your syllabus reflects changes suggested by student feedback.	
6. Your syllabus reflects effective use of instructional methods.	
7. Your syllabus is strategically organized to accomplish course goals.	
8. Your syllabus provides clear and complete information about course goals.	
9. Your syllabus provides clear and complete information about the course schedule.	
10. Your syllabus provides clear and complete information about course requirements.	
11. Your syllabus provides clear and complete information about course grading/assessment.	
12. Your syllabus provides clear and complete information about instructor availability (e.g., office hours, contact information).	
13. Your syllabus sets a positive tone for the course (e.g., uses positive and rewarding language).	
14. Your syllabus is written in the first person with proper pronoun use.	

Note: This self-assessment is adapted and modified from Richmond et al. (2014), Boysen et al. (2015), and Slattery and Carlson (n.d., 2005).

The Purpose, Elements, Evidence, and Examples of a Model Syllabus

Your first time creating or modifying an existing syllabus will quickly cause you to wonder: "What is the purpose of a syllabus and why should I go through this arduous task of creating or modifying it? Instead, why don't I just use one from somebody else who has taught the course?" Actually, there are several very important and impactful reasons to spend time, effort, and forethought on your syllabus. Specifically, best practices in syllabus construction suggest that the syllabus is generally thought to serve as a contract, as a permanent record, as a communication device, and as a learning tool/cognitive map; clearly, meeting all these needs requires considerable planning (Matejka and Kurke, 1994; Parkes and Harris, 2002).

The Model Syllabus is a Contract

As a contract, the syllabus is an explicit document that defines the responsibilities and duties between the teacher and the student (Robinson Wolf et al., 2013).

What elements of a model syllabus are considered contractual? Well, although syllabi are very diverse in organization, typically model syllabi contain a detailed calendar, explicit grading policies, attendance policies, policies for late assignments and make-up exams, policies for revising and redoing assignments, rules regarding academic honesty, and a description of how your university or college institutes the American Disability Act (ADA) policy (Habanek, 2005; Slattery and Carlson, 2005). Gathered from research on syllabi construction, we have summarized and provided examples of best practices for each of these contract syllabus elements in Table 7.2. Additionally, we have included sample syllabi content in Figure 7.1. One sample attendance policy is flexible, whereas the other sample is punitive and inflexible. We hope that your syllabi reflect the clarity and flexibility of the first example.

Considering the importance of these syllabus elements, it is the ethical responsibility of teachers to create accurate syllabi and honor the syllabus contract (American Psychological Association, 2010). For instance, students often ask "What is the policy for late assignments?" or "Can I redo an assignment?" And a model syllabus can answer these important questions. In other words, the syllabus is often viewed as a promise made to students (Bain, 2004) and in some cases a binding contract (Slattery and Carlson, 2005). For example, many colleges and universities require students to sign the syllabus to demonstrate its contractual nature.

There is evidence to suggest that model syllabi frequently include these contract elements. In a study on model teaching competencies, Boysen, Richmond, and Gurung (2015) found that 99 percent of college and university teachers employ syllabi that have clear and concise grading policies and 97 percent of teachers include a clear and concise course calendar. Additionally, Richmond, Morgan, Slattery, and Venzke (2013) found that almost 99 percent of the peer-reviewed exemplar syllabi published by the Society of Teaching of Psychology include student-centered contract elements (e.g., encourage revisions, include both formative and summative assessments, etc.). Moreover, Habanek (2005) found that 100 percent of informative syllabi (i.e., a thorough description of contract elements of a syllabus) include concise and descriptive ADA statements. Therefore, it is truly important to provide clear and complete contract information in your syllabus.

Because a model syllabus can serve as a contract, it is extremely important that contract-related content is concise, accurate, and clear (Richmond et al., 2014). Syllabi should be completely transparent. Unfortunately, unlike the informative (e.g., model) syllabi reported in Habanek's study, this is not always the case. For instance, Parkes, Fix, and Harris (2003) found that out of 200 syllabi across multiple academic domains, 57 percent did not have an attendance policy, 84 percent did not have a statement about academic dishonesty/ethical conduct, 77 percent did not have complete and concise grading policies, and 89 percent did not have an ADA policy. These results are particularly troubling because many of the model syllabi contract elements are what students most frequently pay attention to. For example, surveying more than 800

TABLE 7.2 Best Practices for Creating Model Syllabus Contract Elements

Contract elements	Best practices
Course calendar/schedule	Include dates of class meetings with corresponding course topics, reading assignments, and due dates for all assignments and assessments.
Grading policies	Describe how and what students will be graded on. Include a breakdown of grade distributions, point values, and letter grades. Include information on incompletes and withdraw policies.
Academic misconduct/ dishonesty/plagiarism policies	Often institutions will have a standardized policy for academic misconduct; always include it. However, personalize it by using personal pronouns such as "you." Also, define plagiarism, misconduct, and dishonesty. Explain why academic misconduct is a concern and how you will deal with incidents.
Attendance policies	In most institutions, attendance is required. So, describe how attendance benefits your students. Possibly include information on participation and whether this is graded or not. Describe what students need to do when they cannot make class.
ADA policies	Provide a detailed description of the rights and responsibilities of students with disabilities and how you will accommodate their needs. Often your institution will provide an ADA policy that you should include.
Late assignment polices	Include a clear description for whether late work is accepted or not. If it is, explain how and when students can turn in late assignments.
Revising and redoing policies	Include a concise description of how students can revise or redo assignments. Include a timeline for revisions and what they will gain from their revisions.

Note: These best practices are selected from Cullen and Harris (2009), Parkes and Harris (2002), Slattery and Carlson (2005).

students, Becker and Calhoon (1999) found that grading, attendance, and make-up policies are some of the most frequently attended to syllabi elements. This seems to be especially true for first-year students (Becker and Calhoon, 1999). Thus, if the syllabus is to serve as a contract, properly describing these elements is paramount.

The Model Syllabus is a Permanent Record

As a permanent public record, the syllabus can function as both a record of accountability and documentation; thus, it is important that it be transparent and

Attendance Policy

You are responsible for all information presented in class even on days that you are absent. Absences are generally not excused; however, if absences are necessary, please contact me BEFORE the class. Absences will only be excused if I am contacted prior to class period and for appropriate reasons. In addition, each class missed is 1% off your final grade.

(a)

Attendance Policy

Attendance will benefit you in several ways. Primarily, your understanding of the course material is heightened from double exposure to the material (i.e., in class and in the text). Second, you are responsible for all information presented in class even on days that you are absent. If absences are necessary (which I understand, life happens), please attempt to contact me before the class.

(b)

FIGURE 7.1 (a) An example of a poorly conceived contract syllabus element of an attendance policy; (b) An example of a model contract syllabus element of an attendance policy.

accurate (Richmond et al., 2014). As delineated in Table 7.3, typical permanent record syllabus elements include a focus on course content and requirements. For example, permanent record information includes learning objectives, evaluation procedures, required texts and materials, content, and prerequisites (Parkes and Harris, 2002). Additionally, as you will notice in Figure 7.2, the good example of the contractual syllabus element of attendance policy is flexible yet concise, whereas the example of a poorly conceived attendance policy is punitive and inflexible.

As permanent records, syllabi are constantly open to scrutiny by both students and other members of the college or university community. Case in point, in the age of assessment, the syllabus is increasingly becoming an artifact for evaluation of teachers and courses. For instance, the syllabus can be used for tenure review, merit and promotion, transfer of academic credit, program review, and many other aspects of academic evaluation (Albers, 2003; Parkes and Harris, 2002). Syllabi may also serve the college or university community at large by standardizing content across academic domains (e.g., office hours, learning goals, pre- and co-requisites, application to general studies). Not only is the syllabus a permanent record of accountability, but it may also serve as a permanent record for students to understand what they need to know about a course (Smith and Razzouk, 1993).

Although they are often regarded as optional information in the syllabus, evidence suggests that accurate permanent record elements should be included in syllabi because they increase course transparency. For instance, in Boysen and colleagues' (2015) study on model teaching characteristics, 97 percent of college and university teachers reported that their syllabi provided clear course goals, 75 percent included intentional links of course goals to class activities, 76 percent linked course goals to assessment procedures, 99 percent included instructor information, and 99 percent provided a clear description of course content/requirements. Additionally,

TABLE 7.3 Best Practices for Creating Model Syllabus Permanent Record Elements

Syllabus elements	Best Practices
Course information	Include title and dates of the course, name of instructor of record, pre- and co-requisites, credit hours, and when the course meets.
Course objectives/goals	Write clear and concise course objectives that are directly linked to evaluations of learning. Provide a rationale for the objectives. If applicable, link them to standards within the profession (e.g., nursing, education, or engineering).
Evaluation procedures	Explain how you are going to evaluate students and why. Include a description of both formal and informal evaluations and summative and formative evaluations. Directly tie your evaluation procedures to the student learning objectives.
Course texts and materials	List all texts that the students will be using in the course. This should include both required and optional texts. Indicate whether older editions of a textbook are acceptable. Encourage and describe how students can seek resources outside of those listed in the syllabus. Model discipline style when writing (e.g., APA style for psychology courses).
Course content and topics	In the course calendar, describe which topics will be covered and where students can find the source or reading for each topic.

Note: These best practices are selected from Cullen and Harris (2009), Matejka and Kurke (1994), Parkes and Harris (2002), and Slattery and Carlson (2005).

Richmond and colleagues (2013) found that model syllabi included detailed and concise descriptions of student-centered evaluation methods (e.g., both summative and formative evaluations of learning, evaluations tied to student learning objectives).

Even though evidence suggests that model syllabi should incorporate permanent record elements (e.g., Boysen et al., 2015; Richmond et al., 2013), many syllabi lack these permanent record elements. For instance, the inclusion of student learning objectives varies widely across academic disciplines. In a study by Parkes and colleagues (2003), only 64 percent of the syllabi contained course objectives. Similarly, Homa and colleagues (2013) found only 80 percent of syllabi studied contained learning objectives. Additionally, Robinson Wolf and colleagues (2013) found that only 38 percent of syllabi studies listed prerequisites. Considering the frequency at which the syllabus is used as a permanent record (e.g., evidence for tenure and promotion, transfer credit evaluations, accreditation), it is imperative that model syllabi include accurate and concise records.

Student Learning Objectives

1. Be a critical consumer of statistics.
2. Be able to appropriately and accurately apply statistical knowledge.
3. Be able to read, understand, and integrate psychological research.
4. Understand the importance of scientific problem-solving.
5. Understand the ethical considerations involved in conducting research.
6. Experience the research process by conducting a research experiment.
7. Demonstrate the ability to work collaboratively with peers.

(a)

Student Learning Objectives

Not

1. Become a critical consumer of statistics by understanding the common analyses used in psychology research (assessed by SPSS assignments).
2. Be able to appropriately and accurately apply statistical knowledge to solve problems (assessed by SPSS and project-based assignments).
3. Be able to read, understand, and integrate psychological research (assessed by project-based introduction and discussion assignments).
4. Understand the importance of scientific problem solving (assessed by project-based assignments).
5. Understand the ethical considerations involved in conducting research (assessed by human subjects assignment).
6. Experience the research process by conducting a research experiment (assessed by project-based assignment).
7. Demonstrate the ability to work collaboratively with peers (assessed by peer-group assignment).

(b)

FIGURE 7.2 (a) An example of a poorly conceived permanent record syllabus element of student learning objectives; (b) An example of a model permanent syllabus element of student learning objectives.

The Model Syllabus is a Communication Device

As a communication device, the syllabus can be an incredible opportunity to convey to students how you teach and how this will affect student learning. If you think about it, the syllabus is one of the first interactions between you and your students. In many ways, the syllabus can act as the first impression you have on students. What will this first impression look like? Will students think, "Wow this teacher doesn't care at all. They are just mailing it in!", "Meh," or "Wow this teacher really cares!"? If you are aiming for "Wow, this teacher really cares!", Bain (2004) suggests that the syllabus is an excellent opportunity to garner the trust of your students by demonstrating that the syllabus is more than just a list of assignments and dates.

So you are probably wondering what elements of the syllabus can help you communicate who you are to students and how should you write and construct these elements. As described in Table 7.4, typical communication elements of a syllabus include contact information, teaching philosophy/pedagogy, and student and teacher behavioral expectations (e.g., Landrum, 2011; Matejka and Kurke, 1994). Also, as illustrated in Figure 7.3, a poorly written communication element of student and teacher expectations only lists the expectations for students with a demanding and non-welcoming tone, whereas the example of the model communication syllabus element provides a corresponding and matching expectation for the teacher with each student expectation. But as discussed in the following paragraphs, it is not just about *what* communication elements you put in the syllabus, of equal importance is *how* you communicate about those elements.

Why go through all this trouble of developing a model syllabus? Without a doubt, syllabi are major vehicles of communication and their tone can play an important role in this process. In short, like it or not, the syllabus conveys who you are and what you represent and often can cause students (even before they meet you) to make judgments about you and the course. Therefore, if you want to be a model teacher, then your syllabus should communicate that you are a model teacher. For instance, research suggests that model teachers engage in specific teaching behaviors and have strong rapport with students (see Chapter 4; Keeley et al., 2009; Landrum and Stowell, 2013). Therefore, your syllabus should reflect these traits and skills.

Research supports the notion that students make judgments about teachers based on their syllabi. Two studies best illustrate the impact that the syllabus can have on how students perceive teachers. First, Saville and colleagues (2010) experimentally manipulated two hypothetical syllabi so that one was detailed and one was brief; then, college students rated the hypothetical teacher using the model teaching behaviors represented on the Teacher Behavior Checklist (Keeley et al., 2009). College students rated a hypothetical teacher who wrote the detailed syllabus as more approachable, creative, eloquent, encouraging, enthusiastic, flexible, knowledgeable, prepared, up-to-date, and fair. In a more recent study, Richmond and colleagues (2015) experimentally manipulated hypothetical syllabi as well. In one condition they had students read a syllabus centered students' perspective (as judged by Cullen and Harris's, 2009, learner-centered syllabus rubric) and a syllabus centered on the teacher's perspective. College students then rated the hypothetical teacher on the Teacher Behavior Checklist and the Professor–Student Rapport Scale (Wilson and Ryan, 2013). Students who read the student-centered syllabus rated the hypothetical teacher of this syllabus as being significantly more approachable, creative, encouraging, enthusiastic, flexible, positive, and friendly when compared to those who received the teacher-centered syllabus. As evidenced by these two studies, incorporating the best practices of communication into your syllabus can have a significant impact on students.

TABLE 7.4 Best Practices for Creating Model Syllabus Communication Devices

Syllabus elements	Best practices
Contact information	You should include office hours, office hours location, email address, office phone (some include cell phone), and any other means of preferred communication (e.g., Twitter, video conferencing). Indicate whether you are available outside of office hours.
Teaching philosophy/ pedagogy	The syllabus in its entirety represents your teaching philosophy. As such, it is important to include a brief statement about your philosophy or pedagogy. This should include the why, what, and how of your teaching.
Student and teacher behavioral expectations	This is your opportunity to define what you expect of students. Things like participation, preparedness, enthusiasm, and promptness can be covered. For all student expectations there should be counterpart teacher expectations.
Tone	Incorporating a friendly, warm, positive, rewarding, and supportive tone can be done throughout the syllabus. For instance, write in the first person and use personal pronouns. Use action verbs instead of passive verbs. Use inclusive language rather than exclusive language. Avoid condescending and confrontational language. Use humor when appropriate. In essence, let your personality come out in your syllabus.

Note: These best practices are selected from Cullen and Harris (2009), Parkes and Harris (2002), Slattery and Carlson (2005).

Research also suggests that model syllabi communicate course transparency by providing clear, complete, and inviting information about instructor availability (e.g., office hours, contact information). For instance, Boysen and colleagues (2015) found that 99 percent of teachers reported that they incorporate clear and complete information about instructor availability. Furthermore, Richmond and colleagues (2015) found that students given a model syllabus with clear and complete instructor availability information viewed the teacher as significantly more approachable and friendly than students who received a syllabus without clear and complete availability information.

The syllabus can communicate the culture and climate of a course (Robinson Wolf et al., 2013). Sulik and Keys (2014, p. 151) suggest, "syllabi… do more than communicate course objectives and the means for achieving them. Syllabi (re) socialize students for success in the college setting by establishing student–teacher roles and norms and setting the tone for classroom interactions." As a tool for socialization, the syllabus can be used to establish class norms for behavior and to communicate the methods by which the teacher will meet student expectations

Expectations for Students

a. PLEASE BE ACTIVE AND PARTICIPATE IN CLASS
b. Listen and respect others
c. Be comfortable in taking risks
d. Complete all assignments
e. Turn off your cell phones and/or pagers
f. Be punctual for all classes
g. Discuss class concerns either after class or during designated office hours
h. Be prepared for class by reading chapter prior to lesson

(a)

Expectations for Students & Instructor

Student Expectations	*Instructor Expectations*
a. PLEASE BE ACTIVE AND PARTICI-PATE IN CLASS	a. Be active AND enthusiastic to facilitate student learning
b. Listen and respect others	b. Listen and respect students' views
c. Be comfortable in taking risks	c. Be in class at least 5 minutes before and after class
d. Complete all assignments	
e. Turn off your cell phones and/or pagers	d. Respond swiftly and effectively to student concerns
f. Be punctual for all classes	
g. Discuss class concerns either after class or during designated office hours	e. Turn off cell phone
	f. Grade objectively, consistently, and timely
h. Be prepared for class by reading chapter prior to lesson	g. Be prepared for class
	h. Accommodate differences in students' learning

Please remember if you have any questions, concerns, or comments to let me know right away. I welcome any feedback you're willing to offer.

(b)

FIGURE 7.3 (a) An example of a poorly conceived communication syllabus element of student and instructor behavioral expectations; (b) An example of a model communication syllabus element of student and instructor behavioral expectations.

(Slattery and Carlson, n.d., 2005). As such, it is important to provide student expectations (e.g., be prepared and on time to class, be respectful), and describe what students could expect of you (e.g., be prepared and on time for class, be respectful). Or, as DiClementi and Handelsman (2005) suggest, have students create their own classroom rules by listing ideas and voting on which rules should be used (e.g., how to address the professor, or how to answer questions in the class). Moreover, the syllabus could also be used to socialize students to an academic discipline. For example, if you were a modern language teacher, you would want to model how to write in the discipline (e.g., MLA style) and therefore would write your syllabus using the conventions of MLA style. A graphic design teacher would want to present a syllabus that is especially pleasing to the eye. As the research suggests, always remember that the syllabus will be the first injection of cultural norms of your class, so plan accordingly.

Research also suggests that you need to establish a supportive (Boysen et al., 2015; Perrine et al., 1995), rewarding (Ishiyama and Hartlaub, 2002), friendly, and positive (Harnish and Bridges, 2011) tone in your syllabus. When surveyed, 94 percent of teachers reported that they use a positive tone in their syllabi (Boysen et al., 2015). The next logical question then becomes, *How do I accomplish good communication and set a positive tone?* There are several ways you can accomplish this goal. First, write your syllabus so that students feel supported. Perrine and colleagues (1995) investigated the effects of a supportive statement about helping students in the course vs. a neutral statement. Specifically, they gave college students a supportive statement in the syllabus that read as follows.

> This course is enjoyable, but demanding. There is a large amount of material and it can be overwhelming at times. If you find yourself doing poorly in the course, please come talk to me. Any time during the semester that you have problems in this course, I want to know about it. Together we can try to pinpoint the problem and get you off to a better start.
>
> *(Perrine et al., 1995, p. 45)*

Whereas, students in the other experimental condition received the following statement.

> This course is enjoyable, but demanding. There is a large amount of material and it can be overwhelming at times. Please do not let yourself fall behind. It is very important that you keep up with the readings.
>
> *(Perrine et al., 1995, p. 46)*

They found that students receiving the supportive statement versus the neutral statement reported being more likely to seek out the teacher to discuss course material, grades, and study skills. Additionally, Perrine and colleagues (1995) found that traditionally aged students were more likely than non-traditionally aged students to seek help when a supportive statement was included in the syllabus. The implication of these results is that inserting genuinely supportive statements throughout your syllabus will significantly impact the help-seeking behavior of your students.

Using reward-based, friendly language in a syllabus also effects tone and subsequent student perceptions of the teacher. For example, Ishiyama and Hartlaub (2002) conducted a study comparing rewarding versus punishing language in a syllabus. The example of rewarding language was: "If for some substantial reason you cannot turn in your papers or take an exam at the scheduled time you should contact me *prior* to the due date, or test date, or you will only be eligible for 80% of the total points" (p. 568) versus a more punitive statement such as, "If for some substantial reason you cannot turn in your papers or take an exam at the scheduled time you must contact me *prior* to the due date, or test date, or you will be graded down 20%" (p. 568). They found that political science students viewed the teacher of the reward-based syllabus as more approachable than the teacher who wrote the punishment-based syllabus. Additionally, Harnish and Bridges (2011) conducted a study comparing friendly (warm) versus unfriendly (cold) tone. Examples of an unfriendly or cold tone versus friendly or warm tone include simple things like "office hours" versus "student hours" or "Come prepared to actively participate in this course. This is the best way to engage you in learning the material (and it makes the lectures more interesting)" versus "I hope you actively participate in this course. I say this because I found it is the best way to engage you in learning the material (and it makes the lectures more fun)" (Harnish and Bridges, 2011, p. 323). They found that students viewed the teacher who wrote the friendly toned syllabus as significantly more motivated and approachable; they also assigned the teacher higher student evaluation ratings. In addition, students viewed the subject more positively, saw the course as less difficult, and were more interested in taking another course with the teacher. Considering all of these positive effects, there is convincing evidence that model syllabi should be written in a friendly, positive, rewarding, and supportive tone.

The Model Syllabus is a Cognitive Map and Learning Tool

A model syllabus can provide guidance and strategies for learning in and out of the classroom; thus, it can serve as a cognitive map and a learning tool for students (Parkes and Harris, 2002). As Matejka and Kurke (1994) put it, "Think of your course as an educational adventure... The teacher is the guide and the only one with the cognitive map of the destination, what routes we will take, detours needed, and the method of travel" (p. 117). To be an effective cognitive map and learning tool, the syllabus should include elements such as tips to succeed, student and instructor expectations, common pitfalls/misconceptions that occur in the course, campus resources for assistance (e.g., writing center), and an explanation embedded throughout the syllabus for why they are doing what they are doing (Matejka and Kurke, 1994; Parkes and Harris, 2002). See Table 7.5 for a description of best practices for creating the cognitive map and learning tool elements of a syllabus. We've also provided an example of an assignment description from a model syllabus that is effective as a cognitive map and learning tool, as well as one that is less effective (see Figure 7.4). The model syllabus provides a strong rational to students on the purpose of specific assignments in the course and explains why they should complete the assignments. In contrast, the poorly constructed syllabus element only briefly describes each element of the assignment and focuses on procedural details.

TABLE 7.5 Best Practices for Creating Model Syllabus as a Cognitive Map and Learning Tool

Syllabus elements	Best practices
Success tips	Explicitly explain how students can do well in your course. This may include how much studying and reading time they can expect to do, how to become more effective learners, effective study strategies (e.g., note-taking, use of mnemonics, and elaboration), and suggestions for time management. Provide external aids like websites, optional readings, and study guides.
Common pitfalls and misconceptions	Provide a list and explanation for common misconceptions or pitfalls that occur in the course. For instance, in online classes, students may not set a time to study each week and that contributes to their lack of success in the course. Other examples include not communicating frequently with the teacher to ensure that all is well in the course and common mistakes made in the required coursework.
Campus resources	Provide direction on how students can seek help outside of the course. For instance, list the availability of teaching assistants, tutors, the writing center, the counseling center, and career services. Additionally, refer students to the student handbook for any grievances they may have.
Student-centered focus	Cullen and Harris (2009) have provided an excellent rubric to evaluate your syllabus on how student- versus teacher-centered it is. For example, encourage collaboration, group work, and shared power between the student and the teacher; provide rationale for course assignments and assessments; have students be responsible for bringing additional material to the class; tie grades to learning objectives; and provide both summative and formation evaluations of learning.
Embedded explanations	Throughout your syllabus explain to students why you are asking them to do the required activities. For example, if you have a writing assignment, explain why the students should do it. What do they get out of the assignment?

Note: These best practices are selected from Cullen and Harris (2009), Parkes and Harris (2002), Slattery and Carlson (2005).

There is growing evidence suggesting that teachers should use a student-centered approach to create the model syllabus as a cognitive map and learning tool (Parkes and Harris, 2002; Richmond et al., 2013, 2015). Recall that a student-centered approach puts the student and their learning at center stage rather than the teacher and his or her needs. In order to create a student-centered syllabus, Cullen and Harris (2009) suggest that syllabi should convey instructors'

Course Assignments

MythBusters Analysis: The assignment is designed so that you apply what you have learned in this class to real-world situations. I will explain more about the assignment in class.

Exams: The purpose of the exams is to assess your ability to properly consume research and understand basic concepts in developmental research. You must purchase and bring to class your own Scantron forms (No. 95677) and a #2 pencil. You will have the option of having the multiple-choice portion graded and discussing missed items with me immediately when you hand it in.

(a)

Your Course Assignments ☺

MythBusters Analysis (Student Learning Objectives 1 and 3): This fun and exciting assignment will allow you to observe science in action. By connecting what you have learned in class to real-world problems, you will solidify and reinforce what you have learned. You will watch a short *MythBusters* video clip online and answer several questions in regards to the video. The assignment is designed so that you apply what you have learned in this class to real-world situations.

Opportunities–AKA exams (Student Learning Objectives 3, 4 and 5): The purpose of the opportunities is to assess your ability to properly consume research and understand basic concepts in developmental research. Think of it as your *opportunity* to show me what you have learned! Each of the opportunities could have a series of multiple-choice, true or false, fill in the blank or short answer/essay questions. But I stress depth over breadth, so most of the questions will be focused on application and synthesis of material we have covered in class and in the assigned reading. As it is important to get feedback immediately, you will have the option of having the multiple-choice portion graded and discussing correct and incorrect items when you turn your opportunity in class.

(b)

FIGURE 7.4   (a) An example of a poorly constructed concept map and learning tool syllabus element of embedded explanations for course assignments; (b) An example of a model concept map and learning tool syllabus element of embedded explanations for course assignments.

availability for students (e.g., multiple means of access and open office hours), provide strong learning rational (e.g., rational provided for policies and procedures and tied to student learning outcomes), and encourage collaboration between students (e.g., use of group work). Also, student-centered syllabi should clearly define power and control between students and instructors. One way to do this is to have students responsible for bringing additional knowledge and course information into class (e.g., articles or blogs in popular media that relate to course content). Or you may provide resources available outside of class (e.g., tutoring center). And you should try to focus the syllabus towards achieving student learning objectives (Cullen and Harris, 2009). Finally, student-centered syllabi should include frequent feedback mechanisms (e.g., non-graded quizzes, classroom assessment techniques), policies for encouraging rewriting and redoing, and numerous summative (e.g., comprehensive exam) and formative evaluations of learning (e.g., self and peer-evaluations).

Research supports the importance of taking a student-centered approach to syllabus writing. First, when evaluating peer-reviewed exemplar psychology syllabi, Richmond and colleagues (2013) found that they were predominately student-centered. Between 78 and 99 percent of the syllabi encouraged student collaboration, had well-defined student roles and responsibilities, contained strong learning rationales, tied grades to learning outcomes, provided several feedback mechanisms, and included numerous forms of evaluation of learning. Further, recent research suggests that constructing a student-centered syllabus can influence students' perceptions of teachers (DiClementi and Handelsman, 2005; Richmond et al., 2015). For example, Richmond and colleagues (2015) found that student-centered syllabi can influence perceptions of teachers' model teacher behavioral behaviors (e.g., rapport, approachability, creativity, encouragement, enthusiasm, and flexibility). Additionally, they found that students who received a learner-centered syllabus recalled more elements of the syllabus than students who received an instructor-centered syllabus. Evidence suggests that student-centered syllabi may change student behavior in a class as well. DiClementi and Handelsman (2005) found that when students generated elements of the syllabus such as classroom behavior rules on the first day of class, they had significantly fewer negative class behaviors throughout the semester versus students who had all of the classroom rules imposed by the teacher.

Teachers often think of the syllabus as just a list of dates and policies. However, research is beginning to show that the syllabus can also be an effective cognitive map and learning tool. As such, try to incorporate some of these suggestions into your next syllabus and see how it affects student perceptions of you, the course, and the subject.

The Model Syllabus Requires Planning

Like many great things, evidence suggests that creating model syllabi requires considerable planning (Richmond et al., 2014). There are several ways that teachers can create a model syllabus through explicit course planning. These include the planning of course learning objectives, providing an attractive and readable layout, adapting and changing the syllabus based on student and peer feedback, and organizing the syllabus based on student needs. For a summary description of best practices in planning on writing your syllabus, refer to Table 7.6.

There is ample research that suggests that planning is key to developing model syllabi. First, research suggests that model syllabi require considerable thought about student learning objectives, the instructional methods that will facilitate the learning objectives, and how the learning objectives will be assessed. For instance, Boysen and colleagues (2015) found that 75 percent of

TABLE 7.6 Best Practices for Planning a Model Syllabus

Syllabus elements	Best practices
Course goals and learning objectives	When writing course goals and objectives, think about how they will be evaluated and directly link them to course assignments. Also, link assignments and activities to course learning objectives.
Attractive and readable layout	Carefully consider the font type, size, and style in your syllabus. Use pictures and appropriate humor (e.g., comic strips), headings, borders, shading, and other layout features when designing your model syllabus.
Changes based on student and peer feedback	Strategically organize your syllabus based on what students frequently need in the syllabus (e.g., course calendar, grade distribution, grading policies, late policies) so that they can easily find them. Also, consider the level of the course. That is, a first-year course or general studies course syllabus may highlight the culture of higher education (e.g., how to act appropriately in a class) more than a senior-level course.
Syllabus organization	Each time you teach the course, ask students and fellow teachers to comment on the readability and layout. The following semester that you teach this course, improve your syllabus by incorporating both peer and student feedback.

Note: These best practices are selected from Garavalia et al. (2000); Johnson (2006); Ludwig et al. (2011); Richmond et al. (2015); Slattery and Carlson (n.d., 2005).

teachers reported linking course goals to learning activities, 76 percent linked course goals to evaluations of learning, and 80 percent linked them to course assignments As described previously and in Chapter 6, model teachers should be able to connect every learning objective to specific assignments, learning activities, and evaluations (Ludwig et al., 2011; Slattery and Carlson, n.d., 2005); as such, the model teacher's syllabus reflects this intentional course planning.

Second, keep in mind that model syllabi tend to be attractive and readable (Parkes et al., 2003; Slattery and Carlson, n.d., 2005), so plan to incorporate these elements into your syllabus. For instance Richmond and colleagues (2015) discovered that when a syllabus used more pictures, stylized font, and humor, students viewed the teacher as exhibiting more model teacher characteristics (e.g., rapport, approachability, flexibility) than the teacher who had a plain syllabus. However, a highly stylized syllabus format can contradict discipline-specific professional writing. Therefore, choosing which elements to stylize will largely depend on your academic discipline. Walking the thin line between being a professional and a cool teacher is always difficult.

Finally, organization is key to a model syllabus (Slattery and Carlson, 2005). When organizing your syllabus, it is important to consider the students' perspective (Garavalia et al., 2000). Garavalia and colleagues found that students viewed descriptions of grading and assignments to be the most important elements of a syllabus, whereas faculty viewed these elements as less important. They suggested that teachers would better serve students if the organization of syllabi reflected students' perceptions of what elements are important. Studies consistently find that students revisit the syllabus calendar (e.g., due dates, schedule, assigned readings) and grading policies more than any other part of the syllabus (Becker and Calhoon, 1999; Smith and Razzouk, 1993). Therefore, having these elements strategically placed in the syllabus with easy access may better serve your students. Additionally, Becker and Calhoon (1999) found that students in lower-division courses (e.g., first-year and sophomore) rely more heavily on descriptions of assignments, support services, and academic dishonesty than students in upper-division courses (e.g., junior and senior). Thus, the organization of the syllabus should also factor in the level of the course.

Teachers should consider the structure and order in which students should learn course material (Slattery and Carlson, 2005). Often, in college and university courses, the content needs to build upon itself. For instance, in a college algebra course, typically students are not taught trigonometry before learning about multiplication of polynomials. Therefore, teachers might demonstrate mastery of planning through their course schedules by providing detailed and concise step-by-step schedules. The moral of the story is that when planning to organize your syllabus, consider the student perspectives, what they will likely pay attention to, and the order in which it is best for them to learn.

How Do You Get Your Students to Read and Retain the Syllabus?

As a teacher-scholar, you've now invested considerable time and energy, lost hair, gained weight, and acquired a plethora of other maladies while developing an outstanding model syllabus. How do you ensure that all of your hard work is not wasted? How do you, in fact, get students to read and retain the information you have so laboriously included in the syllabus? Evidence suggests that if you employ a few key strategies, your students not only read the syllabus, they will understand it!

First, test students' knowledge of the syllabus. Raymark and Connor-Greene (2002) found that students required to complete a syllabus quiz knew more about the course and course policies than students who were not required to complete the quiz. However, the quiz should not be purely factual (e.g., The cumulative exam is due when?). Instead, Raymark and Connor-Greene suggest that if you want students to understand and remember your syllabus, you should design a quiz that asks students to answer questions that are typically posed to the instructor. For example, students would have to determine what the syllabus says about whether it is possible to meet with you outside of regularly scheduled office hours? or "Wendy overslept on the day of her first exam. Now she wants to know why you've chosen your particular make-up exam policy" (Raymark and Connor-Greene, 2002, p. 287). Moral of the story: When you assess students on the syllabus early in the semester, they will know how to use the syllabus to answer questions later in the semester.

Second, use communication strategies to make the syllabus more appealing and memorable to students. Thompson (2007) suggests there are several communication strategies to assist you in this endeavor. First, use welcoming strategies when going over the syllabus in class. Strategies include getting acquainted via ice-breakers, stressing your willingness to help, selling the course by pointing out the skills that they will learn, and by using inclusive language (see Table 1 in Thompson, 2007, p. 59, for a complete list). Thompson also suggests that teachers should address students' anxieties about the course, minimize the emphasis on arbitrary rules, and give students choices about course policy when appropriate (see Table 2 in Thompson, 2007, p. 62, for a complete list). Thompson goes on to suggest that reading straight from the syllabus and covering every minute detail should be avoided. Rather, highlight only specific elements of the syllabus and focus students' attention through technology (e.g., PPT, iClickers). Sometimes how you present and attempt to communicate the syllabus will determine how students remember and perceive both you as the teacher and the syllabus.

Third, often the syllabus is discussed on the first day, then put on the proverbial shelf to collect dust. Rather than view the syllabus as a one-shot discussion, research has demonstrated that if you revisit the syllabus (e.g., spend ten minutes in your class to go over student learning objectives and how they are assessed or ethical/plagiarism policies) midway through the semester, students will remember these policies better (Smith and Razzouk, 1993) and follow the syllabus better.

Finally, take control of students' attention to focus it on the sections of the syllabus that you want to emphasize. Students will read and focus on certain aspects of the syllabus without prompting from you (e.g., calendar, grading; Calhoon and Becker, 2008; Smith and Razzouk, 1993), so you should focus your efforts on the elements of the syllabus they tend to ignore. For instance, Smith and Razzouk (1993) found that only 8 percent of students could recall two student learning objectives from their course syllabus (yikes!). So, if connecting student learning objectives to course assignments is important to you, then emphasize this aspect of the course over, say, the grading scale. This rule may apply to any element of the syllabus you believe is important. Another strategy centers on the psychological phenomena known as primacy and recency effects. Often we remember things at the beginning (recency) and at the end of lists (primacy). So, you may want to strategically place items in your syllabus that you want students to remember in these locations. For example, one of us creates syllabi in which the first page always contains the course learning goals and the last page always contains a detailed course schedule; that way, recency will focus students' attention on what they are doing in the class and primacy will focus them on what they should be learning. Along the same lines, descriptions of major assignments start with the learning objectives and end with grading details that students often forget (e.g., late penalties). So remember, just as the organization of the course should affect what students learn, so does the way you organize your syllabus.

In sum, it is extremely important that your students read the syllabus. As we have discussed, there are several methods you can use to cajole your students to read and retain your syllabus. First, test students' ability to actually use the syllabus in practical situations. Second, create welcoming strategies like ice-breakers, send your syllabus out prior to class, and only cover highlighted and often misinterpreted sections on the first day of class. And third, organize your syllabus in such a way that places extremely important information (e.g., course calendar or grading policies) at the beginning and end of the syllabus because this is likely to be what students will remember.

CASE STUDY REEXAMINED: AN OFFER SHE CAN'T REFUSE

So, what should Jocelyn do? How did you answer the questions from the case study at the beginning of the chapter? Based on best practices in syllabus construction, here are our recommendations:

1. *If you were Jocelyn's supervisor, what would you advise her to do?* We would advise her to seek out advice from other teachers who have often taught this course. They are a great resource and can be immensely helpful. Also, politely ask them for a copy of their syllabus for the course. This could be a great starting point from which she could develop her own syllabus. We would also advise her to make the syllabus her own and to inject pieces of her personality into the syllabus (e.g., write in a friendly and supportive tone) and play to her strengths as a teacher.

2. *Based on the description of the syllabus, what elements are missing?* Hmm... where to start? There are many elements missing. First, there needs to be the contract syllabus elements of a course calendar/schedule, attendance policies, late assignment policies, and policies on revising and redoing work. She needs to include permanent-record elements such as learning objectives and details about how she will evaluate student learning. As a communication device, she needs to include elements such as her teaching philosophy and behavioral expectations. As for the syllabus as a cognitive map and learning tool, she should develop tips on how to succeed and provide information on campus learning resources (e.g., writing center).

3. *How would you change the syllabus to reflect your teaching style and expectations?* We would include our own teaching philosophy that communicates the culture of the class. We would list both student expectations for the class behavior along with corresponding expectations of our behavior for the class. We would incorporate our personality by balancing humor with professionalism. We would include detailed descriptions of the student learning objectives and tie them to the assignments that evaluate them.

A Reflection on Your Self-Assessment

After completing the self-assessment in Table 7.1 and reading this chapter, how do you feel about your own syllabus? What are you currently doing that reflects best practices in syllabus construction outlined throughout the chapter? What elements of your syllabus need the most work? Much like the three of us (and Jocelyn), you were likely strong in some areas yet needed to improve in other areas of model syllabus construction. Therefore, once you have identified the areas for improvement, you need to come up with a plan of action for modifying your syllabus. Hopefully, some of the suggestions we've made throughout this chapter will help you in this process and endeavor of constructing model syllabi for your courses.

Summary of Best Practices

Even though each syllabus can be as diverse as the teacher who made it, we have outlined some evidence-based standards by which model teachers can construct their syllabi. Below you will find a brief summary of key points to consider when designing a model syllabus.

- One of the most important purposes of a syllabus is to *define the relationship and responsibilities between you and your students.* To accomplish this task, include clear and concise policies on grading, late assignments, academic dishonesty, ADA compliance, and attendance.
- Remember, as a *permanent record*, your syllabus is not just read by you and your students. Rather, it is used by many constituencies across academia for various official purposes. To achieve transparency, be sure that you accurately list the course information, textbook, learning objectives, and evaluation procedures.
- Your syllabus is your first *communication device*. As such, be sure to communicate who you are as a teacher, what you expect of students, what students should expect of you, and how students can best communicate with you. Finally, tone, tone, tone. Remember to write your syllabus in a friendly, positive, supportive, and rewarding tone. Your students will thank you.

- Remember that your syllabus is a *cognitive map and learning tool*. Provide suggestions for how students can succeed and the common pitfalls students can avoid. Direct them to campus resources that they can utilize to improve learning in your class and in general. Create your syllabus with the perspective of the student in mind (i.e., student-centered focus) by incorporating choice and autonomy.

- Thorough and thoughtful *planning is required to construct a model syllabus*. Slow down and think about the goals for your course and how you can best use instructional methods to achieve these goals. Constantly seek feedback from both students and peers to improve your syllabus. Organize the syllabus in a way that will focus students' attention on the most important information.

- Finally, *test students' ability to use the syllabus* early in the class if you want students to remember and use the syllabus later in the class.

The Very Busy People Book Club: Your Top Five Must-Reads

Grunert O'Brien, J., Millis, B. J., and Cohen, M. W. (2009). *The course syllabus: A learning-centered approach* (2nd edn). San Francisco, CA: John Wiley & Sons.

Nilson, L. B. (2010). *Teaching at its best: A research-based resource for college instructors*. San Francisco, CA: John Wiley & Sons.

Nilson, L. B. (2009). *The graphic syllabus and the outcomes map: Communicating your course*. San Francisco, CA: John Wiley & Sons.

O'Brien, J. G., Millis, B. J., and Cohen, M. W. (2008). *The course syllabus: A learning-centered approach* (2nd edn). San Francisco, CA: John Wiley & Sons.

Roberts, M. (2013). Creating a dynamic syllabus: A strategy for course assessment. *College Teaching*, 61(3), 109–110.

References

Albers, C. (2003). Using the syllabus to document the scholarship of teaching. *Teaching Sociology*, 31, 60–72.

American Psychological Association (2010). *Ethical principles of psychologists and code of conduct*. Retrieved from www.apa.org/ethics/code/principles.pdf.

Bain, K. (2004). *What the best college teachers do*. Cambridge, MA: Harvard University Press.

Becker, A. H. and Calhoon, S. K. (1999). What introductory psychology students attend to on a course syllabus. *Teaching of Psychology*, 26, 6–11.

Boysen, G. A., Richmond, A. S., and Gurung, R. A. R. (2015). Model Teaching Criteria for psychology: Initial documentation of teachers' self-reported competency. *Scholarship of Teaching and Learning in Psychology*, 1, 48–59.

Calhoon, S. and Becker, A. (2008). How students use the course syllabus. *International Journal for the Scholarship of Teaching and Learning*, 2(1), 1–12.

Cullen, R. and Harris, M. (2009). Assessing learner-centredness through course syllabi. *Assessment & Evaluation in Higher Education*, 34(1), 115–125.

DiClementi, J. D. and Handelsman, M. M. (2005). Empowering students: Class-generated course rules. *Teaching of Psychology*, 32, 18–21.

Garavalia, L., Hummel, J., Wiley, L., and Huitt, W. (2000). Constructing the course syllabus: Faculty and student perceptions of important syllabus components. *Journal of Excellence in College Teaching*, 10(1), 5–22.

Habanek, D. V. (2005). An examination of the integrity of the syllabus. *College Teaching*, 53(2), 62–64.

Harnish, R. J. and Bridges, K. R. (2011). Effect of syllabus tone: students' perceptions of instructor and course. *Social Psychology of Education*, 14(3), 319–330.

Homa, N., Hackathorn, J., Brown, C. M., Garczynski, A., Solomon, E. D., Tennial, R., Sanborn, .U. A., and Gurung, R. A. R. (2013). An analysis of learning objectives and content coverage in introductory psychology syllabi. *Teaching of Psychology*, 40, 169–174.

Ishiyama, J. T. and Hartlaub, S. (2002). Does the wording of syllabi affect student course assessment in introductory political science classes? *Political Science & Politics*, 35(3), 567–570.

Johnson, C. (2006). Best practices in syllabus writing: Contents of a learner-centered syllabus. *Journal of Chiropractic Education*, 20, 139–144.

Keeley, J., Furr, R. M., and Buskist, W. (2009). Differentiating psychology students' perceptions of teachers using the teacher behavior checklist. *Teaching of Psychology*, 37, 16–20.

Landrum, R. E. (2011). Faculty perceptions concerning the frequency and appropriateness of student behaviors. *Teaching of Psychology*, 38, 269–272.

Landrum, R. E. and Stowell, J. R. (2013). The reliability of student ratings of master teacher behaviors. *Teaching of Psychology*, 40, 300–303.

Ludwig, M. A., Bentz, A. E., and Fynewever, H. (2011). Your syllabus should set the stage for assessment for learning. *Journal of College Science Teaching*, 40(4), 20–23.

Matejka, K. and Kurke, L. B. (1994). Designing a great syllabus. *College Teaching*, 42(3), 115–117.

Parkes, J. and Harris, M. B. (2002). The purposes of a syllabus. *College Teaching*, 50(2), 55–61.

Parkes, J., Fix, T. K., and Harris, M. B. (2003). What syllabi communicate about assessment in college classrooms. *Journal on Excellence in College Teaching*, 14(1), 61–83.

Perrine, R. M., Lisle, J., and Tucker, D. L. (1995). Effects of a syllabus offer of help, student age, and class size on college students' willingness to seek support from faculty. *Journal of Experimental Education*, 64(1), 41–52.

Raymark, P. H. and Connor-Greene, P. A. (2002). The syllabus quiz. *Teaching of Psychology*, 29(4).

Richmond, A. S., Morgan, R. K., Slattery, J., and Venzke, B. (2013). *How learner-centered are project syllabus syllabi?* A poster presented at the annual convention of the American Psychological Association, Honolulu.

Richmond, A. S., Boysen, G. A., Gurung, R. A. R., Tazeau, Y. N., Meyers, S. A., and Sciutto, M. J. (2014). Aspirational Model Teaching Criteria for psychology. *Teaching of Psychology*, 41, 281–295.

Richmond, A. S., Becknell, J., Slattery, J., Morgan, R., and Mitchell, N. (2015). *Students' perceptions of a student-centered syllabus: An experimental analysis.* Poster presented at the annual meeting of the American Psychological Association, Toronto.

Robinson Wolf, Z., Czekanski, K. E., and Dillon, P. M. (2013). Course syllabi: Components and outcomes assessment. *Journal of Nursing Education and Practice*, 4(1), 100–107.

Saville, B. K., Zinn, T. E., Brown, A. R., and Marchuk, K. A. (2010). Syllabus detail and students' perceptions of teacher effectiveness. *Teaching of Psychology*, 37, 186–189.

Slattery, J. M. and Carlson, J. F. (n.d.). *Guidelines for preparing exemplary syllabi*. Retrieved from http://teachpsych.org/otrp/syllabi/guidelines.php.

Slattery, J. M. and Carlson, J. F. (2005). Preparing an effective syllabus: Current best practices. *College Teaching*, 53, 159–164.

Smith, M. F. and Razzouk, N. Y. (1993). Improving classroom communication: The case of the course syllabus. *Journal of Education for Business*, 68(4), 215–221.

Sulik, G. and Keys, J. (2014). "Many students really do not yet know how to behave!" The syllabus as a tool for socialization. *Teaching Sociology*, 42, 151–160.

Thompson, B. (2007). The syllabus as a communication document: Constructing and presenting the syllabus. *Communication Education*, 56(1), 54–71.

Wilson, J. H. and Ryan, R. G. (2013). Professor–student rapport scale six items predict student outcomes. *Teaching of Psychology*, 40, 130–133.

8

HOW DO MODEL TEACHERS USE STUDENT EVALUATIONS?

At one of our colleges, the topic of grade inflation recently emerged as a concern—an "average" grade of C is now seen as well below average by many teachers and students. In response, the faculty formed subcommittees, performed research, and debated policies. It is likely that inflated evaluations of students have led to similar discussions on your campus. Have you ever encountered similar debate about inflated evaluations of *teachers*? We haven't either. Much like our students, however, teachers seem to all be above average.

Consider Sears's (1983) examination of end-of-semester student evaluations of teaching at the University of California Los Angeles (UCLA). The study took place across four school years, incorporated more than 40 academic departments, and included nearly a third of a million student evaluations. UCLA's end-of-semester surveys asked students to rate their teachers using a nine-point scale with five representing *average* and higher scores being more positive. Average, at least among UCLA professors in the 1970s, was 7.22 on this scale—the average teacher was above average! Sears's findings appear to hold up well; on the campus that recently debated grade inflation, the average teacher receives a nearly perfect student evaluation rating of 4.5 on a four-point scale. Give these trends, do such evaluations have any useful meaning? Can they be used to improve teaching? These are some of the questions we hope to answer in this chapter.

The phrase "student evaluations of teaching" has a fairly specific meaning in the college and university teaching literature. These varied measures consist of students rating a teacher's performance for the dual purpose of (1) improving teaching and (2) informing administrative judgments regarding tenure, promotion, and raises (Cohen, 1980; Spooren et al., 2013). The current chapter will emphasize summative student evaluations of teaching; these are the officially sanctioned evaluations that are administered in every class near the end of the semester.

We place special emphasis on these evaluations because of their importance, ubiquity, and voluminous research literature. However, feedback from students can be gathered informally any time the teacher needs it; this type of formative student evaluation of teaching also plays an important role in model teaching and will be covered in some detail as well. For both types of evaluations, we will outline an evidence-based approach to gathering feedback, analyzing it, and translating the results into improved teaching practices.

Student evaluations of teaching are, arguably, the most contentious topic in this entire book, and it is important to defuse that tension right away. We'll try flattery first—it is pretty awesome that students like us so much! We would like to officially pat you, our colleagues, and ourselves on the back for earning such high average student evaluations. If you are reading this book, we suspect that your teaching evaluations fall well above the midpoint of whatever scale is used to evaluate your teaching. Now, to appease the critics, we will point out that it is more than a little silly to think that the average teacher is above average (Halonen et al., 2012). Clearly, student evaluations cannot define teaching effectiveness on their own. Given the good news–bad news dynamic that has already emerged in this chapter, you can start to sense our pragmatic approach. We treat student evaluations as imperfect measures of teaching effectiveness that, nonetheless, need to be taken seriously. Let's begin with an honest self-assessment. Are you taking student evaluations seriously enough? Complete the self-evaluation (Table 8.1) to get a sense of your consistency with model teaching practices.

TABLE 8.1 Self-Assessment of the Model Teaching Criteria of Student Evaluation of Teaching

Directions: Please indicate on the scale below how often you incorporate these elements/activities to improve your student evaluation of teaching. *Scale: 5 = Always, 4 = Often, 3 = Sometimes, 2 = Rarely, 1 = Never*	*Your score*
1. You regularly solicit summative feedback from students.	
2. You regularly solicit formative feedback from students.	
3. You interpret student evaluations using valid quantitative and qualitative data analysis procedures.	
4. You set goals for the improvement of teaching based on student feedback.	
5. You incorporate student feedback into syllabus revisions.	
6. You incorporate student feedback into changes in course material.	
7. You incorporate student feedback into changes to lesson plans.	
8. You incorporate student feedback into changes in your teaching methods.	

Note: This self-assessment is adapted and modified from Boysen et al. (2015) and Richmond et al. (2014).

CASE STUDY: GARBAGE IN, GARBAGE OUT?

Dr. Olsen is an over-achieving assistant professor of marketing who is just a few years away from going up for tenure. Always wanting to stay ahead of the game, Dr. Olsen made an appointment to speak with her department chair so that she could ask about progress in terms of research, teaching, and service. The chair had glowing remarks about research and service but also said that Dr. Olsen had better "turn things around" in terms of teaching. Shocked, Dr. Olsen asked what the problem was. "Well, you are way below the department averages in terms of your overall ratings. Also, the comments from Advanced Marketing last semester were pretty devastating." Dr. Allan had to admit, she had barely thought about her evaluations because they seem fine to her.

The student evaluation survey administered by Dr. Olsen was not very complex because the Marketing Department had created a new, streamlined survey a few years ago. Teachers administered the survey on the last day of the semester in all of their courses. The survey consisted of just four questions.

Student Evaluation of Teaching Form

Please think about the semester overall in this course and grade your experience using an A to F scale. Then, provide any additional comments that you may have.

1. ＿＿＿ Overall grade for the instructor
2. ＿＿＿ Overall grade for the course
3. ＿＿＿ Overall amount that you learned in this course compared to other courses
4. Additional comments: ＿＿＿＿＿＿＿＿＿＿＿＿＿＿＿＿＿＿＿＿＿＿＿

＿＿＿＿＿＿＿＿＿＿＿＿＿＿＿＿＿＿＿＿＿＿＿＿＿＿＿＿＿＿＿＿＿＿＿＿＿＿＿

＿＿＿＿＿＿＿＿＿＿＿＿＿＿＿＿＿＿＿＿＿＿＿＿＿＿＿＿＿＿＿＿＿＿＿＿＿＿＿

＿＿＿＿＿＿＿＿＿＿＿＿＿＿＿＿＿＿＿＿＿＿＿＿＿＿＿＿＿＿＿＿＿＿＿＿＿＿＿

When the survey's grading scale was converted to numbers ($F = 0$, $A = 4$), Dr. Olsen's average instructor rating was 3.03, and her average course rating was 3.10. The averages in her department for those items were 3.33 and 3.20, respectively. In the Advanced Marketing course, eight out of 20 students provided comments, and they can be seen below.

Student Comments

* I know that Dr. Olsen has only been here a few years, but she is clearly not working out in this department. The other teachers set high

standards for their teaching but Dr. Olsen does not set the same standards for herself. I had her for intro too, and that was just as bad. I think she does not know the material very well herself and cannot teach it well to others. Students just do not have the same opportunity to learn with her. As far as I am concerned, the students were cheated by having Dr. Olsen teach this class rather than Dr. Fox.

- This class should not be required—don't need this information in the real world or in internships.
- Not that interested in the subject, but the class was OK. Good teacher.
- Needs to give more examples during lecture and also a sample of the paper. Other than that, good teacher.
- Good teacher. She gave me a lot of help with the research paper, which was hard.
- Good class. Lots of lecture. Paper was hard.
- I learned quite a bit, especially from the paper.
- The paper assignment is a waste of time. Can't believe I got a C after all that work.

1. *How would you evaluate the Marketing Department's student evaluation survey?*
2. *How should Dr. Olsen interpret her evaluation means?*
3. *How should Dr. Olsen interpret the open-ended comments from students?*

Zombies and Critiques of Student Evaluation Validity: Things That Won't Die

In a widely circulated critique of student evaluations of teaching that was even picked up in the popular press (Kamenetz, 2014), Stark and Freishtat (2014) offered the frank summary that student evaluations "do not measure teaching effectiveness" (p. 19). A full review of validity research on student evaluations of teaching is both beyond the scope of the current chapter and adequately covered by previous authors (d'Apollonia and Abrami, 1997; Marsh, 2007b; Marsh and Roche, 1997; Spooren et al., 2013). Nonetheless, some discussion of validity is necessary because it would be pointless to establish model teaching practices based on measures so easily dismissed as being unrelated to teaching effectiveness.

The psychometric properties of student evaluations can be illustrated using the analogy of a bathroom scale. When getting on and off a scale repeatedly, it should, no matter how pleasing or frightening the result may be, give the same measurement of weight; this represents the scale's reliability. Similarly, student evaluations of teaching should, broadly speaking, be repeatable; results should not be wildly different when assessing the same teacher in the same class on different occasions.

Reliability is absolutely essential for good measurement, but, frankly, nobody is worried about the reliability of teaching evaluations; it is a nonissue because constructing reliable measures is fairly straightforward. Validity, on the other hand, is a trickier issue.

Let's return to the bathroom scale. When a scale gives the wrong weight, it lacks validity. For example, imagine that a scale gave the same wrong weight over and over again. Or, imagine that the readout was somehow reversed and heavy people yielded low weights and light people yielded high weights. In fact, this analogy gets to the heart of some people's main criticism of student evaluations. Namely, some believe that "bad" teachers who offer courses that are "lightweight" intellectually in terms of work and grading become popular and, thus, receive high evaluations. The logic continues that low evaluations are reserved for "good" teachers who are unpopular due to the heavy intellectual lifting required by their courses (Krautman and Sander, 1999; Redding, 1998). We will examine the evidence for this claim later, but the main point is that critics of student evaluations believe that they lack validity; something is being measured, but it is not (at least not primarily) teaching effectiveness.

What do student evaluations measure, if not teaching effectiveness? Establishing the validity of a psychological measure involves subjectivity that can lead to different interpretations—for example, there is still disagreement about what IQ tests measure after more than a century of research on the topic. The essential problem with assessing mental constructs is that measurement can only occur indirectly and, thus, validity relies upon arguments about what, for example, IQ tests or student evaluations should predict. Student evaluations, if they are valid, should predict other measures of teaching effectiveness such as student learning or the evaluations of experts.

Research shows that standardized student evaluation surveys do indeed correlate with a long list of other measures related to teaching effectiveness. Correlates include ratings made by alumni, the favorability of students' written comments, students' scores on standardized final examinations, self-evaluations made by teachers, evaluations made by experts, and repeated evaluations of the same instructor over time spans as long as one decade (Marsh, 2007b). Although the correlations between student evaluations and these measures tend to be moderate at best, research has failed to produce an alternative that functions as a better predictor of teaching-related competencies.

What about the claim that making a class easy is the sure way to become popular and influence evaluations? Research does indicate that students pan courses that are too hard, but they also dislike courses that are too easy (Centra, 2003; Martin et al., 2008). There seems to be a sweet spot for academic rigor. Students do not want courses with impossibly high grading or work standards—no one likes to feel like a failure. At the same time, students also hate to waste time and money on courses that are an academic joke. Where the sweet spot for rigor falls undoubtedly differs by student, discipline, institution, and course; however, it is overly simplistic to assert that making a course easier will uniformly increase student evaluations. Student evaluations seem to relate to how much students feel they got out of the course.

In fact, how much students get out of the course in terms of learning must be considered the ultimate test of student evaluation validity. Meta-analysis—the combination of many studies' results into one overall result—indicates that teachers' student evaluations do have a positive, if small, correlation with student learning (Clayson, 2009). However, there seem to be many factors that cause the correlation to increase or decrease. Consider the complex picture painted by the following study. Researchers examined learning among 839 medical students who were randomly assigned to one of 32 different sections of a surgery course (Stehle et al., 2012). Measures of learning included a standardized multiple-choice test and a standardized clinical examination in which the students had to demonstrate relevant medical skills. Student evaluations consisted of measures of overall teacher quality, overall course quality, and subjective perception of learning. Each of these three student evaluation measures shared a large, significant correlation (0.53 to 0.57) with performance on the clinical examination, but they were unrelated to the multiple-choice test (-0.07 to -0.06). This study illustrates two important summary points: Good evidence does exist for the relation between learning and student evaluations, and measurement of teaching effectiveness is too complex to reduce to a terse all-or-nothing statement.

Let's imagine that some critics are unconvinced by the extensive validity data surrounding student evaluations of teaching (this is true, by the way). What is the worst possible thing the critics could legitimately say about the surveys? They might argue that student evaluations are simply satisfaction surveys—no doubt you can imagine the derision with which critics spit out the word *satisfaction*. Even if the assertion about satisfaction were true, it might not be so bad. Do you want students to be satisfied with your teaching and your courses? Model teachers do. As such, they solicit feedback from students and use the results to improve their teaching.

Asking for the Truth: Collecting Student Evaluations

Aside from certain aspects of syllabus construction, no other aspect of model teaching is more likely to be rigidly dictated by university policy than student evaluations of teaching. The administration of end-of-semester, summative student evaluations has become a universal ritual on college campuses (Spooren et al., 2013). In that sense, teachers generally have no say concerning the fact that official student evaluations are associated with their classes. However, teachers may have some say in the method of administration, especially for online evaluations. In contrast, formative student evaluations occur unofficially and consist of the myriad of ways teachers solicit opinions from students during the semester in order to make midcourse adjustments; teachers have complete control over designing formative student evaluations to meet their specific needs. Model teachers make frequent use of both types of student evaluations.

This is the End: Summative Student Evaluations

Summative student evaluations come at the end of each term in the form of a paper or online survey. The survey is typically standardized so that teachers can be compared to some criterion of quality—be it implicit or explicit. As part of that standardization, there are often rules set by the college for survey administration. Tempting as it may be to manipulate students into giving you a good rating through bribery, bring your delicious baked goods to class on some other day. After all, what good will biased data be in helping you improve your teaching? Furthermore, the increasing reliance on online surveys may soon make such chicanery obsolete.

Despite much hand-wringing among faculty, the gradual shift from paper to online surveys does not seem to have resulted in a reduction in the quality of student evaluation feedback. As is the case with any educational intervention, students are significantly more likely to complete evaluations when they are placed directly in their hands during class time. Research on the topic indicates that response rate for paper surveys range from about 50–80 percent, and online surveys range from 30–60 percent (Benton et al., 2010; Nulty, 2008). Whatever the actual percentage, online response rates are consistently lower (as you will soon see, however, that does not need to be the case). Fortunately, the lower response rate of online evaluations does not seem to affect the numerical ratings assigned to teachers (Fike et al., 2010; Guder and Malliaris, 2010). Nonetheless, receiving comments from as many students as possible is desirable—even a single comment might lead to inspiration for improvement. In terms of student comments, online evaluations have the advantage. Students can type out responses to online surveys on their own time, and this appears to increase the richness of their comments (Guder and Malliaris, 2010).

Response rates of 30 percent for online surveys may seem unacceptably low, but the good news is that response rates can be increased by doing something, just about anything in fact, to get buy-in from students. For example, response rates can be boosted by offering reminders, giving in-class demonstrations of how to access the survey website, and providing incentives (Dommeyer et al., 2004; Nulty, 2008). In fact, one study found that offering an incentive as small as one-quarter of 1 percent of the final course grade led to a response rate of 87 percent (Dommeyer et al., 2004). In our own classes, we obtain 95–100 percent response rates by methods such as (1) mentioning the survey several times in class, (2) conveying the usefulness of student feedback to course revision, and (3) offering very small grade incentives. It is important to note that both the authors and their institutions have different policies about using grades as an incentive to boost response rates. Some view it as coercive; others believe using incentives is ethical because the resultant high response rates ultimately benefit students. Thus, be sure to determine if there are applicable rules at your school before implementing incentives.

As a member of the assessment committee on campus, one of us has occasionally had to inform the college faculty that specific student evaluation items were being altered or retired all together. A common response seems to be "I use that information—I really want it to stay in the survey!" Kudos, of course, to any teacher using feedback from student evaluations, but what these teachers seem to miss is that the official student evaluations are just one possible source of feedback from students, and there is nothing preventing them from asking any and all questions that they deem important. Many teachers fail to consider that they can and should be gathering their own feedback from students. In fact, a really smart teacher might distribute the exact end-of-semester teaching evaluation at midterm and ask students "What do I need to do better?" That would be an example of formative evaluation.

We've Only Just Begun: Formative Student Evaluations

Model teachers solicit both summative and formative feedback from students. Unlike summative evaluations, teachers can completely dictate the administration and uses of formative evaluations. What should this type of formative feedback look like? Lewis (2001b) described the following characteristics as typical of high-quality formative student feedback. First, formative evaluations are ongoing; there should be a continual process of soliciting feedback and making progressive improvements. Second, formative feedback can focus on any teaching topic of value (e.g., lecture quality, assignment clarity, course difficulty). They do not have to follow the rigid structures of standardized student evaluation surveys. Third, and perhaps most important, formative feedback is for personal, professional development. Teachers should design formative feedback so that they can improve their teaching skills (see Chapter 4 for ideas on what teaching skills to target)—performance evaluation and competition with other teachers are beside the point.

Methods for collecting formative feedback are only restricted by the imagination and needs of the teacher. To illustrate their flexibility, we will provide a few examples of how to gather feedback about general teaching ability and specific teaching techniques. Beginning with feedback on general teaching ability, teachers can administer standardized student evaluations of teaching any time they desire psychometrically valid, quantitative data. For example, the Teacher Behavior Checklist (reprinted in Chapter 2) allows students to rate their teacher on a number of model teaching practices (Keeley et al., 2006). In addition, the

---

Instructions: Rate your teacher using the scale below.

strongly disagree	disagree	neither disagree nor agree	agree	strongly agree
1	2	3	4	5

1. My professor encourages questions and comments from students
2. I dislike my professor's class★
3. My professor makes class enjoyable
4. I want to take other classes taught by my professor
5. My professor's body language says, "Don't bother me"★
6. I really like to come to class

FIGURE 8.1   Asterisks indicate items that are reverse-scored (i.e., low scores are indicative of high rapport such that 1 = 5, 2 = 4, 3 = 3, 4 = 2, and 5 = 1). The scale items are from the Professor–Student Rapport scale (Wilson and Ryan, 2013).

Student Evaluation of Educational Quality, which is the most researched student evaluation survey in existence, can be found online and used freely (Marsh, 1982, 1983). Both of these evaluation surveys are fairly lengthy. If you want a more focused measure, you could administer the brief Professor–Student Rapport Scale (see Figure 8.1). Although it is short, it still predicts important student outcomes such as perceived learning and course grades (Wilson and Ryan, 2013).

There is no set way to administer surveys when they are part of formative evaluation. They can be administered face-to-face or online. They could also be administered more than once to monitor change (but be aware of survey fatigue). We do suggest keeping them anonymous so that students feel free to be open and honest. In addition, consider waiting to administer general teaching surveys until after the first major test or paper has been graded and returned—that way students have a sense of their actual learning in the course.

If a teacher desires general feedback, but prefers qualitative to quantitative data, there are even more techniques at their disposal. The classroom assessment techniques outlined in Chapter 6 can also focus on teaching skills (Angelo and Cross, 1993). For example, minute papers, rather than assessing what students have learned, can be refocused on gathering student perceptions of pedagogy. One method that we have found helpful is to ask students the following four questions.

- What is the instructor doing that is helping you learn?
- What is the instructor doing that is *not* helping you learn?
- What are you, as a student, doing that is helping you learn?
- What are you, as a student, doing that is *not* helping you learn?

Please provide me with feedback about today's class. Circle the response that best reflects your opinion.

1.   How engaged were you during today's class?
     totally disengaged   somewhat disengaged   somewhat engaged   totally engaged

2.   How clear were the learning objectives for today's class?
     totally unclear   somewhat unclear   somewhat clear   totally clear

3.   How many of the learning objectives did you fully comprehend today?
     none   some   most   all

4.   How useful was today's class?
     not at all   somewhat   very   extremely

FIGURE 8.2 A formative evaluation technique focused on gathering information about students' perceptions of one class period. This survey is adapted from Angelo and Cross (1993).

What is particularly powerful about the procedure is that it models for students how to provide useful feedback to teachers by emphasizing learning, improvement, and shared responsibility for outcomes. Once again, we suggest collecting responses anonymously using paper or online survey tools. After compiling the frequency of responses, the teacher should go over the results with the class. Explain what action will be taken, or provide the pedagogical rationale for why certain aspects of the class are essential to learning and should not be changed (You can do that for all aspects of your course, right? If not, apply what you have learned from Chapters 4 through 7 to your courses!).

General feedback can be useful, but teachers sometimes need feedback on specific aspects of their teaching. Some of the methods already outlined can be easily modified for that purpose. For example, teachers could create surveys related to one class or one technique (see Figure 8.2).

Of course, the same information can also be solicited using open-ended questions rather than rating scales. For example, teachers who use the interteaching method (see Chapter 4) have students complete the following questions at the end of class discussions.

- Sufficient time provided [for discussion]?
- Quality of the session (on a scale of 1 = *poor* to 10 = *excellent*):
- Topics that gave difficultly, and the nature of the difficulty (e.g., text was unclear, question was ambiguous):
- Topics you would like covered in class [with lecture]:
- What parts [of the discussion] did you find most interesting?
- If a [discussion] question were to be omitted, which should it be?
- Other comments or suggestions? Please give me feedback.

(Boyce and Hineline, 2002, p. 226)

Based on today's discussion, please honestly rate your performance on these aspects of quality in collaboration.

Preparation for discussion (e.g., did the reading and thought about material before class)

poor	below average	average	above average	superb
1	2	3	4	5

Active listening (e.g., paid attention, tried to understand others, asked for clarification)

poor	below average	average	above average	superb
1	2	3	4	5

Contributions to discussion (e.g., shared ideas, moved discussion forward)

poor	below average	average	above average	superb
1	2	3	4	5

FIGURE 8.3 A formative evaluation technique focused on gathering information about students' participation in discussion. This survey is adapted from Angelo and Cross (1993).

Reponses on the survey form the basis of the lecture for the next class and influence the design of later classes; thus, students should be motivated to honestly self-assess what they need the most help with and their satisfaction with various aspects of the class. In addition, students' participation in this process typically counts toward a discussion grade. Although this survey is designed for use in interteaching, it could be easily modified to meet teachers' specific methods and needs.

Formative feedback can also focus on specific classroom activities. The quality of classroom discussion is important to consider, especially for teachers who utilize collaborative learning techniques. To assess students' perceptions of their participation, a brief survey can be administered at the end of class either anonymously or as part of a discussion grade (see Figure 8.3). If a teacher is more concerned with the discussion performance of the class in general, similar questions could be reframed as pertaining to discussion groups rather than individual students (Angelo and Cross, 1993).

Finally, formative assessment can be incorporated directly into existing assignments. For example, questions can be embedded into a quiz or exam (Angelo and Cross, 1993). You might consider adding one or two of the following questions at the end of an exam.

- What did you learn from this test?
- Was there any unexpected material on this test?
- What was something that you expected to see on this test that was not on it?
- If you were going to add one more question to this test, what would it be?

Similar questions could be included as part of just about any assignment. Teachers can make such questions worth no credit, a small amount of required credit, or extra credit. However, be sure to make it clear to the class that there are no right answers to the questions; you do not want students to stress out about finding the right answer or trying to come up with the answer that will stroke the teachers' ego most gratuitously.

In summary, formative assessments are imminently flexible. They can be general or specific, anonymous or named, credit-bearing or not for credit, quantitative or qualitative, student-focused or teacher-focused, and numerous or infrequent. No matter the format, what teachers must keep in mind is that they should only ask for feedback about things that they are willing to change (Angelo and Cross, 1993). After all, the whole purpose of formative assessment is to allow adjustments that improve teaching and learning.

Yes, We are Seriously Going to Talk About RateMyProfessors.com

Google yourself right now. Don't be ashamed, you can tell everyone we made you do it. If you have been teaching for a while, chances are that the first page of results contains a link to an independent, for-profit website offering anonymous evaluations of your teaching ability to anyone with Internet connectivity. RateMyProfessors.com is the most celebrated, and maligned, of these websites due to its inclusion of rating categories such as "easiness" and "hotness." High ratings of hotness earn teachers virtual chili peppers (the authors will let readers do the legwork to figure out if we warrant chili peppers, but we will bask in the glory of fellow psychologist David Daniel who has been rated the hottest professor in America three years running). Despite their limitations, we grudgingly suggest that teachers be aware of what is on these websites.

Why should you pay attention to independent, unsanctioned, and unregulated student evaluations? To begin, like it or not, the information is out there for all to see and use. Indeed, the available evidence suggests that students use the websites and that the information provided can influence their behavior (Davison and Price, 2009; Lewandowski et al., 2012; Kindred and Mohammed, 2005). Furthermore, ratings of teaching quality on the websites appear to be more meaningful than might be expected and can provide some useful information (Addison et al., 2015). For example, high online evaluations in one teaching area predict high online evaluations in other teaching areas (Otto et al., 2008; Sonntag et al., 2009). There is even evidence that website ratings correlate with official university ratings (Sonntag et al., 2009).

Given these characteristics, we suggest that teachers at least be aware of what their ratings are on these websites. If the research is accurate, your online ratings will generally conform to your official evaluations. Thus, you can see it as yet another form of feedback, albeit one that should be interpreted tentatively—especially if the number of responses is low. On the off-chance that your online teaching reputation has been sullied by unrepresentative responses on the websites, you should be aware of that too. Even if nothing can be done to directly change the evaluations, good teachers know the background of their students, and you can be sure that informal rumors about you, online or otherwise, are part of that background.

Interpreting Student Evaluation Scores: More than Reading Tea Leaves

The academe is made up of people with diverse training and talents—one of the authors could leave his office and, within half a minute, knock on the door of faculty members in psychology, English, sociology, religion, communications, Spanish, and history. Given such extensive differences in background, it is rather strange that colleges simply dump raw, statistical reports of student evaluation data into the inboxes of all teachers at the end of each semester. Some teachers know how to analyze data and others do not. Just as problematically, some teachers ignore the analytic expertise they do possess when dealing with student evaluations. Student evaluations are useless or worse if not used correctly; as such, this section will outline some best practices for their interpretation.

Before getting into the rules of interpretation, consider the following scenario. Professor Bellow, who teaches English, heard that you are reading a book on model teaching, and he wants you to take a look at his student evaluations. Professor Bellow's most recent student evaluations can be seen in Figure 8.4. For this evaluation, students rated the courses from one to five with high scores representing more positive evaluations. Once you have looked at Professor Bellow's ratings for English 115, 201, and 302, complete the brief survey pertaining to Professor Bellow's overall performance and his need to improve each specific course. We will return to your evaluation of Professor Bellow later in the chapter, but by way of a preview, were your answers for items 2 through 4 different? If so, you should read the next sections very closely indeed!

At the most basic level, student evaluations are mini research projects conducted on every college class, and this makes them beholden to the rules of survey validity and statistical analysis. When thinking about student evaluations in research terms, the very first consideration is the validity of the survey. Some student evaluation surveys have gone through the rigor of psychometric testing in order to demonstrate their reliability and validity (Richardson, 2005), but many colleges use home-grown surveys that have not been systematically evaluated. If a survey is poorly designed, or even if its validity is simply indeterminate, all bets are off—there is no way to know for sure if the results have meaning or not. Garbage data can only produce garbage results. Teachers must administer valid student evaluation surveys if they want meaningful feedback (Abrami, 2001; Franklin, 2001; Theall and Franklin, 2001).

Student Evaluation Summary and Comparison Mean

Course	My overall effectiveness ratings	Comparison mean: Overall effectiveness rating for my department
	Mean	Mean
ENG 115	4.17	4.31
ENG 201	4.28	
ENG 302	4.02	

Based on the results above, rate your agreement with the following statements.

strongly disagree	moderately disagree	slightly disagree	neither disagree nor agree	slightly agree	moderately agree	strongly agree
1	2	3	4	5	6	7

1. _____ Overall, the instructor appears to be good teacher.
2. _____ The instructor should work on improving ENG 115.
3. _____ The instructor should work on improving ENG 201.
4. _____ The instructor should work on improving ENG 302.

FIGURE 8.4   Fictional student evaluation data for Professor Bellow.

Teachers are left in a difficult position if their college or department uses a student evaluation survey with suspect validity. A good first step would be to consult with someone from the Psychology or Education Department who teaches about testing and measurement; they should be able to provide guidance on the extent to which the survey can be trusted. If the survey is too poor to be trusted, then we suggest administering supplemental surveys with known validity (Richardson, 2005). The previously mentioned Student Evaluation of Educational Quality (SEEQ) stands out as the most highly respected alternative survey. It provides teachers with feedback on the following nine separate factors that map well onto model teaching practices: student learning, enthusiasm, organization, group interaction, individual rapport, breadth of content, examinations, assignments, and overall quality (Marsh, 1982, 1983). A quick search of the Internet will produce numerous versions of the survey already formatted and ready for distribution in classes.

Once a teacher has results from a valid student evaluation survey, the data produced must be interpreted based on the rules of psychometrics and statistics. No doubt, some readers' minds powered down at the mere mention of statistics, but we will try to keep this as painless as possible. Surveys are inherently imperfect. It is never possible to measure people's minds with 100 percent accuracy; a true, perfect score is never produced, and we are always dealing with estimates. Due to error in measurement, even intelligence tests such as Stanford–Binet or Wechsler scales—the very best psychological measures ever created—do not always produce the exact same score if administered twice. As such, the results of student evaluations, most often expressed as means, should not be interpreted as representations of teacher's true scores; they are estimates that must be considered with the interpretive help of statistics.

Because of the wiggle room that results from error in measurement, raw teaching evaluation means should not be interpreted; standard deviations, confidence intervals, and statistical tests must be used as interpretive tools (Abrami, 2001; Boysen et al., 2013; Franklin, 2001). Returning to the case of Professor Bellow, imagine that his overall instructor rating in one class was 4.25 on a five-point scale, and the rating in another class was 4.50. Should he worry about the lower score in the first class? In order to make these raw means meaningful, additional statistical information is needed. To begin, the standard deviation—that is, the average variation of scores from the mean—should be considered. Standard deviations provide some perspective on whether or not differences between means are large or small. Imagine that the standard deviation on the five-point overall instructor rating scale was a whopping 2.00. If that is the case, then the difference between Professor Bellow's means of 4.25 and 4.50 is only one-eighth of a standard deviation, which is a small difference and unlikely to be practically meaningful. However, if the standard deviation was 0.25, the means differ by a full standard deviation, which is a large difference and likely to be meaningful.

Standard deviations are the bluntest instrument of interpretation and should be augmented with confidence intervals (see Franklin, 2001, for instructions on how to compute confidence intervals for student evaluations). Recall that raw means are just estimates of a teacher's true score on a survey. Confidence intervals provide the range of scores that a teacher's true score can be said to fall with a certain level of confidence (typically 95 percent). For example, Professor Bellow's overall instructor evaluation of 4.25 might be said to fall between a score of 3.45 and 4.85 with 95 percent confidence. In a sense, the confidence interval provides guidance on the precision of a mean. The aforementioned confidence interval would not allow a very precise interpretation—the interval is so wide in fact that Professor Bellow's mean could be almost anywhere between the midpoint of the scale and the top of the scale. In contrast, if it could be said with 95 percent confidence that the mean falls between 4.05 and 4.20, that would allow for a much more precise statement that Professor Bellow's score is fairly close to a 4 on the scale.

In terms of interpretation, confidence intervals provide a strong indication of which mean differences should and should not be interpreted. If one mean is within the confidence interval of another, the different is probably not meaningful; however, a teacher's true score on a student evaluation can be said with confidence *not* to include means falling outside of the confidence interval. So, in both of the aforementioned confidence intervals, it can be said with confidence that Professor Bellow's true score is not going to be a 3, and it is also not going to be a 5. Assuming that a score of 5 on the survey indicates a response of *excellent* and a response of 3 indicates a response of *adequate*, Professor Bellow should not be considered excellent, but he should also be considered better than adequate.

Statistical tests are even more precise tools for the interpretation of teaching evaluation means (see Abrami, 2001, for instructions on how to statistically compare student evaluation means). Confidence intervals suggest a potential range of scores, but statistical tests directly determine if the difference between two means is interpretable. A statistical test would say very specifically if the difference between a score of 4.25 and a score of 4.50 is significant. A truism in statistics is that if two means are not different at a statistically significant level, then the difference between them should not be interpreted. In that sense, interpreting differences between raw means is like invading Russia in winter—a classic blunder that should be avoided at all costs.

It is worth noting that some critics question the entire process of interpreting teaching evaluations as means. Some statisticians would argue that responses to Likert scales are actually labels, which prevents them from being used to compute an average (Stark and Freishtat, 2014). To illustrate, you could calculate teachers' average age, but you could not produce an average of their gender—gender is a label. If this is true, the standard method of analyzing student evaluations should be the frequency with which various labels are chosen to describe a teacher (e.g., is a response of *excellent* or *poor* more frequent?).

The statistical fundamentalists may go too far here; about 80 years of psychology research demonstrates that Likert scales can be productively analyzed as means. Nonetheless, the distribution of student evaluation responses is important to consider. If a department average is 4.00, the distribution must be considered to evaluate a mean score of 3.80. If every person in the department gets exactly 4s, then 3.80 might be troublingly low; but if scores are evenly distributed between 3s and 5s, then 3.80 is very close to average (Stark and Freishtat, 2014).

Frequencies can be particularly useful for teachers of small classes where just a few scores can significantly affect the mean. For example, imagine that you are teaching a small seminar class of 15 students. If you received eight responses of *excellent* (5) and seven of *good* (4), the mean would be very respectable 4.53. In contrast, if you had three disgruntled students who give you ratings of *very poor* (1) rather than *good,* the mean drops to a more troubling 3.93. Nonetheless, the most frequent response (i.e., the mode) in both scenarios remains 5—that is, most students found you to be excellent. The lesson here is that frequencies of student evaluation responses can be just as, if not more, informative than means.

Given this review of statistics, let's reconsider Professor Bellow's teaching evaluations. Recall that at the beginning of this section only Professor Bellow's raw teaching means were available. Interpreting differences between raw means

Course	My overall effectiveness ratings		Comparison mean: Overall effectiveness rating for my department		Contrast: My mean vs. the comparison mean at 95% probability
	Mean	95% Confidence Interval	Mean	95% Confidence Interval	
ENG 115	4.17	4.03–4.31	4.31	4.16–4.45	Not significantly different
ENG 201	4.28	4.12–4.50			Not significantly different
ENG 302	4.02	3.89–4.23			Not significantly different

FIGURE 8.5 Fictional student evaluation data for Professor Bellow that is presented in the format suggested by experts (Franklin, 2001).

without further information would be breaking a cardinal rule of statistics and would go against best practices in using student evaluations of teaching (Abrami, 2001; Franklin, 2001). What if you had the additional information presented in Figure 8.5? As illustrated, the confidence intervals between Professor Bellow's means and the departmental mean mostly overlap, and none of the differences are statistically significant. This additional statistical information indicates that no differences between Professor Bellow's student evaluations and the comparison mean should be interpreted; thus, there is no strong reason to believe that one course needs to be revised more than the others.

If you fell into the trap of interpreting small mean differences in teaching evaluations, do not feel bad—you are not alone. Use of raw teaching evaluation means appears to be endemic in higher education. As social scientists, if the authors of this book were serving as peer reviewers of a study that included the interpretation of means without the use of statistics, it would be a kiss of death for that article. However, it is with chagrin that we admit to occasionally using raw data from student evaluation surveys to evaluate our own and others' teaching (invading Russia can be very seductive a times). How does this happen?

Research suggests that teachers and administers interpret student evaluation using the general rule of thumb that higher is better (Boysen et al., 2013; Boysen, 2015a, 2015b). For example, Boysen and colleagues (2013) provided teachers with descriptions of job candidates for teaching positions whose evaluation means differed by less than 0.30 on a five-point scale—too small of a difference to interpret without statistical tests given the typical reliability of teaching evaluations. Participants consistently favored the candidate with higher evaluations. In a second study, department chairs interpreted differences of as small as 0.16 of a point in their evaluations of teachers' need for improvement.

Follow-up research was even more dismal. The inclusion of complete statistical information like that in Figure 8.5 did not reduce faculty members' tendency to over-interpret evaluation means (Boysen, 2015b). Furthermore, even explicit warnings to avoid over-interpretation did nothing to reduce the effects (Boysen, 2015a). The lesson from this research is that teachers must be intentional in their interpretations of student evaluation means and in the monitoring of others' interpretations. As will soon be seen, however, means are not the only data from student evaluations that needs to be treated with care.

Interpreting Written Comments on Student Evaluation of Teaching: Now With 50 Percent Less Crying!

Have you ever had students write a weird, off-topic, or just plain mean comment on your teaching evaluations? We have too.

- "Dr. Boysen dresses like a boss every day of class."
- "You're a good teacher, I just don't like you as a person."
- "Dr. Richmond is nice but not supportive."
- "Professor Richmond is funny but requires to [sic] much work and grades harshly."
- "There was ALOT of material to cover and Dr. Gurung expected you to know all of it. Not the easiest class, but it could have been worse."
- "I learning [sic] a lot from your presentation and enjoyed it Dr. Gurung and I really did not intend to."

Incivility and outright cruelty in students' written evaluations is a concern among faculty (Lindahl and Unger, 2010). However, even when comments are thoughtful and on-target, it is not always clear how they should be handled. It could be a numbers game, and the most frequent comment wins. Alternatively, student passion might be weighted such that the really ecstatic (or hysterical) comments garner the most attention. Perhaps gleaning a general impression of favorability or unfavorability is all that is needed. Or, should comments be ignored altogether due lack of representativeness and objectivity?

Teachers do not generally throw out the written comments on student evaluations. In fact, one survey found that 71 percent of teachers agreed that written comments "help instructors improve their teaching" (Nasser and Fresko 2002, p. 193). Anecdotally, many teachers report that they find written comments more helpful than means of survey items, and at one of our universities the people making decisions about tenure are frank in their assessment of comments as more important than means. All that being said, perception of written comments as important does not guarantee their usefulness. Just as with student evaluations means, misinterpretation can be a serious problem. Experts suggest that comments be analyzed using qualitative research strategies and multiple evaluators (Lewis, 2001b). Qualitative analysis is more than simply eyeballing responses and forming an impression; it involves specific strategies, some of which are outlined below, in order to increase objectivity and ensure that the results are reliable. Having more than one person conduct these analyses increased the reliability of results even further.

Perhaps performing systematic methods of analysis on student comments sounds extreme? Consider the following example. What would you think about Dr. Asch if you read the following comments from his students?

- Dr. Asch is a very cold man.
- He is super-intelligent.
- Dr. Asch is pretty no-nonsense in his teaching.
- Dr. Asch has a lot of expertise.
- He works really hard.
- I found him to be a warm person.

Do these comments make Dr. Asch sound like a good teacher? If you have studied social psychology, then you know where this is going. Do you think your impression would be the same if the comments had been presented with the first and last comments reversed? Classic research demonstrated that people viewed the same personality characteristics in dramatically different ways if the first trait listed was warm versus cold (Asch, 1946). Unless written comments are analyzed systematically, all it might take is one memorable comment—good or bad—to throw off the whole process. Interpretation of written comments will always be more subjective than interpretation of means, but some of that subjectivity can be removed using specific techniques.

There are several simple methods that can be used to make students' seemingly random comments more meaningful. The first strategy is to organize student comments by overall course or professor rating (Lewis, 2001a). Specifically, list all of the comments made by students who gave a rating of *excellent*, then all of the comments made from students who gave a rating of *very good*, and so on down the line to the lowest rating. One advantage of this method is that it provides a sort of implicit weighting of each comment (Lewis, 2001a). For example, if the same complaint that "Test questions have nothing to do with the stuff we do in class!" emerges again and again from students who rate the course as *below average*, then addressing evaluation alignment would stand out as a priority (see Chapter 6). However, if "I hate team discussion! Boo!!! ☹" is a frequent comment among students who rate the class as *excellent*, then revising

Teaching quality	Affirming comments	N	Improvement comments	N
Subject knowledge	• Very informed on research • Answered questions	9 7	• Could not answer all questions	2
Organization	• Lectures flowed well	8	• Too many lecture tangents	3
Respect for students	• Easy to ask questions • Emails students quickly	6 4	• Not enough office hours	2
Evaluation fairness	• Study guide was helpful • Paper rubric was helpful	4 3	• Tests were too hard • Papers graded too strictly	9 8
Clarity	• Material was easy to understand	2	• Material was hard	7

FIGURE 8.6 Sample format for analyzing and organizing open-ended responses from student evaluations.

discussion is harder to justify because the problem was not sufficient to reduce students' positive attitudes about the class. The ability to use this method is, of course, contingent upon on having access to individual surveys, which is not always possible; as previously stated, however, nothing prevents teachers from collecting their own data.

A second method for analyzing comments is to organize them according to the basic principles of good teaching (Lewis, 2001a). Begin by determining the principles you believe are central to being a good teacher (see Chapter 2 on how to be a good teacher). Using the first column of a table, list one principle per row (see Figure 8.6). Then, read each student comment and place them in rows based on what teaching principle the student seems to be referencing. The table can be further broken down into comments that affirm the teaching methods being used and comments that are improvement-focused. One advantage of this method is that it offers perspective on the overall positivity and negativity of comments. The more meaningful advantage, however, is that improvement-focused comments that pile up under one principle clearly suggest it as a teaching area to work on improving.

The topic of improvement signals a transition to the next model teaching characteristic. Just as making instructional changes is inherently part of the assessment process, a key purpose of soliciting feedback from students is to inform instructional change. Model teachers solicit feedback from students, but they also take action based on the feedback.

Making Improvements Based on Student Feedback

Some teachers have rituals related to their student evaluations. For one of us, the ritual is to dive into all of the courses as quickly as possible, getting a general impression of whether the means are above average, below average, or dangerously below average—sort of like ripping off a bandage with one big pull. Once the initial anxiety about the means subsides, the next step is to go over the results more carefully, paying special attention to the comments, laughing or crying as needed. We have heard rumors that other teachers' rituals involve wine—a drastic but festive approach.

No matter the ritual, the important activity is to not only look at student evaluations but use them for the betterment of teaching. Critics often have the loudest voices in the discussion of student evaluations, but, on average, teachers tend to find evaluations useful, and they report making instructional changes based upon the results (Beran et al., 2005; Gravestock and Gregor-Greenleaf, 2008; Nasser and Fresko 2002; Schmelkin et al., 1997). Making such changes is what model teachers do. Model teachers can point to specific modifications inspired by student feedback, be it summative or formative. Changes could be as simple as a modified lesson plan, or they could be as elaborate as an entirely restructured course design.

Does paying attention to student evaluations actually have the potential to improve teaching? There are skeptics. Greenwald (1997) offered an all-too-familiar story. One fall, a course of his received the highest teaching evaluations of his entire career; the next time he taught the course he received career-low evaluations. Despite only slight changes to the syllabus (and presumably no changes in teaching style), the means were separated by the almost unthinkably large margin of two and a half standard deviations. Can measures that produce such varied results be relied upon to improve teaching? Research clearly suggests that they can.

The effect of teachers receiving feedback from students has been the subject of many decades of research. In fact, student evaluation research has been the subject of three published meta-analyses (Cohen, 1980; L'Hommedieu et al., 1990; Penny and Coe, 2004). Generally speaking, research shows that the effect of student evaluations is moderate; receiving feedback increases subsequent teaching evaluations by a little over one-third of a standard deviation. Frankly, that size of an increase is not going to set the teaching world on fire, but it is comparable to the effect size found in other accepted psychological, educational, and behavioral interventions (Lipsey and Wilson, 1993). Increasing teaching effectiveness is a messy business, but it does appear that part of that mess is explained by receiving feedback from students. There is more to the story, however.

If receiving feedback were all that was required to improve teaching, then simply adding student evaluations into the mix of higher education should result in continuous improvement—it doesn't. Following teachers and their student evaluations across long periods of time illustrates a general pattern of stability in scores (Kember et al., 2002; Marsh, 2007a). For example, Marsh (2007a) examined teachers' student evaluations across 13 years. Evaluation means certainly fluctuated, but time alone was not a good predictor of change; this was true of teachers at all skill levels. The evaluations of good, bad, and mediocre teachers remained remarkably stable. The average correlation from year to year was 0.57, which is considered large. Clearly, something is amiss. How can feedback in the form of student evaluations be so stable but also increase effectiveness? The secret lies in how evaluations are used.

Cohen (1980) conducted the first meta-analysis of student evaluation research, and the results provided useful guidance on how to use evaluations. The meta-analysis combined results from 17 separate studies and found that, on average, teachers receiving feedback from students scored at the 65th percentile on subsequent teaching evaluations; this was modestly, but significantly, higher than the teachers who did not receive feedback and scored at the 50th percentile. What was more interesting, however, was the differences that emerged when Cohen further broke down the teachers into groups based on what they did with the student feedback. When teachers consulted with someone else about their student evaluations, their subsequent evaluations rose to the 74th percentile, which was a dramatic increase over teachers who just received feedback (58th percentile) and teachers who received no feedback (50th percentile). It turns out that teachers have to use student evaluations as part of an active process of improvement for feedback to actually have an impact. More recent research has also supported the notion that extra work is needed for student feedback to improve teaching (e.g., Dresel and Rindermann, 2011; Knol et al., 2013).

Based on their meta-analysis of 12 studies, Penny and Coe (2004) made a number of suggestions about how to best work with student evaluations in order to improve teaching. To begin, they emphasized the importance of eliciting quality feedback from students. Teachers should use student evaluations with established reliability and validity. After all, making changes on meaningless data is bound to be fruitless—once again, garbage in, garbage out. After soliciting feedback from students, they recommend explicitly setting aside time to consider and work with the results. It is easy for student evaluations to get lost in the flood of more immediate tasks facing college teachers, but taking time for reflection on student evaluation feedback is essential for improvement.

What needs to be done during time that is set aside to reflect on student evaluations? Penny and Coe (2004) recommend that teachers engage in an honest self-assessment. We have found that it is difficult to be truly surprised by the results of student evaluations—especially in the negative direction. In fact, for one of the authors, a bad student evaluation was a complete surprise just once; it was an honors course, and the fact that the highly intelligent students understood every single topic thrown at them obscured the fact that students understanding and students caring are not one and the same. Mostly, it is easy to tell when the low evaluations are coming because the teaching does not feel like it is working, students do not seem to be learning, or some other dynamic is just plain off. An honest self-assessment of how things went might reveal what needs to change for next time.

The next recommendation is to consult with others about student evaluations. Penny and Coe (2004) suggested several viable options for effective consultation. A common procedure followed in the research literature is to consult with teachers specifically trained to interpret evaluations and provide recommendations for improvement. However, the process should be non-evaluative. Fear of being honest with yourself or the person helping you may prevent an accurate evaluation of areas needing improvement. What should be produced during this process of consultation? Penny and Coe stress the importance of setting goals for improvement. Goals provide direction to and motivation for refinement of pedagogy. They also provide commitment to improvement, which is a key characteristic of model teachers.

Making improvements based on student evaluations is a complex process that involves integration of not only information from this chapter, but from across this book. As such, we propose an evidence-based model for using student evaluations to improve teaching. The model is not unique; it simply reapplies the process that is at the heart of assessment (see Chapter 6) and the scientist-educator model of teaching (see Chapter 2 and Bernstein et al., 2010). Much like assessment, the scientist-educator model emphasizes a continuous process of improvement through the gathering of objective evidence of teaching effectiveness, but both the assessment process and scientist-educator model focus almost exclusively on the achievement of student learning outcomes. In contrast, our model can involve student learning, but it can also involve student rapport, perceptions of fairness, clarity of assignments, and any other aspect of teaching on which students might provide meaningful feedback.

Steps in an Evidence-Based Model for Using Student Evaluations to Improve Teaching

The evidence-based model consists of six interrelated steps. The steps outline a process for gathering, analyzing, and utilizing student evaluation data.

1. Determine an aspect of teaching about which you would like to receive feedback.
2. Select a method for gathering feedback from students.
3. Collect student responses.

4. Interpret the data using the appropriate quantitative or qualitative analysis strategies.
5. Set and follow through with a specific goal for a pedagogical change based on model teaching practices.
6. Collect follow-up data to assess the success of the pedagogical change.

The first steps in the model primarily involve planning. (1) Determine an aspect of teaching about which you would like to receive feedback. What do you need to know? Novice teachers may want feedback about general teaching ability. More experienced teachers may have the basic skills down but need to refine a new assignment or technique. The topic of assessment will be specific to you and your needs. (2) Select a method for gathering feedback from students. The method should match the topic identified in step 1. For example, if feedback on general skills is desired, then standardized student evaluation surveys should suffice. Alternatively, having students anonymously write about "What is going well in this class and what is not going well?" is a less-standardized and less formal way to obtain general feedback. If specific information is needed, teachers will likely have to create their own questions or modify one of the well-known classroom assessment techniques (Angelo and Cross, 1993). When considering assessment methods, however, methods with known validity are preferable. In addition, the data that will be produced should be considered. If rich feedback is required, open-ended questions are appropriate. In contrast, if a teacher wants an overall picture of the relative merits of many aspects of their pedagogy, a wide-ranging survey such as the Student Evaluation of Educational Quality (Marsh, 1982, 1983) will be useful.

The next steps involve the collection and analysis of data. (3) Collect student responses. The method of data collection will vary according to the topic and goals, and teachers should make careful choices about timing of data collection, whether participation is voluntary, survey format (i.e., paper versus online), anonymity of responses, time allowed (e.g., in class versus take-home), and credit for participation. (4) Interpret the data using the appropriate quantitative or qualitative analysis strategies. Responses must be compiled; this leads to numeric and/or qualitative data. In both cases, analysis of the results should follow the suggestions outlined in this chapter for increasing reliability and validity. Specifically, analyze numerical results using good statistical practices, and increase the reliability and validity of qualitative responses through systematically coding.

After the analysis, teachers must utilize the results. (5) Set and follow through with a specific goal for a pedagogical change based on model teaching practices. No matter what type of feedback you receive, the key is to make a specific goal. Without that goal, there will be no direction to improvement efforts. But what goals should be set? For standardized evaluation surveys, this is simple enough; standardized surveys are built to assess model teaching practices, and they can form the goals. If scores on rapport items are low, engage in more immediacy behaviors (see Chapter 4). If scores on fairness of evaluation items are low, revisit the design of evaluations (see Chapter 6). Surveys that teachers have designed themselves to assess a specific aspect of teaching may or may not lead directly to model teaching practices. Imagine an informal assessment of "What is going well..." early in the semester that results in students suggesting that a teacher "lecture more and get rid of small group discussion." Replacing active learning with lecture is not a model practice. As such, alternative responses might be to (a) better explain the rationale behind collaborative learning, (b) base more exam questions on discussion material, or (c) hold students accountable for discussion preparation. The key idea is that model teaching practices should serve as guidelines for any goals that you set for teaching improvement.

Of course, setting and following through with goals is important, but the process does not end there. Collect follow-up data to assess the success of the pedagogical change. Teachers cannot know if the changes that they make to pedagogy are effective unless they reassess outcomes. In relation to student evaluations, this will largely mean giving a follow-up survey to students after some sort of change has occurred; this could occur as soon as the next class period or as late as the next semester. Alternatively, teachers could examine student performance related to whatever aspect of teaching they were attempting to adjust. Did rubric scores increase after providing students with the sample assignment they requested? Did exam scores increase after clarifying what learning objectives would be covered? Have peer evaluations of team members gone up after reviewing the expectations for group work? Across all of these examples, the point is simply to use student evaluations, in all their potential forms, as evidence to evaluate pedagogy.

CASE STUDY REEXAMINED: GARBAGE IN, GARBAGE OUT?

1. *How would you evaluate the Marketing Department's student evaluation survey?* The title of the case should be a dead giveaway here. If the student evaluation is garbage, the information it provides is garbage as well. The Marketing Department appears to have created a truly terrible survey. There is little reason to believe that three questions can accurately assess teaching effectiveness. In addition, the practice of having students grade their teachers, but not explaining what the individual grades mean, leaves the results largely uninterpretable. Furthermore, it is not clear how the grading scale applies to the question concerning students' own level of learning. In this case, Dr. Olsen should abandon all hope in the home-grown survey and adopt one of the many established surveys to inform her teaching and augment data that she submits for tenure (for a review of measures see Richardson, 2005). Without valid data, Dr. Olsen should be very cautious in making instructional changes. However, she is completely free to collect any additional data that would be of use to her. If she collects formative feedback or administers a valid

survey, the resulting information could be extremely useful and more trustworthy than the homegrown department evaluations.

2. *How should Dr. Olsen interpret her evaluation means?* Dr. Olsen's chair appears to have interpreted the fact that the evaluation means are below the departmental average as meaning that there is a reliable and meaningful difference. Raw student evaluation means should not be interpreted. Dr. Allan should calculate confidence intervals for her means and statistically compare them to the average in her department; only with these data can valid interpretations occur. Dr. Olsen should also include these statistics when she reports her evaluations during the tenure process and do her best to see that others follow statistical rules when interpreting her evaluations.

3. *How should Dr. Olsen interpret the open-ended comments from students?* The chair of Dr. Olsen's department seems to have fallen into the common trap of emphasizing one memorable written comment over other comments that better represented trends in the data. In order to analyze the comments, Dr. Olsen could reorganize them into positive and negative categories and then count the number of similar comments. Examination of the comments in this way would reveal that "good teacher" was actually the most common sentiment among students. If she wanted to truly boost the reliability of her interpretations, she could enlist a colleague to independently go through the same coding process so that their results could be compared.

A Reflection on Your Self-Assessment

Now that you have read over the chapter, let's return to your self-assessment. If you are like a lot of teachers, you have mostly been relying on your end-of-semester evaluations. It is time to move toward consistency with more of the model practices. Following the evidence-based model outlined above is a good place to look for suggestions on how to start the process.

Summary of Best Practices

We hope that, even if you are an experienced teacher, this chapter has given you something to consider the next time you wonder what students are thinking about you and your classes—just ask them! By way of a summary, here are some of the things model teachers do in order to take advantage of what students have to tell them.

- Collect formative evaluations data throughout the semester.
- Utilize summative student evaluations of teaching that have established reliability and validity.

- Interpret quantitative data (e.g., means) using statistical tools (e.g., confidence intervals, statistical tests), and avoid making any judgments based on raw means.
- Interpret qualitative data (e.g., written comments) using systematic methods to organize them by meaning and frequency
- Set specific teaching goals, ideally with the help of an expert consultant, based on student evaluations and follow up on the effectiveness changes related to the goals.

Student evaluations of teaching are "consequential, controversial, and inescapable" (Boysen, 2015b, p. 117). Love them or hate them, they will be part of your life if you are a college teacher; our advice is to accept this fact and try to use student evaluations as productively as possible. If you do not buy into the idea that survey questions will ever accurately measure teaching effectiveness, then conceptualize student evaluations as a rough measure of student satisfaction with your teaching and your courses. Only the most staid of teachers have no concern about students' enjoyment of learning, so use student evaluations to increase that enjoyment. Perhaps your beef is with using numbers to evaluate teaching in any way, shape, or form. In that case, dive into student comments headfirst and pay less attention to the means. It is also possible that you find all of the data produced by the student evaluations at your school to be useless. In that case, collect data from students that you do find useful; there is no reason to expect your college to collect all the data that you need to be a better teacher, so institute your own evaluation process. Overall, if model teaching is your goal, then soliciting feedback from students is a necessity.

Simply receiving feedback is not enough to be a model teacher, however; you must also use that feedback to productive ends. Depending on the validity of the survey used, areas of statistical variance in student evaluation means can provide direction to professional development. Do you have means for student rapport that are lower than your peers to an extent that is statistically significant? Then it might be time to work on connecting with students. Are your means for intellectual engagement two standard deviations below the college average? It might be time to make those assignments a bit more challenging. Students' written comments can also provide direction as long as they are examined systematically. Is "goes too fast in lecture" the most frequent comment on your evaluations? Slow down! Perhaps students who rate the course poorly tend to write that they "had no idea what was going to be on the tests." It might be time to clarify learning objectives and make sure they align with evaluations. Do students keep writing "we should have class outside" every semester? That one you can probably ignore. Model teachers do not have to modify pedagogy based on every student whim, but they do take feedback from students seriously enough to make significant changes to their pedagogy.

The Very Busy People Book Club: Your Top Five Must-Reads

Abrami, P. C. (2001). Improving judgments about teaching effectiveness using teacher rating forms. *New Directions for Institutional Research*, 109, 59–87.

Franklin, J. (2001). Interpreting the numbers: Using a narrative to help others read student evaluations of your teaching accurately. *New Directions for Teaching and Learning*, 87, 85–100.

Lewis, K. G. (2001). Using midsemester student feedback and responding to it. *New Directions for Teaching and Learning*, 87, 33–44

Marsh, H. W. and Roche, L. A. (1997). Making students' evaluations of teaching effectiveness effective: The critical issues of validity, bias, and utility. *American Psychologist*, 52, 1187–1197.

Spooren, P., Brockx, B., and Mortelmans, D. (2013). On the validity of student evaluation of teaching: The state of the art. *Review of Educational Research*, 83, 598–642.

References

Abrami, P. C. (2001). Improving judgments about teaching effectiveness using teacher rating forms. *New Directions for Institutional Research*, 109, 59–87.

Addison, W. E., Stowell, J. R., and Reab, M. D. (2015). Attributes of introductory psychology and statistics teachers: Findings from comments on RateMyProfessors. com. *Scholarship of Teaching and Learning in Psychology*, 1, 229–234.

Angelo, T. A. and Cross, K. P. (1993). *Classroom assessment techniques: A handbook for college teachers* (2nd edn). San Francisco, CA: Jossey-Bass.

Asch, S. E. (1946). Forming impressions of personality. *The Journal of Abnormal and Social Psychology*, 41, 258–290.

Benton, S. L., Webster, R., Gross, A. B., and Pallett, W. H. (2010). *An analysis of IDEA student ratings of instruction using paper version online survey methods: 2002–2008 Data*. Retrieved from www.ideaed.us/wp-content/uploads/2014/11/techreport-16.pdf.

Beran, T., Violato, C., Kline, D., and Frideres, J. (2005). The utility of student ratings of instruction for students, faculty, and administrators: A "consequential validity" study. *Canadian Journal of Higher Education*, 35, 49–70.

Bernstein, D., Addison, W., Altman, C., Hollister, D., Meera, K., Prieto, L. R., Rocheleau, C. A., and Shore, C. (2010). Toward a scientist-educator model of teaching psychology. In D. Halpern (ed.), *The NCUEP: A Blueprint for the Future* (pp. 29–46). Washington, DC: American Psychological Association.

Boyce, T. E. and Hineline, P. N. (2002). Interteaching: A strategy for enhancing the user-friendliness of behavioral arrangements in the college classroom. *The Behavior Analyst*, 25, 215–226.

Boysen, G. A. (2015a). Significant interpretation of small mean differences in student evaluations of teaching despite explicit warning to avoid overinterpretation. *Scholarship of Teaching and Learning in Psychology*, 1, 150–162.

Boysen, G. A. (2015b). Uses and misuses of student evaluations of teaching: The interpretation of differences in teaching evaluation means irrespective of statistical information. *Teaching of Psychology*, 42, 109–118.

Boysen, G. A., Kelly, T. J., Raesly, H. N., and Casner, R. W. (2013). The (mis)interpretation of teaching evaluations by college faculty and administrators. *Assessment & Evaluation in Higher Education*, 39, 641–656.

Boysen, G. A., Richmond, A. S., and Gurung, R. A. R. (2015). Model Teaching Criteria for psychology: Initial documentation of teachers' self-reported competency. *Scholarship of Teaching and Learning in Psychology*, 1, 48–59.

Centra, J. A. (2003). Will teachers receive higher student evaluations by giving higher grades and less course work? *Research in Higher Education*, 44, 495–518.

Clayson, D. E. (2009). Student evaluations of teaching: Are they related to what students learn? A meta-analysis and review of the literature. *Journal of Marketing Education*, 31, 16–30.

Cohen, P. A. (1980). Effectiveness of student-rating feedback for improving college instruction: A meta-analysis of findings. *Research in Higher Education*, 13, 321–341.

d'Apollonia, S. and Abrami, P. C. (1997). Navigating student ratings of instruction. *American Psychologist*, 52, 1198–1208.

Davison, E. and Price, J. (2009). How do we rate? An evaluation of online student evaluations. *Assessment & Evaluation in Higher Education*, 34, 51–65.

Dommeyer, C., Baum, P., Hanna, R., and Chapman, K. (2004). Gathering faculty teaching evaluations by in-class and online surveys: Their effects on response rates and evaluations. *Assessment and Evaluation in Higher Education*, 29, 611–623.

Dresel, M. and Rindermann, H. (2011). Counseling university instructors based on student evaluations of their teaching effectiveness: A multilevel test of its effectiveness under consideration of bias and unfairness variables. *Research in Higher Education*, 52, 717–737.

Fike, D. S., Doyle, D. J., and Connelly, R. J. (2010). Online vs. paper evaluations of faculty: When less is just as good. *The Journal of Effective Teaching*, 10, 42–54.

Franklin, J. (2001). Interpreting the numbers: Using a narrative to help others read student evaluations of your teaching accurately. *New Directions for Teaching and Learning*, 87, 85–100.

Gravestock, P. and Gregor-Greenleaf, E. (2008). *Student course evaluations: Research, models and trends.* Toronto: Higher Education Quality Council of Ontario.

Greenwald, A. (1997). Validity concerns and usefulness of student ratings of instruction. *American Psychologist*, 52, 1182–1186.

Guder, F. and Malliaris, M. (2010). Online and paper course evaluations. *American Journal of Business Education*, 3, 131–138.

Halonen, J. S., Dunn, D. S., McCarthy, M. A., and Baker, S. C. (2012). Are you really above average? Documenting your teaching effectiveness. In B. M. Schwartz and R. A. R. Gurung (eds.), *Evidence-based teaching for higher education* (pp. 131–149). Washington, DC: American Psychological Association.

Kamenetz, A. (2014). *Student course evaluations get an "F."* Retrieved from www.npr.org/sections/ed/2014/09/26/345515451/student-course-evaluations-get-an-f.

Keeley, J., Smith, D., and Buskist, W. (2006). The Teacher Behavior Checklist: Factor analysis of its utility for evaluating teaching. *Teaching of Psychology*, 33, 84–91.

Kember, D., Leung, D., and Kwan, K. (2002). Does the use of student feedback questionnaires improve the overall quality of teaching? *Assessment and Evaluation in Higher Education*, 27, 411–425.

Kindred, J. and Mohammed, S. N. (2005), "He will crush you like an academic ninja!" Exploring teacher ratings on Ratemyprofessors.com. *Journal of Computer-Mediated Communication*, 10.

Knol, M., in't Veld, R., Vorst, H., van Driel, J., and Mellenbergh, G. (2013). Experimental effects of student evaluations coupled with collaborative consultation on college professors' instructional skills. *Research in Higher Education*, 54, 825–850.

Krautman, A. C. and Sander, W. (1999). Grades and student evaluations of teachers. *Economics of Education Review*, 18, 59–63.

Lewandowski, G. J., Higgins, E., and Nardone, N. N. (2012). Just a harmless website? An experimental examination of RateMyProfessors.com's effect on student evaluations. *Assessment & Evaluation in Higher Education*, 37, 987–1002.

Lewis, K. G. (2001a). Making sense of student written comments. *New Directions for Teaching and Learning*, 87, 25–32.

Lewis, K. G. (2001b). Using midsemester student feedback and responding to it. *New Directions for Teaching and Learning*, 87, 33–44

Lindahl, M. W. and Unger, M. L. (2010). Cruelty in student teaching evaluations. *College Teaching*, 58, 71–76.

Lipsey, M. and Wilson, D. (1993). The efficacy of psychological, educational, and behavioral treatment: Confirmation from meta-analysis. *American Psychologist*, 48, 1181–1209.

L'Hommedieu, R., Menges, R., and Brinko, K. (1990). Methodological explanations for the modest effects of feedback from student ratings. *Journal of Educational Psychology*, 82, 232–241.

Marsh, H. W. (1982). SEEQ: A reliable, valid, and useful instrument for collecting students' evaluations of university teaching. *British Journal of Educational Psychology*, 52, 77–95.

Marsh, H. W. (1983). Multidimensional ratings of teaching effectiveness by students from different academic settings and their relation to student/course/instructor characteristics. *Journal of Educational Psychology*, 75, 150–166.

Marsh, H. W. (2007a). Do university teachers become more effective with experience? A multilevel growth model of students' evaluations of teaching over 13 years. *Journal of Educational Psychology*, 99, 775–790.

Marsh, H. W. (2007b) Students' evaluations of university teaching: Dimensionality, reliability, validity, potential biases and usefulness. In R. P. Perry and J. C. Smart (eds.), *The scholarship of teaching and learning in higher education: An evidence-based perspective* (pp. 319–383). New York: Springer.

Marsh, H. W. and Roche, L. A. (1997). Making students' evaluations of teaching effectiveness effective: The critical issues of validity, bias, and utility. *American Psychologist*, 52, 1187–1197.

Martin, J. H., Hands, K. B., Lancaster, S. M., Trytten, D. A., and Murphy, T. J. (2008). Hard but not too hard: Challenging courses and engineering students. *College Teaching*, 56, 107–113.

Nasser, F. and Fresko, B. (2002). Faculty views of student evaluation of college teaching. *Assessment & Evaluation in Higher Education*, 27, 187–198.

Nulty, D. (2008). The adequacy of response rates to online and paper surveys: What can be done? *Assessment & Evaluation in Higher Education*, 33, 301–314.

Otto, J., Sanford, D. J., and Ross, D. N. (2008). Does Ratemyprofessor.com really rate my professor? *Assessment & Evaluation in Higher Education*, 33, 355–368.

Penny, A. R. and Coe, R. (2004). Effectiveness of consultation on student ratings feedback: A meta-analysis. *Review of Educational Research*, 74, 215–253.

Redding, R. E. (1998). Students' evaluations of teaching fuel grade inflation. *American Psychologist*, 53, 1227–1228.

Richardson, J. E. (2005). Instruments for obtaining student feedback: A review of the literature. *Assessment and Evaluation in Higher Education*, 30, 387–415.

Richmond, A. S., Boysen, G. A., Gurung, R. A. R., Tazeau, Y. N., Meyers, S. A., and Sciutto, M. J. (2014). Aspirational Model Teaching Criteria for psychology. *Teaching of Psychology*, 41, 281–295.

Schmelkin, L. P., Spencer, K. J., and Gellman, E. S. (1997). Faculty perspectives on course and teacher evaluations. *Research in Higher Education*, 38, 575–592.

Sears, D. O. (1983). The person-positivity bias. *Journal of Personality and Social Psychology*, 44, 233–250.

Sonntag, M. E., Bassett, J. F., and Snyder, T. (2009). An empirical test of the validity of student evaluations of teaching made on RateMyProfessors.com. *Assessment & Evaluation in Higher Education*, 34, 499–504.

Spooren, P., Brockx, B., and Mortelmans, D. (2013). On the validity of student evaluation of teaching: The state of the art. *Review of Educational Research*, 83, 598–642.

Stark, P. B. and Freishtat, R. (2014). *An evaluation of course evaluations*. Retrieved from www.stat.berkeley.edu/~stark/Preprints/evaluations14.pdf.

Stehle, S., Spinath, B., and Kadmon, M. (2012). Measuring teaching effectiveness: Correspondence between students' evaluations of teaching and different measures of student learning. *Research in Higher Education*, 53, 888–904.

Theall, M. and Franklin, J. (2001). Looking for bias in all the wrong places: A search for truth or a witch hunt in student ratings of instruction? *New Directions for Institutional Research*, 109, 45–56.

Wilson, J. H. and Ryan, R. G. (2013). Professor–student rapport scale six items predict student outcomes. *Teaching of Psychology*, 40, 130–133.

EPILOGUE

As we are writing this closing message for our teaching book, yet another semester has begun and there are a host of tasks that need to be done. For instance, in Guy's case, office debris from the previous semester needs to be cleared in order to make room for, well, new debris. In addition to rubrics, advising worksheets, and assessment results, Guy's desk typically houses a ramshackle nest of notes jotted down on random scraps of paper during a year's worth of teaching conferences and workshops. Regan and Aaron have similar collections of post-workshop jottings. Each note elicits a reaction. "Made that change to my syllabus and it worked great!" "Whoa, I can't believe I even wrote that down." "Hey, why didn't I try that out?" Obviously, the last reaction is sometimes tinged with regret. We hope that you can avoid similar regrets when looking back on what you read in this book.

Avoid Teacherly Regret: One Last Self-Assessment

The best way to avoid teacherly regret over pedagogical paths not taken is to use a systematic and intentional approach to professional development. A good first step would be to complete the entire Model Teaching Criteria survey again (see Appendix) and use this tool to identify the areas that you need to work on. If one of the model practices is something you have been meaning to try out, then put it into practice as soon as you can. If you have a number of different items you want to work on, prioritize them or just pick the one that seems like the most fun to work on first. If you need to work on one of the model criteria but feel like you do not know enough to even get started, then track down one of our must-reads on the topic and start learning. The key is to establish a continual process of professional development. In six months, take the Model Teaching Criteria survey again and assess the progress that you have made and the gaps that you still need to fill. Put a reminder on your calendar right now to take the survey again (yes, there must be an app for that). Seriously, we'll wait. In order to keep improving as a teacher you must continually assess the quality of your teaching and set new goals.

Do you have a lot of room to grow before your teaching is consistent with all of the model practices? If your answer is "yes," do not be frustrated. Most college teachers start their careers with little more than enthusiasm for the subject to guide their pedagogy—this was certainly true of us. Having room to grow is only a problem if you never develop. So, start chipping away at the model criteria one area at a time. For instance, revise one course syllabus so that it exhibits all of the model characteristics next semester. Incorporate different types of active learning into specific lessons over the next month. Conduct a formative assessment in your very next class. Email a student to say "Good job!" right now. Becoming a model teacher, just like developing expertise in any area, can be a slow process. But it has to start sometime. So, start now!

What is Stopping You?

We believe that two of the biggest impediments to teaching innovation are inertia and fear of doing things wrong. Inertia is particularly powerful. In a recent class one of us spent way too much time lecturing over a topic not covered in the textbook simply because that is how the class was designed years ago. Were it not for the habit of lecturing on the topic, the material could have been covered outside of class with an assigned video, by assigning readings outside of the textbook, or by asking students to research the topic on their own. Don't base your pedagogy on habit. There are always reasons to wait for next semester, so turn the model criteria into targets for immediate change.

We know what you are thinking, "What if I make a change and it doesn't work?" This is a common fear, but we believe that it is difficult to do real damage with changes intended to improve your teaching. Trust us, no matter how essential you think some aspect of your teaching is, there are people out there who are quite successful teaching the same material in a completely different way. A few semesters ago, Guy completely gave up lecture as a teaching method in an introductory course. He feared that students would revolt and burn effigies of him on the quad, but there was no drama whatsoever. Later on, a colleague from another college reacted to a description of the change by saying "Oh yeah, our whole department agreed to do away with lecture in that class years ago." Similarly, Regan switched all his in-class exams to online tests where students could take it anytime within a window. It reduced student stress and gave Regan more class time to go into greater depth on topics. In actuality, teaching changes are rarely as radical as they feel to us before we make them.

"But if it doesn't work, I will get slammed in my teaching evaluations!" There is some truth to the notion that teaching innovation can lead to, at least temporary, dips in student evaluations. However, in our experience, trying out new teaching techniques actually garners admiration from students, colleagues, and administrators. The key is to be open about what you are doing. Tell students that you are experimenting with a technique that others have found to increase learning; then, ask them for feedback. If you are trying something especially novel or dramatic, run it by the chair and dean to make sure they can support the change. We even invite you to email one of us! We would love to hear your ideas. Even if you technically do not need blessings from students or administrators to teach however you want, they will appreciate your efforts to become a better teacher, not to mention your inclusion of them in the process.

Perhaps you are just too satisfied with your teaching to change. Tenure? Check. Good student evaluations? Check. Students are learning? Check. Well, we challenge you to go beyond good enough. As the story goes, a woman enters her 35th year of teaching with plans to retire in the spring. Before her final fall semester, she goes to the annual professional development workshop. The administrator running the workshop, seeing the teacher among a sea of junior faculty, just has to ask "You are retiring, what are you doing *here*?" To which she replies, "I want this to be my best year of teaching." We hope you have your best year of teaching too—every year.

Appendix

THE MODEL TEACHING CRITERIA SCALE

Directions: Please indicate on the scale below how often you take part in these efforts/activities.

Scale: 5 = Always, 4 = Often, 3 = Sometimes, 2 = Rarely, 1 = Never   *Your score*

Training

1. You teach only courses that are related to your professional degree.	
2. You teach only courses for which you have documented graduate coursework.	
3. You give presentations at regional or national conferences related to content areas taught.	
4. You publish peer-reviewed research related to content areas taught.	
5. You utilize pedagogical training that stems from credit-bearing courses you have completed on teaching.	
6. You present at regional or national conferences on topics related to teaching.	
7. You publish peer-reviewed research related to pedagogical strategies (e.g., SoTL articles).	
8. You participate in continuing education related to content areas taught.	
9. You participate in continuing education related to pedagogical strategies.	
Subtotal	

Instructional methods

10. You use more than one instructional method (e.g., active learning) when teaching.	
11. You strive to be a better teacher.	
12. You promote class discussion.	
13. You are enthusiastic when you teach.	
14. You are professional.	

15. You are prepared for class.	
16. You are happy, positive, and humorous.	
17. You provide constructive feedback to students.	
18. You understand your students.	
19. You encourage your students.	
20. You care about your students.	
21. You treat students fairly.	
22. You communicate effectively with your students.	
23. Your students respect you.	
24. You are approachable.	
25. Your students are consistently engaged in class.	
26. You adapt your instructional methods to individual student needs.	
27. You are receptive to your students.	
28. Your class is enjoyable for students.	
29. You are compassionate towards your students.	
Subtotal	
Course content and student learning	
30. Your course learning goals reflect the breadth of content in your discipline.	
31. You foster the development of student written communication skills.	
32. You foster the development of student critical thinking skills.	
33. You foster the development of student information literacy skills.	
34. You foster the development of student ability to work effectively and collaborate with others.	
35. You foster the development of student oral communication skills.	
36. You infuse ethical issues throughout your teaching.	
37. You infuse diversity issues throughout your teaching.	
Subtotal	
Assessment	
38. You articulate specific, measurable learning objectives in your syllabi or other course documents (e.g., sample lesson plans, a list of course objectives).	
39. You change course syllabi, material, lesson plans, or teaching methods based on formal and informal assessment.	
40. You align class activities, lectures, and reading assignments with learning objectives.	
41. You provide constructive feedback to students is that is related to their achievement of learning objectives (e.g., use of rubrics).	
42. You publically disseminate information about teaching innovations and outcomes (e.g., publications and presentations).	
Subtotal	
Syllabus	
43. Your syllabus reflects an intentional link of course goals to class activities.	

44. Your syllabus reflects an intentional link of course goals to evaluation methods.	
45. Your syllabus reflects an intentional link of course goals to course assignments.	
46. Your syllabus has an attractive and readable layout.	
47. Your syllabus reflects changes suggested by student feedback.	
48. Your syllabus reflects effective use of instructional methods.	
49. Your syllabus is strategically organized to accomplish course goals.	
50. Your syllabus provides clear and complete information about course goals.	
51. Your syllabus provides clear and complete information about the course schedule.	
52. Your syllabus provides clear and complete information about course requirements.	
53. Your syllabus provides clear and complete information about course grading/assessment.	
54. Your syllabus provides clear and complete information about instructor availability (e.g., office hours, contact information).	
55. Your syllabus sets a positive tone for the course (e.g., uses positive and rewarding language).	
56. Your syllabus is written in the first person with proper pronoun use.	
Subtotal	
Student evaluations of teaching	
57. You regularly solicit summative feedback from students.	
58. You regularly solicit formative feedback from students.	
59. You interpret student evaluations using valid quantitative and qualitative data analysis procedures.	
60. You set goals for the improvement of teaching based on student feedback.	
61. You incorporate student feedback into syllabus revisions.	
62. You incorporate student feedback into changes in course material.	
63. You incorporate student feedback into changes to lesson plans.	
64. You incorporate student feedback into changes in your teaching methods.	
Subtotal	
Grand total	

Note: This self-assessment is adapted and modified from Boysen et al. (2015), Keeley et al. (2006), Lammers and Gillaspy (2013), Richmond et al. (2014), Slattery and Carlson (n.d., 2005), and Wilson and Ryan (2013).

References

Boysen, G. A., Richmond, A. S., and Gurung, R. A. R. (2015). Model Teaching Criteria for psychology: Initial documentation of teachers' self-reported competency. *Scholarship of Teaching and Learning in Psychology*, 1, 48–59.

Keeley, J., Smith, D., and Buskist, W. (2006). The Teacher Behavior Checklist: Factor analysis of its utility for evaluating teaching. *Teaching of Psychology*, 33, 84–91.

Lammers, W. J. and Gillaspy Jr., J. A. (2013). Brief measure of student–instructor rapport predicts student success in online courses. *International Journal for the Scholarship of Teaching and Learning*, 7(2), 16.

Richmond, A. S., Boysen, G. A., Gurung, R. A. R., Tazeau, Y. N., Meyers, S. A., and Sciutto, M. J. (2014). Aspirational Model Teaching Criteria for psychology. *Teaching of Psychology*, 41, 281–295.

Slattery, J. M. and Carlson, J. F. (n.d.). *Guidelines for preparing exemplary syllabi*. Retrieved from http://teachpsych.org/otrp/syllabi/guidelines.php.

Slattery, J. M. and Carlson, J. F. (2005). Preparing an effective syllabus: Current best practices. *College Teaching*, 53, 159–164.

Wilson, J. H. and Ryan, R. G. (2013). Professor–student rapport scale six items predict student outcomes. *Teaching of Psychology*, 40, 130–133.

AUTHOR INDEX

Abrami, P. C. 165, 175, 176, 177, 178
Addison, W. E. 3, 36, 37, 173
Albanese, M. A. 54
Albers, C. 143
Allen, D. E. 54
Alsudairi, M. A. T. 21
Altman, C. 3
Ambrose, S. A. 35, 36
American Association of Colleges and Universities 124
American Association of University Professors 14, 37
American Chemical Society 82, 83
American Historical Association 82
American Institute of Certified Public Accountant (AICPA) 84
American Mathematical Society 93
American Philosophical Association 83, 89, 91
American Psychological Association 33, 36, 39, 81, 82, 83, 84, 89, 91, 93, 96, 141
Amundsen, C. 94
Anaya, G. 105
Anderson, H. M. 105, 126
Anderson, L. W. 39
Andrade, H. 124
Angelo, T. A. 125, 170, 172, 185
Anthis, K. 37
Ariovich, L. 113
Arnold, I. M. 127

Arntzen, E. 55
Asch, S. E. 180
Association of American Colleges and Universities (AAC&U) 88, 90
Association of American Educators 93
Association to Advance Collegiate Schools of Business Standard (AACSB) 81, 84, 89, 91, 93

Bain, K. 3, 15–19, 42, 56, 141, 145
Baiocco, S. 14
Baker, S. 37, 93
Baker, S. C. 24, 163
Banta, T. W. 105, 117
Bartozewski, B. 42
Bartsch, R. A. 129, 130
Bassett, J. F. 173
Baum, P. 168
Bean, J. 120
Beatty, J. E. 23
Becker, A. H. 142, 155, 156
Becknell, J. 146, 147, 151, 153, 154
Beidler, P. G. 13, 14
Belenky, M. F. 40
Bell, K. E. 42
Benassi, V. A. 21
Benjamin, L. 52
Benson, T. A. 61
Benton, S. L. 168
Bentz, A. E. 154
Benya, F. F. 92

Beran, T. 182
Berglund, M. B. 69
Bernstein, D. 3, 36, 37
Bhattacharya, G. 59
Bigatti, S. M. 69
Biggs, J. B. 52
Bird, E. 105
Bishop-Clark, C. 24
Bjork, R. A. 37, 41
Black, P. J. 116
Blakemore, O. 37
Bloom, B. S. 39
Blumberg, P. 104
Boice, R. 39
Bok, D. 2
Bonwell, C. C. 52
Bosack, T. N. 113
Boyce, T. E. 55, 171
Boyer, E. L. 24, 129
Boysen, G. A. 2, 4, 5, 15, 25, 30, 51, 64, 96,
   141, 143, 144, 147, 149, 153–4, 176,
   178–9, 188
Bransford, J. D. 94
Brewer, C. L. 81
Bridges, K. R. 150
Bridges, M. W. 35, 36
Briggs, W. L. 25, 66, 69
Brinko, K. 182
Brockx, B. 165, 167
Brookfield, S. D. 11, 22, 23, 30
Brooks, D. W. 39, 41
Brown, A. L. 94
Brown, A. R. 146
Brown, B. R. 106
Brown, C. 80
Brown, C. M. 144
Brown, P. C. 43
Buckley, T. 32, 56, 59
Buskist, C. 56, 59
Buskist, W. 3, 14–15, 21, 32, 37, 56, 59, 61,
   64, 91, 129, 146, 169
Butler, J. M. 56, 66, 69

Cain, T. R. 100, 103, 113
Calhoon, S. K. 142, 155, 156
Carey, B. 43
Carlson, J. F. 141, 154, 155
Carlson, J. R. 129
Carlstrom, A. 41
Casner, R. W. 178–9
Cautin, R. L. 81
Centra, J. A. 14, 166
Chapman, K. 168

Chick, N. 32, 81
Chickering, A. W. 3, 35
Chory-Assad, R. M. 117
Christophel, D. M. 61, 62
Christopher, A. N. 14, 59, 129
Chronicle of Higher Education 104
Churlyaeva, M. 59
Ciccone, A. 129, 131, 132
Clayson, D. E. 167
Clinchy, B. M. 40
Cocking, R. R. 94
Coe, R. 182, 183, 184
Cohen, A. L. 61
Cohen, P. A. 182, 183
Coleman, C. M. 114
Connelly, R. J. 168
Connington, F. 37
Connor-Greene, P. A. 155–6
Cope, M. A. 51, 64
Credé, M. 41
Cronin, T. E. 14
Crooks, T. J. 116
Crosby, J. R. 104
Cross, K. P. 125, 126, 170, 172, 185
Cullen. R. 146, 151–2
Cummings, R. 113
Czenkanski, K. E. 144, 147

D'Andrea, V. 107
d'Apollonia, S. 165
Davis, B. G. 11, 21, 23
Davis, D. 41
Davis, M. H. 104
Davison, E. 173
Dean, K. L. 23
DeWaters, J. 14
Dewey, J. 34
Dickson, K. L. 129
DiClementi, J. D. 148, 153
Dietz-Uhler, B. 24
Dillon, P. M. 144, 147
Dinham, S. M. 32, 34
DiNisi, A. 119
DiPietro, M. 35, 36
Dochy, F. 51, 54
Dommeyer, C. 168
Donald, J. G. 35, 94
D'Onofrio, M. J. 22
Donovan, S. S. 51
Doyle, D. J. 168
Dresel, M. 183
Duch, B. J. 54
Duchastel, P. C. 106

Duell, O. P. 106
Dunlosky, J. 41–2
Dunn, D. S. 24, 81, 93, 163

Eddy, S. L. 51, 53
Edens, K. M. 54
Eison, J. A. 52
Elliott, M. P. 55
Endo, J. J. 69
Englehard, M. 39
Epelbaum, V. B. 69
Epting, K. 59
Epting, L. 56, 59
Essig, L. 64
Ewell, P. T. 100, 102, 103

Farrell, M. 93
Fike, D. S. 168
Fink, L. D. 21
Fix, T. K. 141, 144, 154
Fletcher, C. H. 92
Franklin, J. 175, 176, 178
Frantz, S. M 37, 91
Freed, J. E. 104, 106, 111, 117, 120, 124
Freeman, S. 51, 53
Freishtat, R. 165, 177
Fresko, B. 179, 182
Frideres, J. 182
Frisby, B. N. 61
Frymier, A. B. 62
Fulcher, K. H. 114
Furr, R. M. 59, 146
Furst, E. 39
Fynewever, H. 154

Gagné, E. 106
Gallagher, S. A. 54
Galvan, D. B. 37, 91
Gamson, Z. F. 3, 35
Garavalia, L. 155
Garczynski, A. 80, 144
Gellman, E. S. 182
Gijbels, D. 51, 54
Gillaspy Jr., J. A. 61
Goldberger, N. R. 40
Good, M. R. 114
Goodboy, A. K. 117
Gorham, J. S. 61
Gravestock, P. 182
Greenberg, K. P. 124
Greenwald, A. 182
Gregor-Greenleaf, E. 182
Gremler, D. D. 60

Groccia, J. E. 21
Groh, S. E. 54
Gross, A. B. 168
Grossman, P. L. 34
Guder, F. 168
Guenther, C. 66, 69
Gurung, R. A. R. 1, 4, 5, 15, 21, 23, 24, 25, 30, 32, 34, 36, 40, 41, 42, 80, 81, 85, 92, 94, 96, 141, 143, 144, 147, 149, 153–4, 176
Gwinner, K. P. 60

Habanek, D. V. 141
Hackathorn, J. 80, 144
Hake, R. R. 53
Halonen, J. S. 93, 163
Halpern, D. F. 100, 103
Handelsman, M. M. 25, 66, 69, 148, 153
Hands, K. B. 166
Hanna, R 168
Harden, R. M. 104, 105
Harnish, R. J. 150
Harpel, R. L. 69
Harper, Y. Y. 37
Harris, M. B. 140, 141, 143, 144, 146, 150, 151–2, 154
Hartlaub, S. 149–50
Hattie, J. 24, 41, 127
Haynie, A. 32, 81
Heinich, R. 107, 111
Hendersen, R. W. 37, 91
Herr, L. M. 39
Hestenes, D. 83
Higgins, E. 173
Hill, G. I. 93
Hill, G. W. 56, 63, 64
Hill, W. 39
Hineline, P. N. 55, 171
Hochevar, C. 52, 53
Hoellwarth, C. 53
Hoium, K. 55
Hollander, R. D. 92
Hollister, D. 3, 36, 37
Homa, N. 80, 144
Huba, M. E. 104, 106, 111, 117, 120, 124
Hubbard, A. 51, 64
Huber, M. T. 24, 129, 131, 132
Huitt, W. 155
Hummel, J. 155
Hung, W.-C. 37
Huscher, C. 125
Hutchings, P. 24, 103, 113, 129, 131, 132

Ikenberry, S. O. 102, 103
Ishiyama, J. T. 149–50

Jankowski, N. 102, 103
Jarmoszko, A. T. 22
Jarvis, D. K. 14
Johnson, D. R. 51, 53
Johnson, R. T. 51, 53
Jonsson, A. 124, 125
Jordt, H. 51, 53

Kadmon, M. 167
Kamenetz, A. 165
Kaplan, R. 106
Karpicke, J. D. 42
Kauffman, D. F. 39, 41
Kazemi, E. 125
Keeley, J. 3, 14, 56, 59, 64, 146, 169
Keith, K. D. 81
Kelly, D. 126
Kelly, T. J. 178–9
Kember, D. 183
Keys. J. 147
Kindelberger Hagan, L. 53
Kindred, J. 173
King, P. M. 40
Kinzie, J. 102, 103
Kitchener, K. S. 40
Klein, E. M. 69
Kline, D. 182
Kluger, A. N. 119
Knipp, D. 111
Knol, M. 183
Knowles, M. 35
Kohn, A 37
Komarraju, M. 3, 41, 59
Korn, J. H. 23
Krathwohl, D. R. 39
Krautman, A. 166
Kuh, G. D. 102, 103
Kuncel, N. R. 41
Kurke, L. B. 140, 146, 150
Kwan, K. 183

Lambert, T. 55
Lammers, W. J. 59, 61
Lancaster, S. M. 166
Land, R. 34
Landrum, R. E. 24, 59, 62, 63, 85, 146
Langley, R. 41
Latham, G. P. 106
Lauver, K. 41
Le, H. 41

Lea, S. J. 52, 53
Leach, L. 66, 69
Leary, H. 51
Lee-Partridge, J. E. 22
Lehman, D. R. 40
Leigh, J. A. 23
Leung, D. 183
Levi, A. 21
Lewandowski, G. J. 173
Lewis, K. G. 169, 180, 181
L'Hommedieu, R. 182
Limber, J. E. 42
Lindahl, M. W. 179
Lipsey, M. 182
Lisle, J. 149
Littleford, L. N. 37, 91
Locke, E. A. 106
Loes, C. 92
Lovett, M. C. 35, 36
Lowman, J. 14
Ludwig, M. A. 154
Lumina Foundation for Education 82, 88,
    89, 91, 92

MacFarlane-Dick, D. 117, 119
Maddux, C. D. 113
Magolda, M. B. B. 40
Malliaris, M. 168
Marchuk, K. A. 146
Marek, P. 24
Marsh, E. J. 41–2
Marsh, H. W. 56, 127, 165, 166, 170,
    183, 185
Martin, J. H. 17, 166
Martin, M. M. 61
Martin, R. C. 131
Masterson, J. T. 62
Matejka, K. 140, 146, 150
McCann, L. 94
McCarthy, M. A. 37, 62, 63, 91, 93, 113,
    129, 163
McCroskey, J. C. 61, 62
McDaniel, M. 37
McDaniel, M. A. 43
McDonough, M. 51, 53
McElroy, H. K. 36
McGregor, L. N. 81
McKeachie, W. J. 11, 21, 56, 63, 64, 65
McTighe, J. 21, 117
Meera, K. 36, 37
Mehrabian, A. 61
Mellenbergh, G. 183
Menges, R. 182

Meyer, J. 34
Meyers, S. A. 4, 36, 60–1
Mezirow, J. 22
Middendorf, J. 34
Miele, J. 130
Miller, R. L. 56, 66, 69
Millis, K. 37
Mitchell, N. 146, 147, 151, 153, 154
Mitchell, S. 54
Moelter, M. J. 53
Mohammed, S. N. 173
Molenda, M. 107, 111
Moore, A. 62
Moore, D. L. 105
Morgan, R. 146, 147, 151, 153, 154
Morgan, R. K. 141, 144, 146, 147, 151, 153, 154
Morling, B. 85
Mortelmans, D. 165, 167
Moye, M. 66
Murphy, T. J. 166
Musulkin, S. 59

Nadler, D. 41
Nardone, N. N. 173
Nasser, F. 179, 182
Nathan, M. J. 41–2
National Research Council 39, 41
Nelson, C. E. 24, 85, 94
New Leadership Alliance for Student Learning and Accountability 102
Nicol, D. J. 117, 119
Nida, S. A. 81
Niederjohn, D. M. 113
Nilson, L. B. 53
Nuhfer, E. 111
Nulty, D. 168

Okorafor, N. 51, 53
O'Neil, R. 42
Osborne, R. E. 107
Otto, J. 173
Owen, J. E. 37

Pace, D. 34
Page, M. C. 37, 91
Pallett, W. H. 168
Palmer, B. 66
Palmer, P. J. 23, 30
Palomba, C. A. 105, 117
Parini, J. 30
Parkes, J. 140, 141, 143, 144, 150, 151, 154
Pascarella, E. T. 66, 92

Pascual-Leone, A. 55
Pashler, H. 37
Paulson, K. 102, 103
Penny, A. R. 182, 183, 184
Perrine, R. M. 149
Perry, W. G. 40
Petkova, O. 22
Pierson, C. T. 66
Pogue, L. 62
Pope, D. 55
Prentice-Dunn, S. 36
Pressley, N. 17
Price, J. 173
Prieto, L. 3, 92, 129
Prieto, L. R. 36, 37
Prince, M. 51, 53
Provezis, S. 102, 103
Puccio, P. 81
Puente, A. E. 37, 91
Pugh, J. L. 56, 60, 61, 64
Putnam, A. L. 131

Raesly, H. N. 178–9
Rawson, K. A. 41–2
Raymark, P. H. 155–6
Razzouk, N. Y. 143, 155, 156
Reab, M. D. 173
Redding, R. E. 166
Reddy, Y. M. 124
Richardson, J. E. 175
Richlin, L. 23
Richman, W. A. 113
Richmond, A. S. 4, 5, 15, 25, 30, 53, 69, 96, 113, 141, 143, 144, 146, 147, 149, 151, 153–4, 176
Richmond, V. P. 61, 62
Rindermann, H. 183
Robbins, S. 41
Robertson, S. 55
Robinson Wolf, Z. 144, 147
Rocca, K. A. 62
Roche, L. A. 165
Rocheleau, C. A. 36, 37
Roediger, H. L. 43, 131
Rogers, D. T. 61
Rohrer, D 37
Ross, D. N. 173
Roth, J. K. 11, 13
Rothkopf, E. Z. 106
Royer, P. N. 106
Russell, J. D. 107, 111
Rust, C. 117, 119
Ryan, R. G. 25, 56, 60, 61, 64, 146

Saari, L. M. 106
Salmon, D. 86
Sanborn, U. A. 80, 144
Sander, W. 166
Sanford, D. J. 173
Saroyan, A. 94
Savery, J. 53
Saville, B. K. 24, 32, 55, 56, 59, 61, 146
Savina, E. 59
Schaeffer, G. 59
Scheel, K. R. 36
Schmelkin, L. P. 182
Schwartz, B. M. 1
Schwartz, E. 21, 23, 24, 34, 36, 40
Sciutto, M. J. 4
Scoboria, A. 55
Scribner, M. 23
Sears, D. O. 2, 162
Segers, M. 51, 54
Shaw, K. N. 106
Shea, K. A. 62
Shell, D. F. 39, 41
Shore, C. 3, 36, 37
Shulman, L. S. 32, 33, 34
Sikorski, J. 32, 56, 59
Simmons, F. G. 106
Sipress, J. M. 80, 85
Skotko, D. 59
Slattery, J. 141, 144, 146, 147, 151, 153, 154
Slattery, J. M. 141, 154, 155
Slavich, G. M. 51, 53
Smaldino, S. E. 107, 111
Smith, D. 3, 56, 64, 169
Smith, K. A. 51, 53
Smith, K. L. 114
Smith, M. A. 131
Smith, M. F. 143, 155, 156
Smith, M. K. 51, 53
Smith, R. A. 24, 129, 131, 132
Snyder, J. L. 22
Snyder, T. 173
Soderstrom, N. C. 41
Solomon, E. 80
Solomon, E. D. 144
Sonntag, M. E. 173
Spencer, K. J. 182
Spinath, B. 167
Spooren, P. 165, 167
Springer, L. 51
Stanne, M. 51
Stark, P. B. 165, 177
Stehle, S. 167

Stephenson, D 52, 53
Stevens, D. D. 21
Stevenson, M. R. 91
Stowell, J. 37
Stowell, J. R. 146, 173
Stuhlfaut, M. W. 93
Sue, D. W. 90
Sulik, G. 147
Sullivan, N. 25, 66, 69
Suskie, L. 21, 101, 110, 111, 112, 120, 123
Svanum, S. 69
Svingby, G. 124, 125
Svinicki, M. 11, 21, 56, 63, 64, 65

Tarule, J. M. 40
Tennial, R. 80, 144
Thaler, N. 125
Theall, M. 175
Thomas, C. E. 62
Thompson, B. 156
Titsworth, B. S. 62
Tiwari, A. 54
Towler, A. 25, 69
Trainin, G. 39, 41
Treml, M. M. 129
Trimble, J. E. 91
Troy, J. 52, 53
Trytten, D. A. 166
Tucker, D. L. 149
Tweed, R. G. 40

Umbach, P. D. 92
Unger, M. L. 179

Van den Bossche, P. 51, 54
van Driel, J. 183
Veld, R. 183
Venzke, B. 141, 144, 151, 153
Violato, C. 182
Voelker, D. J. 80, 85
Vogel, D. L. 51, 64
Voigt, M. J. 81
Vorst, H. 183

Wagnor, W. F. 107
Walker, A. 51
Walvoord, B. E. 101, 104, 113, 114
Wankat, P. 94
Webster, R. 168
Weimer, M. 2, 11, 14, 22, 30, 39
Wells, M. 83
Wenderoth, M. P. 51, 53
Wesp, R. 130

Wiggins, G. 21, 117
Wiley, L. 155
William, D. 116
Williams, J. 55
Willingham, D. T 41–2
Wilson, J. H. 25, 56, 60, 61, 64, 146
Wilson, K. 23
Wilson, K. M. 39, 41
Wilson, S. M. 34
Wilson. D. 182
Wissman, K. T. 42

Wolfle, D. 82
Worell, J. 91

Yoder, J. 52, 53

Zajonc, A. 23
Zakrajsek, T. 52
Zepke, N. 66, 69
Zimbardo, P. G. 53
Zinn, T. E. 55, 56, 59, 146
Zinsmeister, D. D. 56, 63, 64

SUBJECT INDEX

Figures are shown by a page reference in *italics* and tables are shown in **bold**.

active learning 4

American Disability Act (ADA) policies 141, **142**

andragogy 35

assessment processes: best practices 133–4; case study 104–5, 115–16; commitments to 102; criteria definitions **7**; embedded assessment plans 113–15, **114**, **115**, 130; and learning goals 101, 102; and learning objectives 105–12; and learning-centered teaching 104, 118; objections to 100–1; as objective/ fair 65; overview of 101, *101*; role of teachers 103; and scholarship of teaching 128–9; self-assessment **102**, 133; using a rubric 124; *see also* evaluations; scholarship of teaching

Association of American Colleges and Universities 88

Association of American Educators 93

attendance policies (syllabi) 141, 142, **142**, 143, *143*

backward design 21, 118, 120

best practices 5

Bloom's Taxonomy 39, 110, 112

classroom assessment techniques (CATs) 125–6, 134

codes of conduct 92

competency, determining 2

concept maps: for classroom evaluations 126; for a concept map *87*; for course content organization 86, *86*; in syllabi *152*

conferences: for maintaining pedagogical knowledge 38; and presentation of research 131

Council for Advancement and Support of Education (CASE) 13

course content: backward design 21, 118, 120; best practices 96; case study 79–80, 94–5; common core guidelines 82; concept map for a concept map *87*; concept map for content organization 86, *86*; conceptual consistency 83; content selection 85–7; criteria definitions **7**; cultural literacy 90–1; Degree Qualifications Profile (DQP) 88–9, 90–1, 92; ethical literacy 92–3; and learning outcomes 83–4; liberal arts skills 87–90; research on 93–4; self-assessment **79**, 95–6; standardization of 80–3; in syllabi 143, **144**; up-to-date literature on 84–5

Degree Qualifications Profile (DQP) 88–9, 90–1, 92

ethical teaching: balanced content 63; in day-to-day practice 62; disciplinary competence 63; ethical behavior of the teacher 65–6; ethical literacy 92–3; experiential learning activities 64; learning objectives 110; objective/fair assessments 65; qualities of 63; respect for students 64; student confidentiality 63–4; teaching behaviors and classroom practices **67–8**; transparent policies 65; up-to-date pedagogical knowledge 37

evaluations: alignment with learning objectives 117; case study 117, 126–7; classroom assessment techniques (CATs) 125–6; concept mapping 126; feedback from 119; grading 116, 119, 120, 124–5, 141, **142**; minute papers 125, 126; muddiest point 125–6; role of 116, 119; rubric for an online discussion forum *123*; rubric for math assignment *122*; rubric for research-based writing assignment *121*; rubrics (analytic/descriptive) 120–5; in syllabi 144, **144**, 150; timing of 125–6; *see also* assessment processes

expert knowledge 32–3

Family Educational Rights and Privacy Act (FERPA). 63

formative evaluations: classroom assessment techniques (CATs) 125–6, 134; embedded into an exam/assignment 172–3; feedback on general teaching ability 169–70, *170*; and the interteaching method 171–2; minute papers for perceptions of pedagogy 170–1; for a one-class period 171, *171*; overview of 163, 167–8; purpose of 169; and specific classroom activities 172, *172*; timing of 170; types of 169–70; *see also* student evaluations of teaching

fundamentals of teaching 20–1

grading: and evaluations 116, 119, 120, 124–5, 141, **142**; grade incentives for student evaluation response rates 168–9; grade inflation 162; policies in syllabi 155

immediacy 61–2

instructional methods: active learning 52–3; best practices 71; case study 50–1, 70; criteria definitions *7*; Definitions, Classroom Examples, and Sources 57–8; experiential learning activities 64; interteaching 55–6; lecturing 56; problem-based learning 53–5; self-assessment 49, **50**, 70–1; student engagement 66–9; teaching qualities and 56–60; varied instructional techniques 51

interteaching: method of 55–6; student evaluations of teaching 171–2

journals: accessing tables of contents 85; for maintaining pedagogical knowledge 37–8; research publication 131; for up-to-date literature and course content 84–5

knowledge: expert knowledge 32–3, 34–5; pedagogical content knowledge 33–5; pedagogical theory and practice 35–8; prior knowledge assessment 35–6

knowledge acquisition by students: Bloom's Taxonomy 39; bottlenecks, conceptual 34; cognitive development and 40; cultural background and 40; learner-centered teaching 39; solidifying knowledge 41; study techniques 41–3; and types of students 39–40; *see also* learning

learning: benefits of scholarship of teaching 132; bottlenecks 34; correlation with student evaluations 167; deep processing 42, 43; defined 41; distributed practicing 43; highlighting text 43; importance of learning objectives 105–6; practice testing 43; self-assessment **79**

learning goals: of the academic department and college 106–7, **107**; within the assessment process 101, 102; and course assignments 113; term 101

learning objectives: ABCD format 107–11; alignment with evaluations 117; and the assessment process 105–12; and Bloom's Taxonomy 110, 112; diversity-related learning 110; evaluation of 111; examples organized according to cognitive level **108–9**; formal sources for 106–7, **107**; importance of 105–6; informal sources 107, **107**; in syllabi 144, **144**, *145*, 153–4; term 101; writing your own 106–12

learning outcomes: and course content
83–4; Degree Qualifications Profile
(DQP) 88–9, 90–1; diversity-related
learning 90–1; liberal arts skills 87–90;
Liberal Education and America's
Promise **88**; term 101; writing
your own 84
learning-centered approaches: and
assessment processes 104, 118; overview
of 39; and respect for student needs 64;
for syllabi 141, 144, 146, 151–3, **151**
liberal arts skills 87–90
Liberal Education and America's
Promise 88, **88**
Lumina Foundation for Education 82, 88,
89, 91, 92

model teaching: characteristics of xiv, xv;
criteria definitions **7–8**; definitions xiii,
2–4; training self-assessment **33**, 44
Model Teaching Criteria 4–5, 193–4
Model Teaching Criteria Scale 196–8

pedagogical training in higher
education 1–2
pedagogy: evidence-based pedagogical tips
36; key principles of 35–6; maintaining
knowledge of 37–8; term 35
philosophy statements 23
policies: academic dishonesty 65; American
Disability Act (ADA) policies 141, **142**;
attendance policies (syllabi) 141, 142,
142, 143, *143*; evaluation policies 65;
grading policies (syllabi) 155
prior knowledge 35–6
professional development: as a continuous
process 193–4; and inertia 194; trying
something new 194–5; *see also* training
Professor-Student Rapport Scale 170, *170*

quality teaching: actions of excellent
teachers 15–19, **18**; award-winning
teachers 13–14; master teachers 14–15;
successful college teachers 14

rapport 60–1
RateMyProfessors.com 173–4
Reinvention Center 38
rubrics (analytic/descriptive) 120–5

scholarship of teaching: benefits to
learning 132; case study 128, 132–3; and
classroom instruction 130–1; compared
to scholarly teaching 129; and empirical
research processes 129–30; professional
benefits of 131–2; and research-focused
faculty 131; and teaching productivity
127–8; and teaching-focused faculty 131;
term 128; *see also* assessment processes
scholarship of teaching and learning
(SoTL) 23–4
scientist-educator model 3, 36
self-reflection: sample questions **22**;
Self-Assessment of What Constitutes
Good Teaching **12**, 24–5; sincere
teaching as 21–3; teacher self-assessment
and student evaluations 183–4;
underlying assumptions of 22–3;
written philosophy statements 23
sincere teaching 21–3
skill levels, evaluating xiv
Society for the Teaching of Psychology
Presidential Taskforce 4
Student Evaluation of Educational Quality
170, 175
student evaluations of teaching: and
academic rigor of courses 166–7;
anonymity of 170, 171; best practices
187–8; case study 164–5, 186–7; and
classroom assessment techniques
(CATs) 125–6, 134; confidence
intervals and 176–7; correlation with
student learning 167; correlation
with teaching effectiveness 166;
criteria definitions **8**; embedded
into an exam/assignment 172–3;
evidence-based model for use of
184–6; formative evaluations 163,
167–8, 169–73; grade incentives for
student evaluation response rates
168–9; as an imperfect measure 163;
interpretation example *174*, 175, 176,
177–8, *178*; interpretation of 174–9;
interpretation of written comments
179–81, **181**; and new teaching
techniques 195; for a one-class period
171, *171*; online vs. paper response
rates 168; Professor-Student Rapport
Scale 170, *170*; purpose of formative
evaluations 169; RateMyProfessors.com
173–4; role of 162; and scholarship
of teaching 24; self-assessment **163**,
187; for specific classroom activities
172, *172*; standard deviations and 176;
statistical tests and 177; and student
engagement 66, 69; Student Evaluation

of Educational Quality 170, 175; summative evaluations 162–3, 168–9; and syllabi language 150; Teacher Behavior Checklist 3, 169; and teacher improvement 182–6; and teacher self-assessment 183–4; types of formative evaluations 169–70; University of California Los Angeles study 162; use of minute papers for pedagogical perceptions 170–1; validity of 165–7, 175, 183

subject-specific expertise 32–3

summative evaluations 162–3, 168–9

syllabi: attendance policies in 141, 142, **142**, 143, *143*; best practices **142**, 158–9; case study 138–9, 157–8; as cognitive maps and learning tools 150–3, **151**, *152*; as communication devices 145–6; as a contract 140–2; criteria definitions **7–8**; fostering student knowledge of 155–7; grading policies 155; language style 149–50; as permanent records 142–4, **144**; planning of 153–4, **154**; purpose of 140, 146; revisiting 156; self-assessment 139, **140**, 158; student-centered approaches of 141, 144, 146, 151–3, **151**; supportive statements 149; transparency 143, 147

Teacher Behavior Checklist (TBC) 3, 15, **16–17**, 59, 146, 169

teacherly regret 193

teacher-student interactions: evaluation alignment and learning objectives 117; formal/informal interactions 69; immediacy 61–2; rapport 60–1; student views on good teaching 19, **20**; syllabi as communication devices 145–50, *148*; use of rubrics for evaluation 124–5

teaching awards 13–14

teaching-centered approaches 104

technology, use of 37

textbooks 84

training: best practices 44–5; campus faculty development center workshops 36; case study 31, 43–4; criteria definitions **7**; graduate courses on teaching 36; self-assessment **33**, 44; *see also* professional development

Writing Across the Curriculum and in the Disciplines 38